To John

Your ...

MW00886645

# Rescued
by
## Grace

By grace you are saved
through faith, and not
of yourselves; it is the
gift of God, not the result
of works so that no one
can boast.

Ephesians 2:8-9

Clifford B. McManis (MDiv, ThM, PhD) is the teaching Elder of Grace Bible Fellowship of Silicon Valley. He is a graduate of The Master's College and Seminary and is on the board of The Cornerstone Seminary in Vallejo, CA where he also teaches Bible Exposition and Apologetics. His previous books include *Christian Living Beyond Belief* and *Biblical Apologetics*.

Derek J. Brown (MDiv, PhD) is on staff at Grace Bible Fellowship of Silicon Valley. He is a graduate of The Master's College and Southern Seminary, an adjunct professor of Systematic Theology for Southern and also oversees an outreach ministry at Stanford University. He previously served as the managing editor of *Journal of Discipleship and Family Ministry,* and has contributed to *Exegesis and Theology in the Protestant Reformation* and *How We Got the Bible Made Easy.*

# Rescued
## by
# Grace

Current Evidence that Jesus
Still Saves Sinners

# Clifford B. McManis
# Derek J. Brown

Rev. date: 03/30/2015

**To order additional copies of this book, contact:**
Xlibris
1-888-795-4274
www.Xlibris.com
Orders@Xlibris.com
701145

# CONTENTS

*This book is affectionately dedicated
to the faithful saints of
Grace Bible Fellowship*

# Commendations for Rescued By Grace

"Scripture commands believers, 'Oh give thanks to the Lord, for He is good, For His lovingkindness is everlasting. Let the redeemed of the Lord say *so*, Whom He has redeemed from the hand of the adversary' (Psalm 107:1-2). This book is a fulfillment of that command. As believers we never tire of hearing the story of redemption told in the fresh forms of every individual who experiences it. My prayer is that through these testimonies, you may join the chorus of those who rejoice in His lovingkindness."

> – *John MacArthur*, *Pastor of Grace Community Church and President of The Master's College and Seminary*

"My favorite authors on grace are Tim Keller, Phil Yancey and Max Lucado—McManis and Brown are now in the upper echelon in this category. This book is a page turner and had me gripped chapter by chapter til the end. It is an extraordinary compilation, beautifully written and spiritually moving. Thousands will shed tears reading these testimonies as God's truth reignites the memories of grace God abounding in their own lives. Knowing Christ personally and trusting His power of grace is a great assurance. Nothing else will fill the void; everything else is empty. *Rescued by Grace* with its treasury of life-changing stories brings it all home!"

> - *Dr. Barry Asmus*, *Senior Economist of the National Center for Policy Analysis*

"Serving Jesus is the highest calling. This book reminds me of that great truth. As a Christian you never know how God might use you as a vessel to touch someone's life in a mighty way. The testimonies in this book will touch many lives just as God sovereignly used me to touch Pastor McManis' life in a gym locker-room in 1985."

-*Calvin Duncan, Pastor of Faith and Family Church, Richmond, VA; former standout of the VCU Rams and missionary for Athletes In Action*

"This book is a powerful testimony to God's forgiving grace at work to meet people where they are and change them into his devoted followers. A book that God can use to bring many others into the kingdom illustrating that God is at work in our world today."

-*Dale Galloway, Author and Pastor of Leadership Development at Scottsdale Bible Church*

"There is nothing more encouraging than hearing personal testimonies of Jesus Christ's transforming power. No matter what you are going through in your life, *Rescued By Grace* will encourage your heart. It is a great book!"

-*Mike Penberthy, former point guard of the Los Angeles Lakers and shooting coach for the Minnesota Timberwolves*

"*Rescued By Grace* is a profound collection of gripping testimonies of searching men and women. Their lives were radically changed by the Holy Spirit, through trials and circumstances. Each was sovereignly guided, irresistibly brought to repentance, and granted faith to embrace Jesus as Savior and Lord. This book is especially for every person, young or old, who is looking for truth and purpose for their lives. *Rescued By Grace* will enlighten, strengthen, and encourage every faithful Christian who desires to be more effective for Christ. I believe this book is needed for the times in which we live and wholeheartedly endorse it, and believe it will be a great tool to bring glory to the Name of our Lord."

-*Dr. Robert Provost, President, Slavic Gospel Association*

# *Acknowledgements*

I would like to thank the contributors of this work who have been rescued by the gospel of Jesus and who were willing to share the details of their life-changing stories. They are testimonies to the power of God's saving grace and compelling witnesses to the truth of Christ as revealed in Scripture. Thanks also to Dr. Derek Brown who wrote the concluding chapter and was my co-editor for the entire project.

Thanks to those who wrote endorsements for the book, who took the time to read the manuscripts in the midst of busy and pressing schedules. Thanks in particular to Rev. Calvin Duncan, who, faithfully and powerfully, preached the gospel to me and took the time to answer my personal questions back in November of 1985...the night I got rescued by Jesus.

Thanks to Rev. Bob Douglas, fellow Elder of GBF, who designed the beautiful book cover.

And thanks most of all to Jesus, the blessed Savior, who came to seek and to save those who are lost.

Clifford B. McManis
Cupertino, CA
March, 2015

# *Introduction*

"Christianity is the most perverted system that ever shone on man." So says the infamous British atheist, Richard Dawkins in his 2006 bestseller, *The God Delusion*. As the most influential atheist since Madelyn Murray O'Hare, Dawkins argues that God does not exist and Christianity is a crude farce...because of the "evidence." Dawkins goes on to audaciously spout that because of "available evidence and reasoning... it is possible to mount a serious historical case that Jesus never lived at all." But even the most secular parochial historians admit that Jesus' existence is undeniable. So much for making assertions based on "the evidence."

How can a self-proclaimed, so-called world class scientist boldly assert that, based on the evidence, Jesus never existed? It's easy—just ignore some of the evidence. Present only partial evidence. Invoke historical revisionism. Be selective in what evidence is under consideration. People do it all the time. That's why our courts ask witnesses to tell the truth, "the whole truth," and nothing but the truth. We need to tell the whole truth, not part of the truth. All the known evidence needs to be considered before rendering a verdict. Dawkins thinks his book is an iron-clad presentation of evidence against Christianity. The problem is he ignores much critical evidence.

Another common way to dismiss truth and reality is to misinterpret or distort the evidence. Dawkins does that as well. Miscreants tamper with the evidence routinely. It is human nature to tinker, embellish, exaggerate, spin and manipulate the "evidence" and in turn distort the truth.

## The Evidence Is In

The truth of the Bible is corroborated by plenty of evidence. The events and people in the Bible were all real and a part of real history. As such, there is plenty of evidence in their wake. The New Testament presents eight lines of evidence to corroborate the truth of Christianity in general and Jesus' teaching in particular. They include internal general revelation, external general revelation, written Scripture, faith, the work of the Holy Spirit, good works, the resurrection and changed lives.

## Internal General Revelation

First is the evidence of *internal general revelation*—or a conscience. Every human born into this world is made in God's image (Genesis 1:26). That image is what makes every human a "person." And that image entails a conscience, an innate moral barometer and an inescapable conscious awareness of God's existence. That's why no one is born an atheist—people become atheists over time as they ignore their conscience, pursue their sin and turn their back on their Creator in willful defiance. Regarding this universal truth that applies to all people, Romans says *"that which is known about God is evident within them, for God made it evident to them" (1:19).* The word "evident" here is related to the word "evidence." And this internal evidence is readily available to all. Further Romans says, *"the law"* of God is *"written on their hearts, their consciences also bearing witness, and their thoughts sometimes accusing them" (2:15).* Every person has a conscience given to them by God the Creator before birth. That is inescapable internal evidence that God exists. The Old Testament attests to this same truth when it says God *"has also set eternity in their heart" (Ecclesiastes 3:11).* That means every human has an innate, unassailable, immediate, internal, personal witness that God is their Creator. That is the human conscience. The conscience is indisputable evidence of God's existence.

*External General Revelation*

Second is the evidence of *external general revelation.* God the Creator has left His fingerprints everywhere, for all to behold. In addition to conscience, and in keeping with the conscience, external creation is undeniable evidence of God's existence and the truth of the Bible. Romans says, *"For since the creation of the world His invisible attributes, His eternal power and divine nature, have been clearly seen, being understood through what has been made, so that they are without excuse" (1:20).* So the created order is evidence of God's existence. And despite what an atheist may say, he sees this truth, understands it and is without excuse. Yes he'll deny it. But the next verse explains why he's in denial: *"For even though they knew God [existed], they did not honor Him as God or give thanks, but they became futile in their speculations, and their foolish heart was darkened" (1:21).* In addition to conscience, creation all around us is evidence of God's existence.

*Scripture*

The third line of evidence for truth presented in the New Testament is *written Scripture*. The critics don't like this, but it's a fact. The Bible is here. It's the bestselling book of all time. There are thousands of extant manuscripts of it in existence today. Those manuscripts are real, ancient, physical, tangible, and empirical. They can be ignored or misrepresented, but they are still evidence. Jesus said written Scripture is "evidence" of who He was and what He taught: *"search the Scriptures...it is these that testify about Me" (John 5:39).* Here Jesus used a legal term in reference to the Scriptures—"testify." In other words, the Scriptures give legal testimony, or are "evidence," regarding the truth of Jesus. The Scriptures are also effectual and persuasive evidence—what they say is determinative and life-changing. John the Apostle said of the Scripture, *"These things I have written to you who believe in the name of the Son of God, so that you may know that you have eternal life" (1 John 5:13).* The evidence of written Scripture enables people to know, with certitude, eternal and spiritual truth...even in our uncertain post-modern world. The Scriptures are inviolable and irrevocable evidence as well, for Jesus declared, *"The Scripture cannot be broken" (John 10:35).*


*Faith*

The fourth line of evidence corroborating biblical truth is *faith*. Yes, that is right... faith. That seems odd and too subjective to many. But Hebrews 11:1 is clear: *"Now faith is...the evidence."* Faith is the evidence! Faith is the evidence of *"things not seen,"* or the evidence of spiritual realities we cannot see but are certain now or will be true in the future. For example, Jesus will return a second time to the earth. It's a fact. The evidence is the faith that God gives us through the truth of Scripture about that subject as it is confirmed in our hearts by the illumination of the Holy Spirit. This verse is talking about a specific and unique kind of faith; a quality of faith; a faith unknown and inaccessible to the world—faith that is a supernatural gift from God given to those who respond in belief when they hear God's divine revelation. This kind of faith issues only from exposure to the content of Scripture, the Word of God or divine revelation (Romans 10:17). It is alien to the natural world. It is beyond human intuition, experience, knowledge, or discovery. Nevertheless, faith is real evidence for "those who have eyes to see and ears to hear."

### The Convicting Holy Spirit

The fifth line of evidence is *the work of the Holy Spirit*. Just before Jesus went back to heaven He said to His Apostles, *"But I tell you the truth, it is to your advantage that I go away; for if I do not go away, the Helper will not come to you; but if I go, I will send Him to you. And He, when He comes, will convict the world concerning sin and righteousness and judgment"* *(John 16:7-8).* This passage is loaded with legal, courtroom terminology. Jesus refers to "judgment" and "convict." He calls the Holy Spirit a "Helper," or literally, "Advocate" which is a formal representative in a court of law. He mentions "sin" and "righteousness" which are words for "right" and "wrong"— the subjects of every hearing and court case. Here Jesus says that the Holy Spirit will carry out a ministry of acting as the prosecuting attorney of the soul, convicting all unbelievers continually about the truth, using divine revelation in tandem with their ever-present conscience. This work of the Holy Spirit is non-stop, universal, real and efficacious. He makes sinners feel guilt. All humans feel guilt. Guilt is evidence that the Holy Spirit is doing His job, just as Jesus said.

### Heavenly Good Works

The sixth line of evidence is *good works* produced by true Christians. Ephesians says that God saves people so that they will do good works on behalf of Christ (2:10). The Bible calls these good works spiritual fruit, or "the fruit of the Spirit"—supernatural manifestations generated by the indwelling Holy Spirit that flow from those who are born-again (Galatians 5:22-23). Only true believers have this capacity. Unbelievers cannot produce these heavenly-quality good works (Matthew 7:15-18). Jesus declared that the good works of believers are tangible evidence for unbelievers who are looking on. Heavenly-generated good works in the life of a Christian are apologetical in nature, used by God to put Himself on unmistakable display before those in the world. That is what Jesus meant when He said to believers, *"You are the light of the world. A city set on a hill cannot be hidden.... Let your light shine before men in such a way that they may see your good works, and glorify your Father who is in heaven" (Matthew 5:14, 16).* Good works in the life of a Christian are evidence.

### The Resurrection of Jesus

The seventh line of evidence is *the resurrection of Christ.* Paul the Apostle, who was formerly a Christian killer, became an evangelist, missionary, church-planter and pastor for the cause of Jesus. He went into the pagan city of Athens, Greece and preached the gospel to secular philosophers in the Areopagus on

Mars Hill. Paul told the crowds there that they needed to repent of their sin against their Creator (Acts 17:30) because *"He has fixed a day in which He will judge the world in righteousness through a Man whom He has appointed, having furnished proof to all men by raising Him from the dead"* (17:31). God has "furnished proof"—that is "evidence." God will "judge"—that is legal, courtroom terminology. The "proof" or "evidence" is Jesus' resurrection. The resurrection of Jesus was a historical event witnessed by hundreds of eyewitnesses (1 Corinthians 15:6-7). Eyewitness testimony/evidence is accepted in the courtroom today. A naysayer can dismiss, marginalize, misinterpret or distort the evidence of Jesus' resurrection, but it is authoritative, binding, irrevocable evidence nonetheless. And it will be the standard by which God judges every soul in the next life.

*Changed Lives*

The eighth and final line of evidence *is the changed life of a saved sinner.* Virtually all religions speak of having some sort of religious or mystical "experience," but only Christianity and the Bible teach about the possibility of a changed life from the inside out—a change of nature that is ontological, instantaneous, permanent and a work initiated and wrought by God the Savior. It is a supernatural work that He does, not something we do (Titus 3:3-7). The Bible describes it as a "regeneration" whereby God's Spirit brings the dead human soul to life (Romans 8:10). The Bible says every person is spiritually dead the moment they enter this world and as a result are separated from God on a personal level (Ephesians 2:1). They are dead spiritually because every person has inherited Adam's sin at conception (Psalms 51:5). Every person is religiously "still born." As such, Jesus said every person needs to be "born again"—or born "from above" (John 3). Every person needs God's help to give them spiritual birth to overcome their bondage to inborn sin and separation from a holy God. No spiritually dead person can accomplish this on his own—it's beyond human capability. Jeremiah declared, *"Can an Ethiopian change his skin or a leopard its spots? Neither can you do good who are accustomed to doing evil" (13:23).*

The good news is that God sent Jesus into the world to accomplish this very thing. Jesus came to save people from their innate sin that condemns them, to give them spiritual life, to regenerate their dead souls, to remove the separation that they had with their Creator, and to give them a new nature—a divine nature (2 peter 1:4). This transaction happens only when a person believes in the gospel of Jesus and repents of sin. When they do, in that moment that person is "born again." They become a new person on the inside—they are brought instantaneously from death to life. God animates them by putting His Holy Spirit in them, to live and indwell them all their life on earth. This miraculous reality is called "justification" or "salvation" and happens in a moment of time. It is not a process. The sinner becomes a saint, and their spiritual eyes are opened for the first time—they have new godly desires, aspirations, sensitivities and thoughts. They experience love, joy, peace, patience, goodness, kindness, gentleness, and self-control deep in their soul for the first time. On the inside they have truly become a new creation, a new person. God radically has changed them. It defies human explanation. Scripture says of this life-changing reality, *"If anyone is in Christ, he is a new creation. The old has passed away; behold, the new has come. All this is from God" (2 Corinthians 5:17-18).*

This supernatural, miraculous, personal, spiritual, eternal change that God does in a person's life is evidence that Christianity, Jesus and the gospel are true. Primarily it is evidence—undeniable evidence—to the believer who has been changed. The born-again believer actually experiences the evidence, which is continual and ongoing. The most potent evidence known to man is evidence that can be experienced—real, true, personal, supernatural, eternal evidence given by God. And that is the blessed lot of every soul who becomes born again: *"You have received the Spirit of adoption as sons, by whom we cry, 'Abba! Father!' The Spirit Himself bears witness with our spirit that we are children of God" (Romans 8:15-16).*

This truth is beautifully and poignantly illustrated in John chapter nine when Jesus healed a man who had been born blind. Jesus healed the man on the Sabbath. The Jewish leaders and Pharisees already hated Jesus and wanted to kill Him (John 5) so they wanted to discredit the miracle about the blind man when they heard about it. They did not care about the evidence. No one in the history of the world had ever restored the sight of a man who was born blind (John 9:32). But Jesus did on this occasion.

The Jewish leaders interrogated the man who was healed, trying to trip him up, asking "Who healed you?"

When he answered, "Jesus did," they became infuriated and *"the Jews did not believe that he had been blind" (9:18).* Then the Jewish leaders intimidated the man's parents and threatened to kick them out of the synagogue if they defended the miracle of Jesus. Evidence and eyewitnesses did not matter to the critics. They had a pre-conceived agenda of malice that dictated the outcome. Despite the intimidation, the threats and the rebuke, the man who was healed could not deny the evidence—Jesus had changed him, and no one could take that away. As a result the man believed in Jesus and even worshiped Him as the God-Man! (9:38).

Every time Jesus transforms a sinner into a saint, that changed person becomes incarnate evidence of gospel truth. When Saul the Jewish Christian killer was transformed into Paul the Christian Apostle, *"all who heard him were amazed and said, 'Is not this the man who made havoc in Jerusalem of those who called upon His name?'"* (Acts 9:21). Every time Jesus changes a doubter into a believer, that believer is living evidence of God's truth. Paul said of Christians,

> *You yourselves are our letter of recommendation, written on our hearts, to be known and read by all. And you show that you are a letter from Christ delivered by us, written not with ink but with the Spirit of the living God, not on tablets of stone but on tablets of human hearts (2 Corinthians 3:2-3).*

The book you are holding is about lives that Jesus has changed; lives Jesus has rescued. Transformed lives that now serve as letters or epistles of God's grace that we hope will "be known and read by all." Each changed life is "evidence" corroborating God's truth. The atheists and skeptics dismiss, marginalize and even ridicule such a suggestion. But God the Creator counts each saved, transformed, rescued soul as eternally precious.

Our prayer is that you are blessed by the true stories herein. If you are a Christian we believe that you will be tremendously edified, that your hope in the gospel's power will be renewed, that your prayer life for others will be invigorated and that you will have fresh cause to give God and His Christ all the glory. If you are not a Christian and you are reading this book, we welcome you; and we ask you to read the whole thing, be open and see what you think. We'd love to hear your thoughts.

# 1

# *Jesus to the Rescue*

*"For the Son of Man has come to seek
and to save that which was lost"
Luke 19:10*

**W**hy did Jesus come into the world 2,000 years ago? That is the most important question in the world, and yet countless wrong answers have been proposed all throughout history. Even in His own day many were confused about why He came. The question of why Jesus came is directly related to who He is. Who is Jesus? Answer that question, and you will also answer the question of why He came at the same time.

*Who Is Jesus?*

After three years of public ministry, at the end of His life, Jesus asked His disciples the most important question in the world. He asked them, *"Who do people say that the Son of Man is?" (Matthew 16:13)*. They told Him that people were confused and gave mixed replies. They said many of the Jews thought Jesus was John the Baptist. Some thought He was Elijah the prophet. Others thought He was Jeremiah the prophet reincarnated, or one of the other prophets (16:14).

The masses were confounded about who Jesus was—even after watching Him publicly minister first-hand for three years. One Jewish ruler thought He was just a good teacher or rabbi (Luke 18:18). His own younger siblings at one time saw Jesus as nothing more than an ego-centric, local popular ring-leader (John 7:3). John the Baptist, Elijah, Jeremiah, an Old Testament prophet back from the dead, a good human teacher, a popular small-time ringleader—all these wrong answers came from people who were sympathetic to His ministry, for the most part.

Then there were those contemporaries of His that despised Him who had other misguided theories about who Jesus was. These contrarians were mostly from the religious establishment in Israel. These influential "leaders" hated Jesus and came up with nefarious monikers of their own that they assigned to Him.

Some of them implied He was an unclean, half-breed Samaritan bastard-child born of an immoral mother (John 8:41, 48). Others said Jesus was demon-possessed (John 8:48). Many of the Jewish leaders denounced Him as being "insane"! (John 10:20). Herod Antipas, the wicked, Idumean wanna-be-king thought Jesus was nothing more than a trickster and illusionist (Luke 23:8). The Pharisees accused Him of being a lowbrow carouser (Mark 2:16). The scribes and chief priests accused Jesus of being a deceiver and a political agitator (Luke 23:2). The Jewish high priest said He was a blasphemer worthy of death (Matthew 26:65). For this last false accusation, Jesus would eventually be executed on the cross. Samaritan, bastard, offspring of Satan, psychotic, huckster, carouser, deceiver, agitator, blasphemer? It defies the imagination as to how Jesus' very own people came to such a wrong-headed diagnosis of who He was and why He came! John the Apostle's summary statement is certainly apropos when he wrote, Jesus *"came to His own, but those who were His own did not receive Him"* (John 1:11).

## Jesus through History

From the outset, many hostile to Jesus distorted who He really was by conjuring up and proliferating caricatures and stereotypes about Him. Church history has done the same. History is rife with wrong ideas as to Jesus' identity and the purpose of His coming. In the early centuries of the Church, believers were constantly warding off ill-conceived and unbiblical notions of Jesus' identity that were trying to worm their way in among the faithful. The two most common were Arianism and Modalism.

Arianism, from Arius the Alexandrian Bishop (AD 250-336), undermined the deity of Jesus, alleging that Jesus was a created being and not eternal like the Father. Modalism suggested that God is one person, not three distinct persons, and that the one God revealed Himself in different forms or modes at different times. Modalism taught that at the incarnation God the Father became the Son, existing in a different mode but as the same person, to accomplish a specific purpose. God is one person who just changes roles when necessary—like one man might act as a husband, father and brother depending upon his function. A third century theologian, Sabellius (ca, AD 215), is most noted for popularizing an early form of a modalistic view of Jesus.

Arianism and modalism have recycled time and again throughout history under different names and personalities, but all from the same heretical genus. These Christological heresies even abound today, inside and outside the Church, as ignorant musings about the Christ are thoughtlessly spouted in contradistinction of what the Bible actually says about Jesus, and counter to what Jesus actually said about Himself. More clouded caricatures and stereotypes.

One of the most influential and pervasive wrong views of Jesus bequeathed to the world by Church history is called the "moral influence theory." First systematized by the controversial medieval philosopher, logician and monk, Peter Abelard (1079-1142), the moral influence theory proposed that Christ's death was primarily an *example*—an act of sacrificial love that was to serve as the paragon of all good human works. In this view Christ's death is not primarily a legal, penal substitution offered as a spiritual sacrifice to appease God's wrath against sinners, as the Bible teaches it to be. Rather, this appealing but jaded view says Jesus' death was more like the work of a martyr—a good example for all people to follow. Jesus was primarily a "do-gooder" and we all need to do good too, to the best of our ability.

## User-Friendly Jesus

Over the centuries this view has been adopted, modified and nuanced to the point today, where no longer is Jesus' death the main point of emphasis, but only His life (and usually it's not His life as portrayed in the Bible, but some conjured up pseudo-life of Jesus fabricated in the mind of someone's ingenuity run amuck). As a matter of fact, many ignore the purpose of Jesus' death altogether and speak only of His morally exemplary life as a mere man that all should emulate. Remember the popular rock opera musical, *Jesus Christ Superstar*, by Andrew Lloyd Webber that came out in 1970? It portrays a rendition of who Jesus was, but excludes entirely the resurrection of Christ! To promote Jesus without His resurrection, is no Jesus at all. Talk about missing the boat. Thomas Jefferson would serve as another prime example of Jesus as moral do-gooder. Jefferson wanted to showcase Jesus' moral teachings and kind deeds, but tried to jettison all of His miracles and calls to repentance from sin.

Jesus the "do-gooder" is preached today by many politicians who are looking to amass votes during their campaigns as well as by liberation preachers, social gospel profiteers, and by popular civil-rights activists. They all propagate "Jesus the man" –Jesus the pacifist, Jesus the social engineer, Jesus the moralist, Jesus the socialist, Jesus the community organizer, Jesus the environmentalist, Jesus the political liberator, Jesus the equal-rights spokesman, Jesus the education czar, Jesus the soup-kitchen manager. But Jesus was actually none of these.

*The Evidence*

Despite the malaise of confusion in His own day, in history, and even in our day, there is no mystery about who Jesus is or why He came. The Bible makes it crystal clear. Scripture gives an iron-clad testimony. God's Word speaks with certainty about who Jesus is and why He came. There is no need for a "quest" to find the historical Jesus, for He has been manifestly revealed already to the world. Two thousand years ago John the Apostle, who was a relative of Jesus and one of His best friends, who was also an eye-witness to Jesus' ministry, death and resurrection, wrote the following about the certitude of knowing who Jesus is:

> *What we have heard, what we have seen with our eyes, what we have looked at and touched with our hands, concerning the Word of Life* (the historical Jesus)—*and the Life was manifested, and we have seen and testify and proclaim to you the Eternal Life, which was with the Father and was manifested to us...Jesus Christ (1 John 1:1-3).*

John said He "heard" Jesus preach; that is verbal evidence. John "saw" Jesus personally; that's "eyewitness" evidence. John even "touched" Jesus; that is "hands-on," empirical evidence. John said he had other eyewitnesses with him—"we"—that is corroborated evidence. We have manuscripts of John's letter that are almost two-thousand years old; that's written evidence. The verdict is unshakable—the New Testament tells us exactly who Jesus is and why He came.

The Bible is 100% reliable in helping us learn the truth about Jesus. As a matter of fact, there is no other source to go to when trying to figure out anything true at all about Jesus. Everything we know to be infallibly true about Jesus is found only in the Bible and nowhere else—not in archaeology, not in other religious books, not in Church tradition or Creeds, not in ongoing dreams and revelations, not in historical research. Any second-hand source purporting to offer information of the works and identity of Jesus must be subjected to and vetted by the Bible. The true, historical Jesus can only be found in the

Bible—that's what He said! *"Search the Scriptures...it is these that testify of Me" (John 5:39).*

*Jesus On Jesus*

Jesus revealed His identity in the three-plus years of His public ministry. He was clear in what He said. Consider some of the main truths He gave about Himself.

First, Jesus claimed to be eternal! Only God is eternal, and this is the very truth Jesus ascribed to Himself. This is most explicit in John 8:58 where Jesus proclaimed publicly in Jerusalem, before multitudes, including the Jewish religious leaders, that He was as eternal as God the Father. Jesus told them His name was "I AM," which was the personal name YHWH God called Himself in revealing His identity to Moses at the burning bush in 1400 BC (Exodus 3:14). God goes by many names in the Bible, but when God called Himself "I AM" to Moses it meant something specific and unique. "I AM" in the Hebrew language means, "the self-sufficient Eternal One." And in John 8 Jesus claimed that name for Himself. The Jewish leaders knew Jesus was claiming to be eternal, so they immediately picked up stones to stone Him for blasphemy (John 8:59), for they believed only Almighty God was eternal—and they were correct. They were wrong in failing to recognize Jesus too was eternal.

As an eternal being, Jesus is un-created, self-sustaining, and never changing. He existed before angels were created. He was alive before the world was brought into being. He has always existed. He has been around longer than the universe. There was never a time when He did not exist. He has existed since eternity past with the Father and the Holy Spirit. He explicitly affirmed this mind-boggling truth just before His death when He prayed to the Father in John 17. He said to the Father, *"Now, Father, glorify Me together with Yourself, with the glory which I had with You before the world was"* (v. 5). Here Jesus said that He existed in eternity past in equal status and glory with the eternal Father, before He came to earth through Mary, before the world was created. Jesus is eternal. In Revelation 22:13 Jesus said, *"I am the Alpha and the Omega, the first and the last, the beginning and the end."* Here He claimed to be eternal in three parallel phrases. Indeed, *"Jesus Christ is the same yesterday and today and forever"* (Hebrews 13:8).

Second, Jesus claimed to be God! When Jesus called Himself, "I AM," He was calling Himself a name of God. In John 10:30, in another public setting in Jerusalem, Jesus said, *"I and the Father are one"* (John 10:30). From the context it is clear that Jesus was claiming equal status, power, glory, authority and even an equal nature with God the Father. The unbelieving Jews got the message clearly when He said this, because they immediately picked up stones to kill Him for blasphemy. They screamed at Him in response, *"You make Yourself out to be God!"* (John 10:33). Jesus also claimed to be *"the Son of God"* (John 10:36). This was a technical phrase Jesus used that meant He had the same nature, essence and being as God the Father—in other words it was a claim to deity. For this claim His detractors once again accused Him of blasphemy, for they accurately interpreted Him to be making a claim to deity—equality with God. As God, Jesus is the Creator (John 1:3), all-powerful (Isaiah 9:6), omniscient (John 21:17), sinless (Hebrews 4:15), worthy of worship (Matthew 2:11), and the only way to heaven (John 14:6).

Third, Jesus claimed to be the Judge of every soul! After Jesus healed a man on the Sabbath, the Jewish leaders accused Jesus of breaking the Mosaic Law. Jesus then told them that they had no right to Judge Him, for He was the Judge of all men. On judgment day, the Father won't judge anyone, but Jesus will be the Judge of every soul (John 5:22). On the last day, every soul will appear before Jesus in heaven and they will humbly address Him as, "Lord, Lord" (Matthew 7:21). Then He will render His sovereign, omniscient verdict, consigning them to either eternal life in heaven or to eternal damnation in hell (Matthew 7:23; 25:34).

This is why the Apostle Paul referred to Jesus as the Christ *"who is to judge the living and the dead"* (1 Timothy 4:1). Every human who has ever entered this world, and breathed one breath will inevitably face Jesus Christ as Judge—and His verdict will be just, binding and eternal. Acts 17:30-31 is clear:

> *Therefore having overlooked the times of ignorance, God is now declaring to men that all people everywhere should repent, because He has fixed a day in which He will judge the world in righteousness through a Man whom He has appointed, having furnished proof to all men by raising Him from the dead.*

So from His own lips Jesus made it clear that He was the eternal God and Judge, equal in glory to the Father—a stark contrast from the contrived caricatures and stereotypes posed by His enemies.

*Why Jesus Came*

Scripture is clear about Jesus' identity and it is equally clear about why He came into the world 2,000 years ago. Jesus did not come to simply be a good man or moral example. His main purpose in being born was to die! His death defines the very nature of His ministry.

The first prophecy in the Bible was given 6,000 years ago and it highlights the meaning of Jesus' death (Genesis 3:15). The greatest chapter in the Old Testament is an extended exposition on the meaning and nature of His death (Isaiah 53). All four Gospels accentuate and showcase the act and meaning of Jesus' death. Virtually all twenty-seven books of the New Testament explain Christianity as an application of Jesus' death to the life of a believer. In summarizing the heart of his ministry, Paul said he preached primarily about the death of Jesus—*"we preach Christ crucified"* (1 Corinthians 1:23). And again in Galatians 6:14 he exclaimed, *"But may it never be that I would boast, except in the cross of our Lord Jesus Christ, through which the world has been crucified to me, and I to the world."*

Jesus came to die—but what is the purpose and meaning of His death? The answer to that question is actually the theme of the whole New Testament, and actually the theme of the whole Bible. The meaning of Jesus' death can be summarized in a few purpose statements given in the New Testament.

First of all, Jesus came to die in order to fulfill the will of the Father. Jesus said, *"I have come down from heaven, not to do My own will, but to do the will of Him who sent Me"* (John 6:38). In the night He was betrayed, Jesus knew He was about to die and He prayed to the Father, *"not as I will, but as You will"* (Matthew 26:39). Jesus knew the Father sent Him into the world to die. It was God's plan from eternity past that Jesus would be crucified. Jesus did not die as a helpless victim at the last minute when His plans went awry. It was no surprise that the Jews rejected Him, that one of His Apostles betrayed Him, that the eleven other Apostles scattered when He was arrested, and that He was hung on a tree as an accused criminal. All those things were orchestrated by God the Father before the world existed! God determined that Jesus would die before the foundation of the world (1 Peter 1:20). Jesus' death was God's will. Jesus came to do only God's will. He fulfilled that mission to the last detail.

Second, Jesus came to die to provide a ransom for sinners. In Mark 10:45 Jesus proclaimed about Himself, *"For even the Son of Man did not come to be served, but to serve, and to give His life a ransom for many."* Jesus was the greatest self-less servant that ever graced the planet, as He sacrificially ministered to people wherever He went. But His greatest act of service was His sacrificial death on the cross for sinners. The greatest need people have is forgiveness of their sins before a holy God. That need was satisfied by Jesus' substitutionary death.

Jesus considered His death as a "ransom." A ransom was the price paid to free a slave. According to the Bible, all people are born into this world slaves to sin and Satan. Romans 6:17 says all unbelievers are "slaves of sin." Wickedness, evil and all unholiness have mastery over them, and usually they don't even know it, or they deny and dismiss it.

The Bible also says that non-Christians are slaves of Satan and his demons! Unbelievers live their lives *"according to the prince of the power of the air, of the spirit that is now working in the sons of disobedience"* (Ephesians 2:1). Jesus said all who don't know Him personally are *"slaves to sin"* (John 8:34) and children of the devil (John 8:44). Satan is the false god of this world who supernaturally blinds unbelievers spiritually so that they cannot even perceive reality for what it is (2 Corinthians 4:4).

Because the slavery to sin and Satan is of a supernatural nature, only God has the power to liberate sinners from this spiritual death-grip. As punishment for sin, all people were sentenced with this spiritual death, or separation from God (Romans 5:12-14). And the only thing that can liberate them is a supernatural, heavenly ransom of shed blood. Only death will appease a holy God (Romans 3:23). And Jesus' death is that ransom that satisfied God's requirement.

The ransom that Jesus paid was His perfect life, given sacrificially on the cross in death. And the ransom was paid to the Father, who is a holy God. The Father was satisfied, even pleased with Christ's death and resurrection (Isaiah 53:10). Jesus' substitutionary death provided all that God required to earn forgiveness on behalf of any sinner who trusts in Jesus' death and resurrection. The price of Jesus' death has the power to liberate any sinner from slavery to sin and Satan. Trusting in Christ and His sacrificial work on the cross is the only thing that enables a wretched, evil sinner to become a sinless, holy child of God.

A third reason Jesus came to die was to destroy the works of the devil. Hebrews 2:14 says Jesus became a man so that *"through death He might render powerless him who had the power of death, that is the devil."* Satan is real even though most unbelievers try to deny it. You can say, "I don't believe in gravity!" but you will still splat on the ground if you jump from a ten-story building while repeating that refrain.

Satan is powerful, supernatural, invisible, finite, 100% evil and hell-bent on opposing God, Christ, truth and the gospel (1 Peter 5:8). His most powerful weapon is death. His power of death is delegated to him and limited by God's oversight (Job 1-2). Jesus' death conquered Satan's greatest weapon—death— by rising from the dead three days after His crucifixion. Jesus' substitutionary death and resurrection provides supernatural power for all who believe in Him, providing them eternal life and future bodily resurrection, sounding the final death knell for death once and for all.

A fourth reason Jesus came to die was to rescue sinners. Jesus said, *"The Son of Man has come to seek and to save that which was lost"* (Luke 19:10). The first time Jesus came was NOT for the purpose of condemning sinners—all humans were already condemned because of God's judgment that was previously issued in Genesis 2 and 3. God has already rendered the sentence for sin—*"the wages of sin is death"* (Romans 3:23). God decreed in the Old Testament, *"Behold, all souls are Mine... The soul that sins will die"* (Ezekiel 18:4). What every sinner born today needs is a spiritual, eternal rescue of the soul from sin, Satan, death, the world and eternal hell. And Jesus came 2,000 years ago to fulfill that mission. Jesus came to earth to die for sinners.

This is the same thing John 3:16-17 talks about:

*For God so loved the world, that He gave His only begotten Son, that whoever believes in Him shall not perish, but have eternal life. For God did not*

*send the Son into the world to judge the world,*
*but that the world might be saved through Him.*

In other words, Jesus came to be the Savior of the world. God is holy and must punish sin, but He is also love and has provided a way to rescue sinners from their sin—through Jesus the Savior. "Savior" is actually the meaning of Jesus' name. When Mary was pregnant, an angel of God told Joseph to name the Child "Jesus": *"She will bear a Son; and you shall call His name Jesus, for He will save His people from their sins"* (Matthew 1:21).

As the seeking Savior, Jesus is the one who initiates salvation. He proactively, continuously pursues sinners. As sinners, we never seek after God—our inclination is to run from God (Romans 3:11). That is what Adam and Eve did when they first sinned—they felt guilt, ran from God and hid in the bushes (Genesis 3:7-8). Jesus has been chasing sinners out of the bushes for 2,000 years. And every time Jesus rescues a sinner and they become a born-again, forgiven, saved soul, adopted into the family of God, there is great rejoicing in heaven. The main one celebrating with each rescue is God Himself! (Luke 15:10)

*The Rescued*

The rest of this book is about modern day stories of desperately lost sinners who have been graciously and miraculously rescued by Jesus the Savior. Jesus is the eternal Creator and Judge, equal in power and glory with God the Father and God the Holy Spirit. He left heaven's glory to rescue the lost that He loves. He continues rescuing today. He is *"indeed the Savior of the world"* (John 4:42). He is *"not wishing for any to perish but for all to come to repentance"* (2 Peter 3:9). The invitation He gave 2,000 years ago still stands for anyone who will listen and heed:

> *Come to Me, all who are weary and heavy-laden, and I will give you rest. Take My yoke upon you and learn from Me, for I am gentle and humble in heart, and you will find rest for your souls. For My yoke is easy and My burden is light (Matthew 11:28-30).*

# 2

# *Rescued From Religion*

*"God is spirit, and those who worship*
*Him must worship in spirit and truth"*
*John 4:24*

*I* was born the youngest of ten children into a Roman Catholic home in the heart of south Denver, Colorado—the year was 1966. I spent eighteen years in the same neighborhood, in the same house, in a low to middle-class area. 340 South Sherman was actually dead-center in the middle of an old, traditional Catholic parish.

*All Things Catholic*

My old, Amityville-horror looking, three-story brick house that was built in the late 1800's was less than half a block from the rectory where the priests lived, the convent where the nuns lived, St. Francis Elementary school (where I was educated and began my illustrious sports career), St. Francis high school, the

Catholic social hall and the massive old cathedral-like church building where I attended Mass for the first fifteen years of my life. The Murphys on the left and the Durans on the right side of our house were Catholic. The Murphy's dog, Diablo, was Catholic. Mr. Burke, the city councilman across the street, was Catholic. It seemed like everyone in the neighborhood within a six block radius all attended the same Catholic church we did. Even the produce man at Safeway across the street, my buddy Mark Vigil, was a proud multi-generational Roman Catholic.

On Sunday mornings from 7:30 AM until 1:00 in the afternoon, a non-stop stream of parishioners, dressed in their Sunday best, walked down the sidewalk right in front of our house, shuffling faithfully to and from "Mass." Catholics don't "go to church"—they "go to Mass." I knew many of them by name. And everyone's favorite US President was John F. Kennedy— the only Roman Catholic President in American history. It's no wonder I did not even know what a "Protestant" was until I moved from that neighborhood when I was eighteen as I went off to college.

*My Parents*

My mom grew up in a very devoted Catholic home where the priorities included going to Mass weekly (grandma Miriam went every morning!), fasting during Lent, praying to Mary on the rosary, venerating icons of Mary and the saints that were sprawled around their home, and rooting tirelessly for the *Notre Dame Fighting Irish*, grandpa's *alma mater*. My dad was one of twelve children and grew up in Idaho Springs on a farm in a non-religious home. He converted to Catholicism later in life when he fell for my mom as they met on the dance floor. He was an instructor for the *Arthur Murray Dance Studio* and mom was one of his students—a young, single, beautiful, talented student at that...and very Catholic. She was committed to her religion and dad quickly realized that he would not get the girl without adopting her faith—so he did.

Most Catholics I have known over the years are pretty ignorant, and nonchalant, in their knowledge and approach to their own Catholic faith. Not so with my dad. He actually became a hard-core fanatic for the Catholic faith upon his conversion in his twenties. He figured if it's true, and there was no salvation outside of the Catholic Church, then he should jump in with both feet. He studied all its history and doctrines and embraced all of it with a rare zeal. He tried his best to implement all its requirements, dogmas and decrees. He became very "religious." And he tried to make his family do the same. He sent nine of his ten kids to private Catholic parochial schools at great cost, hard work and sacrifice. The family routinely said the rosary together in the evenings, around his bed, on our knees. During Lent we had to attend Mass daily at the early 6:00 AM service! I hated Lent. Icons and statues of Mary, Joseph and the saints were in every room of the house. A large picture of the "Sacred Heart of Jesus" and the massive, ten pound Catholic Bible (that was rarely touched or opened) were perched front-and-center as holy relics in the family living room for all to see and venerate.

*Rituals*

During Lent we had to "give something up" like chocolate or lying or cussing as a penitent work to shave some years off of the inevitable eons we would spend in the burning fires of purgatory after we died (purgatory comes from the word "purge," "to purify"). I always wanted to "give up" homework, or Lent itself, but that never was received as appropriate. Also during Lent we could not eat meat on Fridays and had to eat fish instead. I hate fish. We had to fast on Sundays for three-plus hours before communion. All six McManis boys were obligated to serve terms as altar boys during the junior high years. The local priest was invited over to the house often to bless the premises with "holy water." All ten McManis kids received the sacraments of infant Baptism, Holy Communion, Penance, and Confirmation. We all had "God-parents" too, whom we inherited when we were eight days old. We did not know them very well as we got older but they always brought cool Christmas presents.

I have vivid memories of solemnly venerating the statues, pictures, icons and crucifixes throughout the house. I shared a bedroom with five of my older siblings, and in our room alone we had an entire five-shelf bookcase with various statues of Catholic saints on it and a crucifix or two. It was a veritable mini-Catholic shrine. We were taught that if at any time, one of the statues of the saints should fall to the ground, then we were to delicately pick up the statue, kiss it, and then reverently put it back on the shelf. Being that we had a full-fledged NERF basketball court set up in our room, with non-stop aerial dunks from the top bunk bed, and continual long-rang three point shots flying through the air, the icons were perpetually flying off the sacred shrine of shelves onto the hard tile floor from errant jump shots and diving, aggressive full-court man-to-man defensive maneuvers.

If an icon broke when it fell then we had to have a funeral for it! My older sister was the funeral coordinator. She'd get a shoe box and put Joseph's head, hammer and other body parts in the box, seal the lid; we'd all dig a hole in the backyard, lower the coffin, cover the body with slate rock to keep our German shepherd from digging it up, pat down the dirt, say a Hail Mary and an Our Father, and then make a cross of twigs and stick it in the ground above the grave. Being about five years old, I always hoped Joseph would get healed or go to heaven some day. We must have buried him five times over the years. Because we were young and trained this way from birth, such sacred, peculiar, fastidious protocol seemed normal to us. We knew nothing different.

## Catholic School

To complement and protect the strict Catholic indoctrination we were receiving at home, we were sent to *Saint Francis de Sales Elementary School* to be educated by the stern Sisters of St. Louis. Conveniently for my parents, the school was two buildings away from our house. Inconveniently, it was private schooling so it cost money, and we were pretty poor. My dad was a self-employed painting contractor, who worked all day six days a week, twelve hours a day. Mom took care of ten children and also worked Monday to Friday from 7:00 am-3:00 in the afternoon as a secretary in the local public school. Both parents had an amazing work ethic that they bequeathed to all of their children. They worked non-stop mostly to make ends meet but also to pay for private Catholic schooling. My dad was philosophically opposed to secular public education.

I had "Religion" as one of my core classes all eight years I attended *St. Francis*. We never studied the Bible in Religion class, but rather Roman Catholic dogma and tradition—man-made religion. The emphasis was on works-righteousness, external behavior modification and guilt, not on God's grace and the need for internal heart transformation. It was in Religion class that I was taught to memorize the "Hail Mary" prayer and a host of other Catholic recitations. I was taught to pray to dead saints. I learned about the seven sacraments, purgatory, mortal and venial sins, and the Pontiff.

I was exposed to Mary's supposed sinlessness, her purported perpetual virginity and that she was to be prayed to, adored and venerated—her approval was key to escaping the fires of a long purgatory. I was told in Religion class that during the Mass the elements (bread and real wine) were literally turned into Jesus' body and blood by the priest when he prayed. That blew me away as a little kid. At the time I believed it.

It was from Sister Grata in second grade Religion class that I was told Mother Theresa was the holiest person who ever lived and that she may be the only person who would ever by-pass purgatory. It was in fourth grade Religion class that Sister Francis told us that the universe was two billion years old and that God used evolution to create Adam and Eve. In sixth grade Religion class the boys were being primed to become altar boys in seventh grade, which I did. The one main perk of being an altar boy was occasionally being excused from Sister Joan's boring math class during the week to serve the priest at an occasional funeral. If Mike Shaw and I timed it right, we'd show up before the priest got to the church and "prepare the elements" for the funeral Mass, and usually be able to pilfer in a few swigs of the sacramental wine before anyone noticed some had been missing. It was in eighth grade Religion class that Sister Eleanor taught us there is no salvation outside of the Roman Catholic Church.

*Religions of the World*

While I was getting systematically educated in all things Catholic at school, things at home were going awry religiously. Between my third and eighth grade years, my older siblings began leaving the Catholic Church one by one as they entered high school. Their parents' faith was not their own. The first time it happened it rocked our house. That was when my oldest sister, at age eighteen, became a Mormon. Then another sister became a Mormon a few years later. That devastated me because my second oldest sister was my best friend at the time—so I became quite confused.

Then the next oldest sister became a Jehovah's Witness. And my oldest brother became a practitioner of Transcendental Meditation (TM) and a devout follower of the Maharishi Mahesh Yogi—the eastern guru who was introduced to America by the Beatles and George Harrison. And another older brother became a black belt in taekwondo and a proponent of Taoism. And another older brother stopped going to church. And another older brother began exploring the various philosophies of the world. In addition, alcohol and marijuana became commonplace behind the scenes. All this seemed to happen within a five to six year period. My dad became angry and felt betrayed by his children. As a young elementary kid who looked up to and loved all my older siblings, I became thoroughly confused about religion...and skeptical. To make it all the more confusing my dad started getting into Dianetics, or Scientology, big time. Ironically, my dad was furious with all the children who compromised their Catholic upbringing but saw not conflict between L. Ron Hubbard's kooky metaphysical musings and his Catholic faith. He believed they complemented each other.

By eighth grade I figured, "If no one in my family can figure out the true religion, then there probably isn't one." So at about that time I became a self-professed agnostic/atheist, and lived accordingly all through my high school years.

*Hoop Dreams*

Upon graduating in eighth grade, I continued my Catholic education under the Jesuit priests, the spiritual descendents of the militant Ignatius of Loyola (1491-1556), of Counter-Reformation fame. I attended a large all-boys high school known for its rigorous academic standards and top-notch athletic program. It was the top school in Colorado, expensive and far from my house. I did not go there for the Catholic education. I had good grades, but I went there for one reason—to play for the top basketball program in the state. By this time basketball had become my god and was quickly replacing Catholicism as my religion of choice.

I was a pretty good point guard by ninth grade and had one goal in life at the time—I wanted to play college hoops. I practiced year-round, several hours every day. Hoops was all-consuming. I also had to figure out a way to pay for my school since my parents had little money. So I made a deal with the school and in the summer before ninth grade they allowed me to work eight hours a day all summer long, every Saturday during the school year, and three days a week after school all year long to work off the tuition. I must have painted every building on that college-size campus by the time I was done...at age fifteen. I did that for about two grueling years...while maintaining a 3.83 G.P.A. And to boot, I had to take the city bus across metropolitan Denver to get here, three-plus hours total every day, rain, snow or shine. But I thought it would all be worth it once I made the hoops team en route to my college career.

Then the day finally arrived—basketball try-outs, October 1981. My high school was so big they had six boys' teams. All ninth graders had to try out and fight for just twelve spots on the freshman team. On the first day seventy guys showed up for tryouts—with the likes of the six-foot-five freshman, Mike Garnett, younger brother to Bill Garnett who was then the six-nine power forward for the Dallas Mavericks! I was overwhelmed. They were mostly rich kids, and here I was, this scrawny unknown "poor white trash." But I believed I wanted it more than any person out there on the court. On day two I made the first cut—down to twenty-two players! The rest of the week I dominated...or so I thought, and several of the other players trying out thought so too.

### Shattered Dreams

The following Monday the names of the twelve who made the team would be posted in the cafeteria for all to see. I was confident I was a shoe-in—probably starting point guard. I'll never forget the literal pain in my gut and the loss of breath I had when I looked at the list of twelve names, written in red ink on a yellow lined piece of paper...and my name was not on it! I stared at it in unbelief for a good ten minutes as others were pushing me, looking over my shoulder trying to read the list. I literally went into shock. I went to *this school* for one reason— to play basketball. And I got cut.... The rest of the day was a fog, and I went reeling emotionally for the next several months. I had no real faith so I had no internal source of strength to help me to recover or deal with the devastating blow. I actually wouldn't recover from this for several years. God used this disappointment to humble me like never before.

## Transfer

After getting cut I began my exit strategy and asked my parents if I could transfer to a smaller Catholic school where I knew some guys on their team so I could play there. They agreed, and so I transferred to a smaller Catholic high school in the east part of Denver. After losing a year of eligibility, I made the team as a junior, became the starting point guard and captain of the team, was BMOC (big man on campus) and ended up being a big fish in a little pond the next two years. We had some talented players and we were very competitive. Basketball-wise, transferring met my goal. As for the rest of my life...it was falling apart and I was spiraling out of control.

Being a Catholic school, I had to have a Religion class at my school as I did in my previous schools. We also had chapel every Wednesday. Since I started high school I became skeptical of the Catholic religion and as time went on I grew incredibly cynical as well. In high school I had categorically rejected "Catholic Christianity." But I had to keep enduring those Religion classes, year after year, going over all the same Catholic dogma and tradition—but never the Bible.

## Immorality

Looking back I am surprised at how secular, and immoral, my two Catholic high schools were. In my school alcohol reigned supreme on the weekends, especially for the juniors and seniors. All the talk during the week was about the big football game Friday night and then where the party would be so everyone could go get hammered on beer. It was shocking when I first became aware of its prevalence as a young, naïve freshman. My new high school was worse! It seemed like all the students (there were only 450 in the school) lived for the weekend, to party, get drunk and engage in immorality. I had guys from my football ball team having illicit liaisons with the female English and Chemistry teachers. And teachers who smoked pot with the students—it was like *Animal House* for teens. I wish I was exaggerating. It was very sad.

Needless to say, in that kind of overtly profligate environment my moral, spiritual and thought life plummeted to rock-bottom. I tried to find my identity while at my new school, tinkering with almost everything at least once. I tried hanging with the "cool" kids—but they were too cool, and too shallow, for me. I tried a short stint of hanging with the academic nerds, but they were too boring and didn't like sports. I tried alcohol and got drunk once when I was seventeen, to the point of passing out—I decided never to do that again. And I didn't. But, not because it was immoral and a sin (Ephesians 5:18), but because it would undermine my athletic career and my pursuit toward college hoops.

God actually used basketball to providentially protect me from destroying myself through alcohol, drugs and immorality like all my peers seemed to be doing. I needed to stay focused, healthy and disciplined for basketball competition. One example of this providential protection stands out—April of my senior year in high school. I went to visit the Catholic *Benedictine College* in Atchison, Kansas on a basketball recruiting trip. After the first work-out on Saturday morning with the *Benedictine* varsity players they all escorted me over to student housing to "show me dorm life." We all crammed into one of the player's rooms. Someone promptly shut the door behind us and locked it. Another player quickly grabbed a towel and stuffed it in the crack under the door, so that the room became air-tight and hermetically sealed. A couple others opened the small fridge and started passing out the Budweiser while a couple other players got the marijuana bong out, filled, lit and ready for puffing. It went swiftly around the semi-circle of players, as each one enthusiastically took a big "huff"...and then it got to me. I was shocked. I declined the booze and the weed and told them I'd like to leave. They recognized my fear and quickly started spraying Lysol into the air and on our clothes and let me go. Right there on the spot I knew I would not be going to that school to play college hoops—these guys were not serious about basketball, but were very serious about partying and "livin' the college life."

*Romance*

My senior year I had my first actual girlfriend. She was a sophomore volleyball player. Prior to that time I never really had a girlfriend because my school was an all-boys school, I was grotesquely self-conscious and introverted, and I was actually quite homely looking—mostly because since birth I had always appeared anorexic. My mom called me "skinny bones" my whole life, and for good reason. I was scary skinny. But drinking protein shakes and working out religiously for four years during high school started to pay off finally in my senior year when I began to look somewhat like a normal, fully developed *homo sapien*—at least my girlfriend thought so.

We dated for three months. I was totally infatuated with her and I thought she was the "one" for me. But the feelings weren't mutual and she dropped me like a hot rock after three months and started dating some other guy (with bigger muscles) behind my back. When I found out I was devastated. Almost to the same degree as when I got cut from the team in my school.

This was the second major blow in my life that God used to humble me and show me that there would be no fulfillment in this life apart from a personal relationship with Him. But at the time I did not see that so I continued to turn my back on God, calling myself an atheist. I also went into a short time of severe depression because of the rejection from my girlfriend. It is the one and only time in my life I remember crying and heaving in my mom's arms for an extended period of time as she helplessly tried to make me feel better, not knowing what to say to console me. I was eighteen. I would be reeling emotionally over the next year as a result.

### Invasion of the Gospel

When I was seventeen I met a guy named Paul while playing a pick-up game of hoops. He was six feet four, ten years older than me, incredibly friendly and extroverted, an amazing shooter and an evangelist. Through a mutual friend we ended up playing hoops a lot together. He had a heart for me, saw himself in me, and made me his project "for Jesus." Over time he shared his faith in Christ with me, his love for the Bible and genuinely cared for me. He had a unique sense of purpose, joy and peace I had never really seen before—he was different. I wanted to be just like him and I wanted what he had. But at the time, I did not know that that would mean denying myself, taking up my cross, and following Jesus (Matthew 16:24).

It turns out that "Tall Paul" grew up in a Catholic home similar to mine, loved hoops, and even went to the same high school I was attending. He had a great sense of humor, as did I. And he liked to have clean, silly fun, even at age twenty-seven. Within six months of our friendship he shared the gospel of Jesus Christ with me. I had never heard it before! I was seventeen and had never heard the biblical gospel. I knew in my gut and in my soul that it was true the first time he explained it. I knew I was a wicked sinner (Romans 3:23), I knew God was real and my Creator (Romans 1:19-20), I knew that Jesus was Lord and Judge (Romans 10:9-10), I knew that I could not get to heaven apart from Christ (John 14:6), and I knew the Bible he was quoting from was true.

But EVERY TIME he would ask, "So Cliff, since you believe all these things, would you like to pray to Christ and ask Him to come into your life and save you from your sins?"

And I would say, EVERY TIME, without hesitation, "No, not now." He was amazingly patient with me. I said "No" because I wanted to remain as lord of my life and I did not want to give up my sin—even though I knew the truth. I was the person in Romans 1 who Paul describes to a T: *they knew God, but did not honor Him as God.* I was like the demons, who know God exists and even shudder, but refuse to bow the knee to Him because of their love for evil (James 2:19). Paul kept praying for me, loving me, being patient, sharing his testimony and being a Christ-like example to me. Then he started dating my sister.... She was a new believer. So they both started praying for me.

Paul was involved with various sports outreach ministries, including *Athletes In Action (AIA)* and the *Fellowship of Christian Athletes (FCA).* At the end of my senior year in high school Paul invited me to a large, two day high school *FCA* evangelistic sports camp in beautiful Estes Park, Colorado. I reluctantly agreed to go. I won the free-throw competition there, but I had a rotten attitude the entire time. I was subjected to several evangelistic messages over the course of two days and was very uncomfortable hearing them. God's truth was convicting my wicked heart...and I did not like it. I was in Paul's "huddle," or discipleship group, of about seven other high school boys that he met with for prayer and discussion three times a day—I refused to participate. I sat on the top bunk and watched them as they met down on the floor being all "religious."

I distinctly remember the main message on the last day with eight-hundred of us teens in the audience, as a famous Christian athlete gave his testimony and "preached" from the Bible. I don't remember what he talked about, but I do remember going to the very back of the facility, literally in the last row, where I mocked him the entire time he was talking. I was being sarcastic, insulting and cutting—I thought it was funny. I can't believe now what utter, hard-hearted mockery I was spewing from my mouth in disbelief as the faithful servant of God preached the gospel and God's Word. God, in His mercy, did not strike me down dead on the spot for being a blasphemer—although I deserved it. God, and "Tall Paul," continued to be patient with me.

### College Hoops

In His goodness, God allowed me to go to *Westmont College* in Santa Barbara, California where I hoped to play college hoops. It was a Christian college and I had no business going there— by this time I was thoroughly worldly and wild. Pretty much had a seared conscience. In September, 1985 I tried out and

made the team! The head coach was the highly respected Chet
Kammerer. Chet was a solid believer and eventually went on to
be an assistant for the *Lakers* and is currently the Vice President
for Player Personnel with the Miami Heat. Coach Kammerer
welcomed me to the team as a walk-on and said I would have to
keep working hard year-round to earn playing time. He said I
had the potential to make it happen.

But I did not want to "work hard." I had a new-found freedom
in college that I did not have growing up in a strict, religious
Catholic home, and so I wanted to have fun. And I did. I went
back to Coach Chet the next day and told him I did not want to
play but wanted to focus on other things. So I quit. To this day
I believe that was one of the dumbest decisions I ever made in
my life.

I did have fun, but only for a short time. For the next
month I had so much fun, staying up all night, ditching all my
classes, ditching chapel, hanging with friends on the weekends,
frequenting the beach minutes away, daily pulling pranks on
fellow dorm mates—I thought it was "camp" *Westmont*, instead
of an academic institution to which I was paying big bucks in
order to earn a degree. The pranks got so out of control that
I got busted by the Resident Director, was put on probation,
and had to do work-duty for two weeks as my punishment. If I
messed up again then I'd have to withdraw from the school. It
was pretty humbling.

*Athletes In Action*

It was November 1st, 1985, 7:30 PM and the *Westmont
Warriors* were hosting the *Athletes In Action (AIA)* men's
basketball team for the first game of the season. I was not suited

up for the home-opener because I quit three weeks prior to what could have been my first collegiate game. I was in the crowd though because I loved to watch basketball and I also had my tail between my legs after getting put on probation. I did not want to get kicked out of school. The *AIA* team was composed of former NCAA Division 1 players who all knew Jesus Christ personally. They were a Christian evangelistic basketball team. It intrigued me because guys like Reid Gettys were on the team. Gettys was the six-seven, dead-eye shooter who played for the Houston Cougars alongside Akeem Olajuwan and Clyde the Glide Drexler—"Phi Slamma Jamma." He was drafted by the Chicago Bulls one year after Jordan. And there were other big-time studs on Reid's *AIA* team that thoroughly impressed me.

*AIA* went on to beat *Westmont*, but at half-time I was caught off guard when several of the *AIA* players talked the entire time on a microphone for twenty minutes at center court. They gave their testimonies, telling us how Jesus saved them and meant everything to them and that all of us students needed to repent and believe in Jesus too for the forgiveness of sins and entrance into heaven. I was awe-struck. These guys were not sissies, but studs of the first order. I was speechless when they finished. Unlike my senior year in high school at the *FCA* camp when I mocked the preacher, this time I said nothing but listened intently.

*Preacher Man*

After the final buzzer I talked briefly with some friends and then headed down on the court toward the front exit...when out of the blue came a deep, thundering, authoritative voice some fifteen feet away, beckoning me. It was one of the *AIA* players. When I quickly turned to look at him, he fixed his eyes on me and demanded, "Come on over here, boy, and listen to my testimony!" I sheepishly complied because he was huge, and muscular, and intimidating. He had a circle of about twenty other students around him as he was open-air preaching on the gym floor. I was amazed by his testimony as he went on preaching for another ten minutes after I joined the circle. He then made a call for repentance and dismissed the crowd. After everyone left I approached him and asked him some follow up questions.

We talked for another ten minutes and then he said, "Son, I need to go to the locker room before the bus leaves me behind. If you want to keep on talkin' then follow me." So we headed for the locker room and we talked some more about Christ, the Bible, sin, salvation, the devil, heaven, hell. Finally, he cut to the chase and went for the jugular and asked, "Do you believe everything I'm tellin' you?"

I said, "Yes."

Then he said, "Well, then you need to ask Christ to come into your life and save you and change you. You need to repent to Him and believe in Him. We can do that right now in a prayer. How 'bout if I lead you in a prayer to Jesus."

I said, "Yes!"

And so he prayed up a storm and I prayed a short prayer too, asking Jesus to save me. Instantly I was supernaturally changed—I literally felt or experienced the difference. Invisible spiritual blinders fell off my eyes and I was suddenly overwhelmed with a peace and joy I had never experienced in my life. I was nineteen years, one month and twenty-eight days old that moment when I was born again at 10:17 pm in the smelly locker room of *Westmont College* in Santa Barbara, California.

The preacher, or evangel, that night who preached the gospel to me was Calvin Duncan, the star all-American basketball player from *Virginia Commonwealth University.* He was drafted by the Chicago Bulls in 1985 (one year after Michael Jordan) and was offered $800,000 a year...but declined the offer to join *AIA* and go "preach for Jesus" where there were eternal, heavenly rewards and riches! After praying with Calvin, I felt like I could fly. I ran upstairs, ran through the gym, tears coming down my face, no one around, happier than I had ever been in my life. I ran back to my dorm room and hunted down every born-again student I could find telling them I just got saved. It was awesome!

*Rescued*

Through the power of the simple gospel of Jesus, God had made me a totally new creature just as He promised in His Word (2 Corinthians 5:17). "Tall Paul" had been praying for two-plus years after he first shared the complete gospel with me in high school, and it had finally come to fruition. My transformation was dramatic, day and night—an instant, radical one-eighty. Everyone who knew me previously instantly saw the difference. As a brand new believer I immediately had a voracious appetite for reading the Bible—and that's what I did for hours on end, every day for the next several months. I had to make up lost ground for wasting nineteen years of my life. And Roman Catholicism created an appetite for religion and faith but could not fill the void, so I felt religiously anorexic needing pure spiritual milk and meat from God's Word so that I could grow and mature.

I read the whole Bible from cover to cover. It was glorious! It fed my soul, opened my eyes, gave me joy, convicted my heart and provided practical wisdom for living. With a first-time, fresh read through the Bible a few things struck me in significant ways. One was that it was clear that I could not save myself; I could not do any good deeds to eradicate my sin, assuage a holy God or earn salvation. Unlike what the Catholic Church taught me, salvation was a gift from God, initiated by Him through the truth of Scripture and applied to the heart through the work of the Holy Spirit. Ephesians 2:8-9 quickly became a favorite passage for me. And so was Titus 3:5-6 which says,

> He saved us, not on the basis of deeds which we have done in righteousness, but according to His mercy, by the washing of regeneration and renewing by the Holy Spirit, Whom He poured out upon us richly through Jesus Christ our Lord.

In addition to learning that salvation was by grace and not through human works, I also learned that I had salvation now in this life, and I could be secure in that truth. Catholicism teaches that no one can know in this life the certainty of salvation. But Scripture is crystal clear that if you are truly saved, then you can know that with iron-clad certainty and assurance right now:

> He who has the Son has life; he who does not have the Son of God does not have life. These things I [John the Apostle] have written to you who believe in the name of the Son of God, so that you may know that you have eternal life (1 John 5:12-13).

I also learned that praying to Mary, statues and dead people was idolatry and a sin condemned by the Bible (Exodus 20:4-5; Deuteronomy 18:11-12; Isaiah 26:14). I was surprised how little the Bible says about Mary—as a Catholic I was taught to believe that she was pre-eminent. I was shocked to learn that Mary was a sinner and had other children after Jesus was born. Those are just a few examples of how the Bible set my thinking free.

Since salvation God has been continually growing me, refining me and molding me. He has blessed me by giving me a believing and faithful wife and four blessed children. He gave me the privilege of going to *The Master's College* and *The Master's Seminary* where I was able to study the Bible under dozens of godly mentors to help prepare me for life and vocational ministry. Though I walk with feet of clay, and am a finite and fallen sinner still, God has allowed me to teach His Word in many different venues, as a seminary professor, as a missionary around the world, and the highest privilege of all—being one of His under-shepherds in the local church where I feed His sheep alongside fellow under-shepherds.

I thank the Father for sending His Son into the world 2,000 years ago to seek and to save sinners, and I thank God Jesus found and rescued me.

# 3

# *A Higher Wisdom*

*"For as the heavens are higher
than the earth, so are My ways
higher than your ways and My
thoughts than your thoughts"
Isaiah 55:9*

**M**y name is Anne and I was born in Minneapolis, Minnesota, where both my parents were born and raised. In their youth my parents attended one of the many Lutheran churches scattered throughout the city. Both their families stayed true to their Scandinavian culture and had their children confirmed and married in their local Lutheran parish. When my parents began their married life they dropped their participation in church, so my brother and I grew up un-churched in our early years.

My only memory of church was attending a beautiful towering, stained-glass Lutheran church with my aunt and uncle when I would have sleep-overs with their two daughters who were the same age as me. I was in awe of the beauty and vastness of the place and enjoyed attending with my cousins.

## Growing Up

My next memory of church was when my grandmother visited us for a few weeks after my grandpa died. By this time we had already shocked our extended family by leaving the generational nest in Minneapolis and moving to San Jose, California in the 1970's so my dad could pursue his career in computers. Grandma insisted on getting my brother and me to church while she was there and so we walked every Sunday to a neighborhood church where Grandma left us at the Sunday school classroom while she attended the main service. The class was run just like my fifth grade class at school, homework and all, so I quickly decided that was *not* for me. When Grandma left, I did not return.

When I started high school, my parents decided to join a church. They were worried about how "wild" California high schools were and decided it would be good for me and my brother to be in church. Having just moved to Santa Clara, California, my parents were looking to meet new people, too, so we joined the nearby Presbyterian Church.

The youth group was fun and it was an easier way to meet new friends than in my large high school. Soon the youth group leader took me down to the kitchen basement, gave me a Bible and asked if I wanted to accept Jesus as Savior. I said "Yes," and we prayed. I took my Bible home and was satisfied I was now a Christian and part of "the group." My life remained unchanged and my whole motivation for attending church continued to be entirely social. When I would hear about the older kids partying with alcohol and pot after youth group I did not see much conflict in it.

My second year of high school I joined the cheerleading squad. For the first time in my ten years of schooling I received the attention of others, especially when I wore my short-skirted cheerleader outfit to school to advertise for the football game that day. My social circle enlarged. I was very pleased with the way life was going.

### Blessed Evangelists

The only thing I was uncomfortable with was these two girls at school who would repeatedly invite me to an on-campus Bible study during lunch. I politely declined but they would not stop inviting me. I had no interest in going; they met in the cafeteria sitting in a circle of chairs in front of everybody! "Somebody might see me there!" I thought. Still, they were incredibly kind girls and I felt bad about continually refusing them. Then one day the girls told me that a teacher had offered her classroom for their Bible study. Would I consider going now? I felt I should go at least once, just to be nice, especially since the Bible study was now private and I could attend without worrying about others seeing me. I found I liked the group. The students were kind and sincere; I was drawn to them.

One week, half way through the year, one of the girls who attended the lunch-time Bible study offered to pick me up on a Tuesday night to join them at their youth group. Upon arriving, we squeezed into a huge room with some 400 high school and college kids. When worship started I stood frozen in shock. I was surrounded by hundreds of kids who were raising their arms and worshipping their hearts out. At my youth group most of the kids kicked back and were "too cool" to sing along with the leader. These students didn't care who saw them or what people thought, they loved Jesus with abandon. I remained wholly overwhelmed the entire evening. But I left hooked. I couldn't wait to go back!

*Convicted*

When summer started I accepted an invitation to attend an outdoor Christian conference called "Jesus, West Coast." We camped out for two nights and my dad, unsure about this Christian event and the fact it was a group of boys *and* girls, came along to supervise. The second night we were enjoying the music and preaching and were rather sad to be going home the next day. I was especially excited to hear the band about to come up after the speaker of the evening and wished he would finish his message, when suddenly out of the blue, in my head, I clearly heard the words, "Anne, you need to be saved." Like a tree I stood rooted to the spot. "What?" I thought to myself. In the span of a second or two I created a mental religious checklist: attending church-check; had a Bible-check; at a Christian conference-check. "What more was there for me to do to be saved?"

With gentleness, I heard the words again, "Anne, you need to be saved." And God in His mercy gave me understanding. I had never accepted Jesus as my LORD and SAVIOR. Up until this moment HE had been my avenue of social connection, of fulfilling the need to be part of a group, of feeling good about myself. In an instant I understood I was missing the boat big time. God loved ME and was offering HIMSELF to Me! I was LOST without HIM and didn't realize it! It was an epiphany moment for me that changed the course of my eternity. I began to sob over the enormity of God's love. For Jesus to personally reach out and make Himself known to me, an unremarkable, selfish sixteen-year-old year old girl. My group of friends surrounded me in my tears. "What's wrong?" they asked nervously.

"I am saved!" I choked out. And truly, I was transformed. When I walked out of that place I saw with new eyes, comprehended my world with new understanding, and left a changed person. At my old Presbyterian youth group I shared my salvation experience, and at school in the fall I talked about the Lord with whoever would listen. At home I cleaned out my room, filling a bag full of books, music and other belongings that no longer reflected my new life. I read my Bible daily and relished it! Some of my high school and Presbyterian youth group friends decided I had experienced some weird spiritual "high" at the conference but would be back to "normal" in no time. By God's grace, my skeptical friends were wrong and I did not revert back to my old ways. I continued to follow Christ.

*Family Life*

Four years after salvation I married my husband DJ, a native of Mountain View, California. The testimony of God's grace in my life is not just about how He saved me at age sixteen, but also how He has worked in me and sustained me after salvation over three decades of being a wife and mother. After marriage, DJ and I soon had Christa, our oldest child; then came Mark, Grant, Scott, then Tryna, my baby girl who lived only ten days. She was born with half a heart. Then came Erik, and Ryan. Not to be forgotten are the two babies lost during pregnancy. So after nine pregnancies and seven births I have five surviving children. Sounds like a hundred years ago, doesn't it?

When my second child was born I was overwhelmed with love for this little boy just as I was when my daughter was born. The intensity of my love for my children amazed me. With that love I suddenly had a fear just as intense. What if something happened to them? How could I ever bear it? I tried not to think about it. Little did I know that in the future, not only would I experience the loss of two babies through miscarriage but I would bury two more children.

### Baby Tryna

When I was in my mid-thirties I was half way through my fifth pregnancy. My other children were ten, eight, five, and two-and-a-half. My husband and I were having a routine ultra-sound of our baby. It was a girl! We were thrilled! Our ten year-old was the only girl and she had been praying for a sister through all three of her brothers' births. Then the tech passed over her little heart. Our minds did not want to acknowledge what our eyes could see. Our baby had only two chambers to her heart. The diagnosis was death within forty-eight hours of her birth or sooner. The top heart surgeon on the west coast at that time came to the same conclusion after extensive study of her heart. Heart transplant, for complicated reasons was not an option. This was the beginning of my boot camp of faith.

First, my husband and I did what we knew to do; we prayed. We asked others to pray. We begged God daily to heal our daughter and we cried. As my stomach grew and I was faced with all the usual comments of, "Congratulations!" and "How exciting," I was dying on the inside. One evening in my regular cry sessions in the shower I told God I could not endure it. This was too hard.

This is where Jesus extended His hand of love. I saw in my head a flashback of me and my dad when I was a little girl. My feet were standing on his feet with my little arms wrapped around his legs as he walked around the room. With this picture, I heard in my heart the Lord say, "I know this is too hard for you. Step up on my feet and hold on, I will do the walking."

Jesus knew I couldn't bear this; He knew I needed assurance of His love to trust Him in my pain. And that was what He gave me. I clung to this picture of me with my feet on His feet and my arms wrapped around His legs. It gave me comfort and helped me to bear those days. At that time I clung to the promise of 1 John 4:18, *The Living Bible Translation* reads,

> *We need have no fear of someone who loves us perfectly; his perfect love for us eliminates all dread of what he might do to us. If we are afraid, it is for fear of what he might do to us and shows that we are not fully convinced that he really loves us.*

In the midst of all those difficult days, my dread did leave me. I trusted in that picture of Jesus' tender love for me and His understanding of how weak I was. But I fiercely *did not* give up hope for my daughter's life.

When baby Tryna was born we continued to pray for her healing. I can still see my husband walking around our house with our baby in his arms praying out loud, sometimes *loudly* for hours and hours asking the Lord to heal our precious little girl. Tryna lived ten days and died in our home, in my husband's arms with me talking words of love and stroking her little face. This is where my boot camp of faith got harder.

The morning after she died, lying in bed with my breasts engorged with milk and no baby to nurse, my grief felt like a thousand pound blanket. All I wanted to do was imagine that she wasn't dead and all the joy I would be having. It was Christmas Eve. We planned to take family pictures. I had a darling Christmas dress picked out for her, and on and on my wishing went. These imaginings plagued me in the days that followed. I wanted my baby back and I couldn't let go.

*Divine Comfort*

This is where Jesus, whom I knew loved me, extended His hand of counsel. I imagined a picture of a large, very deep, dry well with a bench at the bottom. I had put that bench there and I was resolutely sitting on it. It was my 'well of wishing things were different.' I also saw a ladder extending all the way to the top. Jesus had put it there and He was leaning down over the edge and encouraging me to climb out. Again, He had given me what I needed, but receiving that help was a whole lot harder. When Tryna was alive I had hope the worst would not happen. Now my heart was broken and there was no fixing the outcome. At first I could not climb that ladder which I termed the "ladder of acceptance." I came to understand that I needed to know *not only* that Jesus loves me; I needed to *accept* God's sovereignty by trusting His wisdom. That ladder in my "wishing well" represented steps of acceptance and in that acceptance was peace.

Sometimes I would get part way up the ladder and feel some peace with God and what He had allowed to happen and then I would waver and be right back down in my well of wishing things were different. Sometimes I flatly refused to even try to climb that ladder because that meant letting go of what I wanted and accepting God's sovereignty in a way I did not want to. If I chose to trust God to the point of accepting even the death of my child, what else did He have planned for me? I did not want to give up that much control. I slowly came to realize I needed to know *in my whole being* the depth of God's love which enabled me to let go of the plans I wanted and accept His sovereignty no matter how painful. Remember our verse, *"If we are afraid, it is for fear of what He might do to us and shows that we are not fully convinced that He really loves us."*

I will be honest with you. I climbed up and down that ladder thousands of times and have spent much time on that bench. But Jesus never gave up beckoning me to climb out of that well, every tiny bit of progress I made I could feel His pleasure and encouragement. Jesus wanted me to climb that ladder of acceptance for my good because of His love for me.

I learned that as long as I wrestled with control of my life, I shortchanged myself on the peace that surpasses understanding (Philippians 4:7). Jesus did love me, I could trust Him; I did not have to be afraid. I made it my aim not only to accept God's complete sovereignty but truly to be at peace with it. I eventually did come to peace with it. This did not mean I stopped longing to be with my daughter or stop missing her. It is God's way for mothers to love and long to be with their children, but I was at rest with her death and accepted it without wishing my story were different.

## Greater Challenges

Eight years after Tryna died, in January 2005, our delightful and talented thirteen-year-old son, Grant, was diagnosed with cancer behind his left knee—an incredibly rare cancer that few had ever seen and even fewer had recovered from long term. Our doctor at Kaiser was very honest. The cancer was called Synovial Cell Sarcoma and was not always responsive to treatment. Even when it was, the cancer often came back. We resisted this diagnosis. We knew God could do miracles. Our daughter Christa had been miraculously healed of an incurable liver disease when she was nine, astounding the doctors at Kaiser Hospital and Stanford. That is another story.

Days before, just two hours before the lab called to confirm the cancer, Grant came to me and said, "Mom, God just spoke to me!" Grant had never said this to me before. Grant told me God impressed upon him that it *was* cancer, but that he would be *ok*. I was stunned. Teenagers always believe that nothing terrible will happen to them, even when they act stupid. Especially teen boys! So we started chemo. Because the cancer was bad, we were told the treatment would make Grant very sick. This was an understatement. He was in the hospital two out of every three weeks. The first week he had chemo; the second week he was so sick he had to be on IV fluids and antibiotics and the third week he was home to recover. Then repeat. DJ and I swapped sleeping at the hospital and spending time with him during the day. We had the family in as much as possible as Grant liked having family with him.

By the end of May it was obvious that the chemo was only marginally working. It was killing the cancer cells but the tumor was still significant so, as we were expecting, the doctors suggested that Grant's left leg be amputated above the knee for the best odds at eliminating the cancer. We told Grant this had to be his decision as he would have to live with it the rest of his life. He was completely for it. He wanted to live and if this was the best chance for that—the leg had to go. He was given a few weeks to strengthen his chemo-ravaged body and in June his leg was amputated.

The day after Grant lost his leg he asked for Scott to come. Scott was his closest sibling and inseparable best friend. Scott would often spend eight to ten hours at the hospital with Grant. As homeschoolers, the two had always done everything together. Walking through cancer was no different. By the third day Scott was wheeling Grant through the hospital doing 360's!

*Courageous Faith*

This is the extraordinary part. Grant never complained or pitied himself. Not when he lost his hair, not when he became skeletal and so weak he could not sit up without help. Not when he lost his leg. Grant did not even complain to DJ and me in private. This was astonishing to DJ and me and we often commented on it to ourselves. How could a teenager experience such unspeakable suffering and loss and not complain? This had to be a supernatural gift of the Holy Spirit. He is called our Helper (John 14:26) and this is the most dramatic demonstration of help I'd witnessed myself.

By day four we were home with Grant on crutches. Within an hour of arriving home, DJ's dad came by to take the cousins and siblings out to fast food for lunch. I asked Grant if he would like to go. He thought about it and said, "Well, everyone will see me one-legged sooner or later, I might as well get it over with."

I said, "Now Grant, people will stare. How many one-legged people have you seen?"

His response was, "I might as well get used to it." So off he went. Grant was completely forward thinking. He did not look back. Not an hour, not a day. There were no "what ifs" and no "if onlys." It was amazing for me to see—especially as his mother. I asked Grant how he managed to stay positive and uncomplaining.

He said, "Mom, I only focus on what I can do something about."

I had long tried to do this but here was this thirteen-year-old kid actually living it in the most difficult and uncertain circumstances. He really did focus only on what he could do and not what he could do nothing about.

Within a few weeks we were back doing chemo. Grant's suffering is too difficult to describe. Having to deal with the pain of amputation, his phantom foot pains were horrendous, and the vomiting and weakness of chemo. I cannot think on it for more than a few moments. Still Grant did not complain. He lived in the present and embraced even the smallest pleasures such as a visit from a brother or sister or guessing the words on "Wheel of Fortune." We found out daytime TV really does stink except for "Wheel" and "Jeopardy."

By August he had a simple prosthetic leg and all the chemo his body could handle for a lifetime without doing damage to his heart. We had a break. Grant dived into life. His prosthetic leg was good only for walking on level ground so often he went with crutches. He helped at *Vacation Bible School* and *AWANA* and went boogie-boarding at the beach. On his flute he decided to learn the music scores for "Pirates of the Caribbean" and "Lord of the Rings." He taught himself guitar. We went on a long postponed family vacation to Yellowstone and the Grand

Tetons. Grant hiked, climbed, and swam as fast as his siblings. I often heard passersby comment, "Did you see that one-legged kid? Can you believe he passed me up!"

For a time Grant appeared cancer free. We had a party. Grant took up hand-bells to replace the youth musicals where he could no longer dance. He learned to trampoline, climb a tree, dive off the high dive at our local public pool and ride a bike all on one leg. Grant cherished life and poured love and gratitude into his family and the Lord. His hair grew back and he liked it better than his old hair.

## Continuing the Battle

Then came spring of 2006. Grant's oncologist called. His latest scan showed tumors in the lungs. A few very tough cancer cells had simply scurried off, hidden and then traveled to the lungs where blood and oxygen was well supplied. There would be no medical cure, yet Grant continued with life unfazed. There were new drugs that could possibly slow or stunt tumor growth for years. Again, Grant was all for it as long as it did not make him so sick he could not enjoy life. He wanted to live. This meant clinic treatments Monday, Wednesday and Friday for three to four hours.

He eventually had three lung surgeries to remove the tumors. Grant continued to live life with a mission; a life filled with service to God through *VBS* and *AWANA* and in the community where he volunteered weekly at El Camino Hospital. He interviewed at the YMCA and became their first one-legged swim instructor. He advanced to the adult bell choir at Valley Church in Cupertino. He got his driver's license and decided to take some classes at *Foothill Junior College*. He continued with flute lessons and put on mini-recitals for the family.

We were on our knees imploring God to give us one more miracle and preserve Grant's life. He had fought so hard to live and lived so vivaciously in spite of crippling surgeries and treatments. We went to many church meetings and asked for healing. Grant grew more abandoned to God, lifting his hands in worship and prayer. He held no bitterness. He focused entirely on today and tomorrow and left his fate completely to God. Still he wanted to live. He wanted to live.

In the summer after his junior year of high school we said he could get a dog. This had been a desire of his for many years. At the end of two tiring weeks of *VBS* we picked up the *shih tzu* ("lion dog" in Chinese) puppy of his choice. He named her *Suki* which is a Japanese term of affection that is sometimes used as a nickname like a nurse Grant had during treatments. Friday afternoon we picked out collars, her food dish, and other supplies. We had fun. Then Grant went for a check-up with dad. Everything on the EKG and blood counts looked good. His cancer was still progressing despite his clinic treatment, but presently he seemed healthy overall.

When he went to bed that night I came in and kissed him, laid my hands on his chest and prayed. That was the last time I looked into his eyes or spoke with him. About 4:00 AM I got up to use the restroom and, as Scott was away at camp, I decided to peek in on Grant. He was in his usual sleeping position, but I could not hear his gentle snore. I came up close. He was still warm, but did not stir when I gently shook his shoulder. I half wailed and half yelled. DJ shot out of the bedroom and so did

Mark. I told Mark to call 911. Within minutes the paramedics were there. Grant wanted to live.

I needed to know there was no possibility he could be revived. We were ushered out and when his room quieted down, I poked my head in the door and asked, "Is there any hope?"

The medic responded, "No Ma'am, there is no hope." They left. I laid across Grant and hugged and kissed him and talked to him. Grandparents and family members did the same. When everyone felt they had enough time, we called the coroners and they wheeled his body away on a stretcher. I went in and laid on Grant's bed and sobbed for three days, saying his name over and over again. When I got up, I could no longer read. Somehow that gradual aging of the eyes that makes it hard to read had happened in three days. I never regained that vision.

*Sorrow and Loss*

My grief was so deep I questioned how I could live the rest of my life with such sorrow. I had walked this road with baby Tryna but she died at ten days old. Grant was weeks away from his seventeenth birthday. I could not bear the reality of living without my son in my life after such a long time. This is where God remains faithful.

How did Grant do it? For three-and-a-half years every worst-case scenario happened to him over and over again. I realized Grant's hope was not in his circumstances. His hope was in *Who God is*—that God is good. That He loves us, and that His wisdom is higher than ours. Grant chose faith and hope no matter what. I had to choose the same. What was the alternative, to live a life in despair and heartbreak? What would that do to my kids, my neighbors? I wanted them to experience a God who could carry them through any nightmare like He had for Grant. The people in and outside my family would surely experience heartbreak and loss sometime in their lives. I wanted them to turn confidently to God. Also, my other kids needed a mother, a mother who was there for them physically and emotionally. How could I short-change them? They had already lost a brother and a sister. I wanted my remaining kids to live godly, happy, emotionally healthy lives. I could not wallow in how I felt. I had to live life above my shattered hopes and heartbreak. This is my journey now. I choose faith and hope. *I choose it.* God is good. He loves me. His wisdom is higher than mine.

### Sustaining Grace

Life after Grant's death has been hard. My sorrow was so intense at first I dealt with flu symptoms on and off for over a year before I realized it wasn't the flu. It was my physical reaction to deep loss. Now it is bouts of intense fatigue. Yet, I smile at my kids and husband. I plan fun activities. I continue to serve at the church. I cook and bake and share with my neighbors. But it is not by my strength I do this. Not by a long shot. It is living the power of 2 Corinthians 5:7: *"We walk by faith and **not** by sight."* I choose faith and hope.

Romans 5:5 says, *"and hope does not disappoint because the love of God has been poured out within our hearts through the Holy Spirit who was given to us."* How can I say that? My hope to see Grant grow up and have a full life was terribly disappointed. I face daily the disappointment of seeing Scott grow up without his best friend, of never seeing Grant or hearing his voice. The disappointment of holidays, family photos, birthdays and more without Grant. But I remind myself. I *tell* myself, "Where does my hope lie? Does it lie in the circumstances of my life, or the lives of my family? Does it lie in what I hope will happen or what I hope won't happen. Is my hope in my spiritual or physical strength to accomplish what I want in my life? If that is the case then my hope has been unilaterally squashed, *repeatedly*! No. I choose to place my hope and faith in Who God IS. He is good. He loves me. His wisdom is higher than mine." This hope got Grant through every devastating loss till he woke up in Heaven. This hope has power. This hope never changes.

Many have said, "Oh you have gone through so much, I hope life gets easier for you." I anticipate no such thing. All four of our aging parents are nearby and will soon require our help. My husband has pain issues that often keep him flat on his back. When my daughter died I prayed, "Please, God never let me go through this again." I have learned...*finally*...not to place my hope where hope is uncertain—where hopes may fail and disappoint. I place my hope only in *Who God is*: God is good. He loves me. His wisdom is higher than mine. Come what may, no matter what. This hope will not fail. My faith will not be shaken. God is good. He loves me. His wisdom is higher than mine.

I am still in awe of the depth of God's love for me, for all of humanity, and I am even more grateful than ever to my beloved Savior. Now married almost thirty years, and on my twenty-eighth year of raising a houseful of children, I have been serving the children of my church since my firstborn went into the nursery, hoping to make an impact on those who are "hearing" but not "understanding" the love and transforming power of God's plan of salvation.

# 4

# *No Soldier Left Behind*

*"Hear, O LORD, and be gracious
to me; O LORD, be my helper"
Psalm 30:10*

$M$y name is Robert Anderson and I was born on October 29, 1971. The following is my testimony of faith in Jesus Christ. When I was a young child I can remember clearly a time playing in my backyard, looking into the clear blue sky with the full radiance of the sun and wondering who God was. It would be many years before I fully understood who He was and my need for Him through the good news of the gospel.

*Growing Up*

I was born at Port Hueneme (pronounced "why-nee-mee"). It was a naval base in a small beach city surrounded by the city of Oxnard in southern California. I was the youngest of three kids. My two sisters and I were raised in a military family and we moved many times over the years of my youth. It came with the usual challenges of moving from city to city and starting different schools, leaving friends behind. We had lived in Maryland close to the famous Arlington Cemetery and over the years lived in Santa Ana, Riverside, and Visalia, California.

My father made a career in the military, serving twenty-three years in the Marine Corps. He had served in multiple military conflicts, including holding the shores of Cuba until Russia pulled its nuclear missiles out during the "Cuban Missile Crisis" of 1962. He also did two tours in Vietnam. From 1965 to 1966 he was close to Da Nang and operated out of Saigon from 1969-1970. While there he served with the Marine advisors helping train the South Vietnamese fight against the Viet Cong, the communist faction of Vietnam. He had also served with a specialized unit called MAC-V-SOG. I can remember him being gone often during his service and at year intervals at times. I always missed him and had wanted to spend more time with him as a young boy. I knew it was his job, but it was hard for me to understand why his job kept him away so much. My father struggled with memories of war and at times I could hear screams of his memories while he slept. At the time it was frightening to me as a child not understanding the effects of war on a man. During this time he struggled with many issues including alcohol, trying somehow to cope with devastating memories of war.

This was a dark period for the whole family. There were many low points in our family during this time, but I still loved my father dearly and I loved my family. During the low points I can remember thinking I wanted to do things different when I had a family. I didn't want the turmoil within my family that we lived through. Unfortunately, when I grew up I would repeat some of the same mistakes I swore I would never make. Yet, despite his weaknesses, my father was a good role model for me in several ways. He was a hard worker and honest. He was also very generous with his money and showed me kindness, but he left the religious and spiritual training to my mom.

*Religious Life*

I also had a loving mother. She raised us in the Roman Catholic Church. When I was very young I believed that reciting prayers, and going to Confession and Mass made me accepted in the eyes of God. We didn't go to Mass every week, but I did both my First Communion and Confirmation through the Catholic Church. As I grew older I didn't see the church showing the mercy and love it talked about. It was always giving out harsh rebukes for not doing some ceremony or for reciting a memory prayer incorrectly. To me, everything at church (Mass, prayer, Confession, worship) seemed mechanical and repetitious. I was taught about Jesus and did understand that He was the Son of God, but I did not understand the good news of the gospel outlined in 1 Corinthians 15:1-3 which says,

> *Now I make known to you, brethren, the gospel which I preached to you, which also you received, in which also you stand, by which also you are saved, if you hold fast the word which I preached to you, unless you believed in vain. For I delivered to you as of first importance what I also received, that Christ died for our sins according to the Scriptures, and that He was buried, and that*

*He was raised on the third day according to the
Scriptures.*

I was unaware of what salvation was or its importance for this life and the life to come. I didn't know much of the Bible, but I believe God was moving in my life even though it would be many hard years before I would surrender it to Him. External religion did not transform me or give me what I needed so I continued to look for fulfillment elsewhere. I was hanging with bad company and I also did not know how to deal with the difficulties of life. So I started using drugs at the age of thirteen.

At about this time I was also introduced to the occult and embraced it with curiosity and enthusiasm. I remember attempting to put a spell on a girl that I liked, thinking I could force her to like me. It was real, demonic and even affected me physically. When I performed this spell it made me ill and I remember it kept me up all night vomiting. Providentially, my sister Tina came into the bathroom and for no apparent reason asked me what the hand-woven band around my wrist was. I explained that it was part of the spell ritual cast on the girl I liked. Aghast, my sister immediately cut it off my wrist. The rest of the night I was fine as if I had no illness. I began to see that an evil, satanic realm does exist in this world. After that encounter I never attempted rituals like that again.

### Party Life

However, as time went on my use of drugs and alcohol increased. When I was fourteen I started playing bass in a punk rock band. By sixteen I was drinking and getting high on marijuana almost daily, and anything else I could get my hands on, including speed, crack-cocaine and LSD. I got hooked on LSD, using it weekly as it became my favorite drug. I spiraled out of control. Most of my close friends were all involved in criminal activity, some with felonies, and some with jail time. Although we would likely not have admitted it, we were all addicts to drugs and alcohol. I had a few girlfriends and some were involved with occult activity. Our band travelled throughout California playing at parties and underground club venues during most of my high school years. These places were filled with lost souls like me and some were as close as family. They had come from broken and abusive homes and altogether terrible circumstances. They were ostracized, vulnerable and looking for identity and community, even if it was among dangerous and unhealthy prospects.

At this point in my life I was starting to question all authority and developed a negative outlook on all forms of law and government. My music and lifestyle was all that seemed to keep me happy, although inside my soul I was deeply miserable and discontent. It was like a misery that I somehow enjoyed in some twisted way. Lost and spiraling out of control in my sinful nature, I somehow adapted to and tolerated this depraved state of existence. I can remember numerous times being pulled over by police for illegal activity, like trying to buy drugs and stealing beer. But time and time again the Lord showed me mercy in that I was never prosecuted. So many times I was in dangerous situations and yet God showered me with grace...when I least deserved it.

These events, along with others, would be used to lead me to understand my need for the Lord. It is amazing to look back on it now and see that the Lord was working all along to lead me to where He wanted me to be. I remember my oldest sister,

Tawna, who was saved during my high school years, inviting me to church. I had noticed how her attitude and lifestyle had changed so much for the better. She had also given up a life of vices; then she began serving the Lord at her local church. She would always be there for me when I would show up at her place and she would let me know she loved me and was praying for me. I knew that if I continued down the path I was on that I would either end up in jail or worse.

### Scared Straight

I thought the military would clean me up and provide purpose I so desperately needed in my life, so at age seventeen I joined the Marine Corps in June of 1989 and left home to Marine Corps Recruit Depot (MCRD) in San Diego. Training was crazy hard and I thought to myself the first night, "What did I get myself into now?" Because my father was a Marine I thought I knew what to expect, but nothing can prepare you for this type of training and environment. I had never seen such exacting discipline, been so tired, pushed so hard physically and mentally, or expected to be absolutely perfect in everything. A hair not shaved off my face, wax in my ear, a piece of lint or one thread on my uniform out of place, dirt found on my rifle with a q-tip, all came with unpleasant consequences. But I highly respected those Drill Instructors (DI's) who not only trained me, but modeled their expectations for me. It was clear that whatever my DI asked, they could do ten times better, faster, and with greater efficiency.

During the third phase of boot camp we were on a twelve-mile forced march in full combat gear. It was hot and with all the gear we had on it just made it worse. I could see guys passing out while in formation and needing immediate medical assistance.

One of our DI's that was with us ran by full speed carrying a five-gallon water jug toward the fallen private. I was so tired, but I was amazed at the speed, strength, and stamina that Sergeant Hazlett had. It was a brutal march. I even broke my foot but did not realize it until a week later.

Normally my feet would swell after these types of marches due to the distance and weight carried, and the swelling would soon go away. However, after one week my left foot did not recover and was still swollen. The training was intense and we were conditioned not to complain, so I didn't. We were supposed to focus completely on the given mission or task. I eventually got a cast on my left foot for a few days, but had it quickly removed when my senior DI, Sgt. Williams told me I would be transferred to a medical platoon if I left it on. This meant I would need to stay in boot camp until I healed and then be transferred to a platoon that was in third phase to complete my training.

This was a huge setback and very discouraging. I wanted to graduate with the platoon I started with and that I had come to know as my brothers. Once I cut my cast off I was told I didn't need to finish the final PFT (physical fitness test) since I already passed the most recent one with high scores. The only thing I needed to pass was final drill—on a broken foot using my boot as a cast. Again God's goodness was shown to me, a lost sinner. God continued to temper and humble me while also loving and showing me His compassion. I managed to complete the last few weeks of boot camp on a broken foot. After graduation I was able to stay at MCRD to help in the battalion office while my foot healed before continuing my grooming at Marine Combat Training (MCT) at Camp Pendleton (an extension of the infantry school).

*The Spirit Moves*

During my first years in the military, my second sister, Tina, became a Christian. She immediately started ministering to me by sending me a Bible with messages concerning my spiritual welfare. She told me that I needed to understand the good news of the gospel, the wonderful truths of God's Word, and that I needed a relationship with Christ Jesus who could save my soul from deserved judgment. I didn't want to hear it, but I did love and respect her so I kept the Bible and notes she sent me. I continued living in sin and was unwilling to surrender my life to the Lord Christ. The Lord was using my sister to convict me, expose my sin and my need for a Savior as He was preparing to bring me to faith in the wonderful truth of the gospel. She was persistent in sharing God's truth and grace with me.

For years my sister lived a lifestyle of heavy partying, drinking, and drug use prior to her salvation. Now all of a sudden she was a changed person. I could not deny the amazing work the Lord did in her life. The faith she professed was genuine, and I knew it. She had freely given up that shallow party lifestyle and now possessed true joy and contentment as she raised her new children with her husband.

*Off To War*

Prior to my first deployment I met my Misty through a friend in my unit that went to high school with her. Due to my many rough edges, she was not a fan of me during our first encounter. The Lord moved again and placed me in the first Gulf War at the age of eighteen. I was on my first overseas deployment (West PAC) with my unit and had stopped in the Philippines. There was a US base there in Subic Bay that we would do training at and get supplies. Again, in usual fashion, I would be out as often as I could drinking heavily and being with the girls of Olongapo outside the base. We were doing gun maintenance on base when we heard Kuwait had been invaded. The Gulf War had begun. I knew we would be leaving soon and the next day we were on our way there. My sister continued to minister to me throughout the conflict. Maybe even more due to the seriousness of the region I was in. I still have the little Bible she sent to me on my nineteenth birthday (October 29, 1990) with the following message:

> *Bobby, Russ and I pray every night for your salvation. We pray that you would study the Bible and come to know Christ in a personal way. As you talk to your best friend, God wants you to talk to Him. When you love someone you want to talk with him. God knows what you need before you ask but when you pray to Him about everything you are building a relationship.*
>
> *Love,*
> *Russ & Tina*

She also included the following verses for me to look up:

> *"As it is written, 'There is none righteous, not even one'"* (Romans 3:10);
> *"For all have sinned and fall short of the glory of God"* (Romans 3:23);

*"But God demonstrates His own love towards us, in that while we were yet sinners, Christ died for us. Much more then, having now been justified by His blood, we shall be saved from the wrath of God through Him"* (Romans 5:8-9);

*"Therefore, just as through one man sin entered the world, and death through sin, and so death spread to all men, because all sinned"* (Romans 5:12);

*"For the wages of sin is death, but the free gift of God is eternal life in Christ Jesus our Lord"* (Romans 6:23);

*"That if you confess with your mouth Jesus is Lord and believe in your heart that God raised Him from the dead, you will be saved; for with the heart a person believes, resulting in righteousness, and with the mouth he confesses, resulting in salvation"* (Romans 10:9-10); and Ephesians 6:10-18.

She ended with, "Hide God's Word in your heart."

You would think that with such a clear call to repentance, my dire need for salvation, and the fact that I was in a war zone with my life on the line, I would have turned my life over to Christ. But I did not! Yet the Lord was patient, still working on my heart.

*Hell On Earth*

It was at this point in my life that I started to think of how short life really was. We had trained for war but you are never fully prepared to be in a hot zone, especially at such a young age. We spent the next few months training hard in the extremely elevated temperatures of the Gulf. I was in top physical condition at the time, but still had trouble for the first month adapting to the extreme heat.

On one occasion I passed out during training and suffered from headaches. After about a month I started to adapt to the 140-plus day temperatures. We trained in Oman and Saudi Arabia with their Marines. On the ship we were responsible for the ship's security and at times joint training with special units (Force Recon-SEAL teams) as aggressors. Mostly, I think, for their benefit. There were more than forty US war-ships in the area with multiple carriers. We conducted "air and mine watches" daily. On multiple occasions we had targeted mines for EOD (Explosive Ordinance Disposal) teams to come in to destroy. The explosions in the water were huge, creating splashes and waves thirty feet high. I could only compare it to war footage from the Pacific in WWII. So much was going on all around and yet we were being protected by the Lord of Hosts.

It was eerie at night to watch the many oil fires make the sky red and our ships cut through the oil-drowned sea that was once beautiful blue gulf water. It felt and looked like hell on earth. God used these frightening realities of war to remind me of my lovely Christian sister who had told me of my need of salvation found only through Christ.

After a month of sorties consistently bombing Kuwait and Iraq the ground war had begun. Immediately word came down that we had a mission. We were told half of our battery would be sent by helicopter under the cover of night to a designated location to fire onto the enemy and draw their fire away from the infantry unit tasked to take out the missile sites that were of strategic value. The first platoon of our battery that used the smaller 105 mm guns was tasked with this mission. Our 155 mm guns were not selected, but they needed four additional volunteers from our second platoon to help out.

Everyone in our unit wanted to help in this war effort, but this mission left a bad taste in everyone's mouth. It was clearly very dangerous. I thought it was a suicide mission. The task was to fly by helicopter under the cover of darkness to an island the size of a football field to fire 300, 105 mm rounds onto a much larger island (approximately 1000 yards away) just off the coast of Kuwait in order to draw enemy fire toward us. While this took place, an infantry platoon landed on the island we were firing on to neutralize a strategic missile site. There was no place to maneuver once we started to take fire until the chopper returned to extract us. A much as I cared for those I considered brothers in my unit, volunteering for this risky operation was not my first choice. Three had already volunteered from our platoon, but no one else did. I can remember specifically thinking to myself, "God if you are here with us and want me to go, then I will not protest if I'm selected."

## Spared From Death

To my amazement I was immediately selected out of the pool of fifty men in my platoon. At that point I determined to do all I could to support this effort and prepped with the rest of the team. As I looked around, in shock that this was all very real and imminent, I could see we prepared together like clockwork. The men of my unit that were not selected for this mission prepared all the ammo, fuses, crates of shells, gun powder, and 105 guns that we would take with us as we flew out that night. We were given satellite images of our target area and flown by CH 53 choppers to the USS Okinawa. From there we would leave in a few hours under the cover of darkness to unleash everything we had as a diversion for our infantry team that would land shortly after to neutralize the enemy targets. We were all prepared and on standby with less than two hours to deploy.

Captain Lowrey arrived in the staging area and informed us that there was a press leak on our mission. The enemy knew we would arrive that night. He also informed us that the command had estimated sixty percent casualties from our team if we left that night. So we were put on standby for the next three days. We were told we had to be ready to deploy at a moment's notice for the same mission if called upon. The days passed and to our amazement, the Iraq detachment of the 440 Marine brigade at our missions target location (Faylaka Island) had surrendered without our mission taking place or a shot fired. Units from our thirteenth MEU (Marine Expeditionary Unit) captured and processed 1,400 POW's. Quickly the war came to a close and Kuwait was liberated. This was a big turning point in my life and I knew the Creator of heaven and earth had spared not only our lives, but the lives of our adversaries.

*Coming Home To Chaos*

I would like to say that at this time I became a son of Christ by placing my faith in the gospel, but God was still doing work in my life. After ten months of being deployed I returned to the states. As time passed I continued to live in sin even though my life was once held in the balance. I lived once again as though there was no judgment of my soul awaiting my death. Still, my soul was troubled as I remembered the words of my sisters as they ministered to me, and I never forgot the mission that almost took my life during the war.

After the war I returned and continued seeing Misty who I knew one day would be my wife. I took some time of leave to visit my family and connected with some of the same guys I hung with in high school. We got drunk and early the next morning I found myself at a house of someone I didn't even know. A fight erupted for some reason and my friend was smashed through a glass table, and somehow we immediately fled the scene.

The next thing I remember was being in a vehicle, driving through the night. Not long after I saw a police car cross the intersection in front of me. I then realized that I had been driving down a one way street the wrong direction for some time. The police officer immediately turned around with his lights on. He started coming for me, so I floored it, trying to escape. Turning quickly down an alley, I realized I would only be caught soon and be in serious trouble. I panicked and then fled to a nearby parking lot. My friend and I quickly jumped out of the car and hid behind a nearby dumpster. We waited, breathing heavy, what seemed like forever until we were confident the police were out of sight. Our escape had been successful—or so we thought. We decided to come out to see if we could drive away for the escape, but out of nowhere two police cars appeared and we were arrested on the spot.

I asked the police if they would lock my truck and I told them that I had just returned from the Gulf War. They booked us and put us in the "drunk tank" in the city jail. I did not know if I would get a DUI (Driving Under the Influence), how long we would be in jail, or if they would contact my command. I didn't sleep all night. This was another major low moment of my life. I knew I never wanted to be in jail again. The Lord was again gracious to me and they released us the next day without any charges.

Not long after I returned to base, I was drinking with some Marines from my unit. We were on our way back to the barracks when I was pulled over by the base MP's. Not thinking straight, we still had open beer cans in our laps from the ride home. I was cited for driving under the influence with a high blood alcohol level and given a DUI. That night I found myself in the base brig on main side. Again the Lord was gracious, and even though I lost my driving privileges on base for a year, I was not punished by my command under the USMJ (Uniform Code of Military Justice). Also, because this DUI was on base, it did not reflect on my civilian driving record, so I was free to continue to drive off base.

My DUI was followed by another incident involving my soon-to-be wife and a friend from my unit. We had all been drinking and swimming in a popular swimming hole down at a nearby river. The water was high and we started swimming down the rapids when suddenly I was pulled under into a water-hole. I couldn't get out or rise to the surface since the water resistance was so strong and pressing down on me. After trying and trying to get to the surface for air I realized the only way out was to pull myself around the rock next to me so the current would push me down-stream. I should have drowned, but I didn't. I know the Lord had again protected me that day and was still working on my heart.

*Guilt Sets In*

Soon after, Misty and I were living together with her friend in the city of Vista close to the base. I was feeling guilty living with her without being married. I knew it was wrong. The fact that I felt guilt was evidence that the Lord was again changing my heart. I finally proposed to her and we got married on January 13, 1993. I had six months left in my enlistment and had just been promoted to Corporal (E-4).

At this time I was considering reenlisting or heading to college. This was when Walter, a close friend, and I began working out a lot and devised the brilliant idea to start using steroids and other enhancing drugs to supplement our training. It wasn't long before we were heading south of the border to acquire steroids. I lied and told Misty we were going shopping for her—truly a lame plan, and it came back to bite me with a vengeance.

We picked up some steroids at a Tijuana vet shop and hid the cargo around our waist on the return across the border. This must have been attempted a million times by other fools, because we were immediately caught by customs officers during our re-entry process after we claimed we had nothing to declare. We were searched and everything we had was confiscated. We were held until our command was contacted. I then had to call my poor wife and explain my stupidity. This time we really messed up and the charges were felony level with a possibility of a court martial.

*Driven To Scripture*

After having a very unpleasant review with a base Marine lawyer and having to go through the NJP (Non Judicial Punishment) process which included standing in front of the Battalion Colonel, I received a reduction in rank to Lance Corporal (E-3) and extra duty. I was not fined by the military because I had recently married and because I had already paid fines to customs. Again the Lord showed me much grace and my heart was becoming softer as He continued to show me my need for Him. I was discharged honorably a few months later after my four year enlistment ended. Even though the Marine Corps had taught me a lot about myself and others, it did not fix my heart's sick condition. I needed Christ Jesus.

Misty and I moved back to my home town, Visalia, where we started to attend my sister's church. I started to study Proverbs and Ecclesiastes in the Old Testament. They are books on practical wisdom for life. The truths and wisdom of God in these writings pierced my soul and had a profound personal affect on me. I had recently started working and going to school. It was around this time, in the summer of 1993, that I repented and became a Christian by putting faith in Jesus Christ, and then was baptized. The Lord used my sister's prayers, her diligent pleas with the gospel, and the difficult events in my life (as well as others not mentioned) to change my heart and save my soul from the unimaginable judgment of God's holy wrath that I deserved.

*A New Creation*

I was instantly changed at salvation. The very first thing the Lord helped me with was my speech. I had used many colorful metaphors in every sentence I spoke and almost overnight the Lord had removed it. He had also made me successful in my studies in school even though I had done so poorly in high school. I was eager to share the gospel with others and what God had done in my life. My heart and attitude towards my wife and others changed for the better day by day. I was being conformed to His image as He started the sanctification process in my life. As believers, we are His workmanship, or masterpiece, (Ephesians 2:10), but we still have feet of clay with an ongoing inward war against indwelling sin to struggle with (Romans 7:14-25).

As a new Christian I longed to be without sin in my life, but it was clear from the Scriptures that as the Lord changed me from the inside out, I would still battle with sin every day of my life until I went home to heaven to be with Him. As a new believer I still struggled from some of the sinful patterns I developed from my youth. As I wrestled with sin and my faith I would think to myself, "There is no way I would ever return to my old life, where else would I go?" always coming back to, "Only to You will I run and trust, Lord Jesus." The first two years were very trying as the attacks from Satan, the enemy, were fierce. But greater is He that lives in me, than he who is in the world (1 John 4:4).

The Lord is the Author of Life and the Savior of men's souls. He was faithful (as He promises) and delivered me from patterns of sin; He healed my marriage, and blessed me with three wonderful children—Nathaniel, Moriah and Joshua. And though I am now His son, He continues to change me to be more like Christ day by day.

It took a lot to bring me to faith and I wish the road had not been so painful, but I know the Lord knew what He was doing. I am always blessed when I hear the testimonies of those brothers and sisters as they share their amazing journeys to faith in Christ. As remarkable as the events in my life were that brought me to faith, every testimony of a soul that comes to faith is significant. The youth who is saved by faith without the need of so many difficult circumstances is no less significant or amazing. I am equally convinced that many have had a tougher road than me. I love Him because He first loved me. He is worthy of our praise, for we were bought with a very high price (Acts 20:28). All honor and glory belongs to the Lord of Lords, King of Kings, Lord of Hosts, Jesus the Christ!

*Because he has loved Me,*
*therefore I will deliver him;*
*I will set him securely on high,*
*because he has known My name.*
*He will call upon Me,*
*and I will answer him;*
*I will be with him in trouble;*
*I will rescue him and honor him.*
*With a long life I will satisfy him*
*And let him see My salvation*
*(Psalm 91: 14-16)*

# 5

## *Finding True Love*

*"We love because He first loved us"*
*1 John 4:19*

$F$ully redeemed; faithfully refined; forever loved. This is my identity in Christ. But it was not always this way—before I knew God, I was a lost soul. All my life, I longed for love, but my view of love was a twisted one, bred by romantic novels and popular culture. To make matters worse, I looked for my so-called love in all the wrong places. In my selfish pilgrimage to find love, I hurt myself, people who loved me, and most of all, I hurt God. Like the Prodigal Son, I left those who loved me in search of what I thought would bring me pleasure, but the happiness was short-lived.

I suffered major consequences as a result of my own doing. Though I deserved eternal damnation because of my sins, God did not abandon me. My parents did not leave me. My earthly father welcomed me home, and my heavenly Father secured my eternal home in heaven. I have received complete forgiveness for all my past, present, and future sins, all because of the grace that God imparted to me through the sacrifice of His Son on the cross. I am now freed from the bondage of sin, because of Jesus' resurrection and His victory over death. Finally, I learned what True Love really is, and it was given to me freely when I least deserved it (Romans 5:6). God's love for me extends beyond redeeming me from my past — He cares so deeply for me—He sanctifies me daily, and He promises me life everlasting in His future kingdom. Though I still go through trials and tribulations in life, I now have true, supernatural deep-seated joy because of the eternal hope that I have in Jesus Christ.

## Lost In Hong Kong

Please allow me to walk you through my journey in search of my True Love. I was born in Hong Kong, when it was still under British colonial rule. For a time, our household consisted of four generations: my great grandmother (from my paternal grandmother's side), my grandparents (from my father's side), my parents, my uncle, and me. Multigenerational housing was, and still is, very typical in Hong Kong, and we loved our lively home. My father's side was Catholic, and my mother's side was agnostic. Religion was never a point of strife in my house, since my paternal grandmother was the matriarch *and* the devoted Catholic who made sure we attended Mass with her every week. Though my mother was not religious, she was a submissive wife who supported my father in everything. Financially, we were not wealthy, but what we had was sufficient. My parents both worked hard to support the family, and we never had to worry about food or shelter. Because of this, life was pretty simple for me as a child. My only expectations were to go to school and to get good grades. Even so, my own sinful nature was already emerging during my childhood years.

As a young girl, I was naturally selfish, and my status as the only child exacerbated my need for attention. My grandmother especially loved me, because she had two sons and had always wanted a daughter. Since my parents both worked on the weekdays, I spent a lot of my time with my grandmother, who spoiled me rotten. Many of my memories about my childhood are dominated by my grandmother who poured most of her attention on me. Because all my family members showered me with so much love, I unknowingly allowed selfishness to fester in my heart.

In addition to selfishness, another sin began taking root in my heart at a young age. I have always been a big bookworm, and my avid reading accelerated my reading skills and vocabulary to levels well above my peers at the time. I became interested in studying Chinese poetry and classic novels in early elementary school age. By the time I was eleven, I was bored with the typical children's literature. So I started exploring literature that would both challenge and tantalize me, and unfortunately I started being deeply drawn to a couple of authors whose work consisted mostly of unhealthy, unrealistic, and dramatic romances. My family was fully aware of my obsession over these books. However, neither they nor I foresaw the stronghold that this kind of twisted love would have on me. We had no idea that it would almost cost me my life.

In school, I earned good grades, but I had a difficult time with my social life at first. I was enrolled in an all-girls Catholic elementary school, where I had religion classes and strict rules to follow. Neither one was an issue for me, but I struggled socially in the first few years. While I got along with almost everyone, I had a hard time in the first few years formulating a core group of friends with whom I could play consistently. It was not until I reached the fifth grade that I finally befriended a group of girls with whom I felt comfortable. Unfortunately, this was short-lived, as I discovered I would soon leave everything I had ever known to start a new life in a place I never knew.

To everyone born in Hong Kong, 1997 was an all-important historical year. It marked the end of British sovereignty in Hong Kong. Many citizens of Hong Kong had fears of what our beloved city would become once the Chinese government took over. Because of this, many who had the connections and the financial means to do so made the difficult decision to emigrate out of Hong Kong. In the years preceding 1997, some of my friends and extended family moved to Canada, the United States, and Australia. Since my mother's family was in northern California, my parents, too, started having talks about settling in the United States. Naïve as I was, I imagined a place where school would be much easier, I would have more free time to read my romantic books and spend time with my grandmother, and everything would just be...better. No one prepared me for the difficulty of the traumatic transition, the learning of a whole new culture, and the unexpected shifting family dynamics. But no one could have predicted all these things ahead of time either.

## A Difficult Transition

In the fateful year of 1995, my parents, my grandmother, and I packed up all our possessions and headed for our new lives in northern California. We spent the first few days with my mother's family touring different places and buying things that we needed to get settled. We had a blast. Unfortunately, the vacation bubble burst quickly for all of us.

During our transitional period, life was extremely stressful for each of my family members. Reality kicked in hard for my grandmother, who went from an autonomous, social butterfly in Hong Kong, to a restricted senior citizen with no driver's license. The closest bus stop was located a mile away from our house. Compared to being surrounded by friends and family in Hong Kong, she had no friends or close relatives in the United States. She grew lonely quickly, and she started spending much of her time watching television. It was also evident that her health followed her mental well-being into deterioration. Meanwhile, my parents had struggles of their own as they were both looking for work. All of a sudden, everyone became so busy adjusting to the new life that I felt much more distant from my family.

The tipping-point of the changes happened when my mother announced that she was expecting a new child. I did not handle this news well. Overwhelmed by the changes of my new environment, the surge of teenage hormones, and dramatic shifts in the family dynamics, I exploded on my mother. In my immaturity, I blamed many things on her. I was jealous that my would-be brother would take my parents even further away from me. It was around this time that my relationship with my mother became very sour, and I was often angry with her. I was like a wounded animal that wanted care and love, but would howl at everyone who tried to come close.

With only two weeks left in the sixth grade, I became the foreign new girl in a school where practically everyone grew up together. Though I had English classes in Hong Kong, the emphasis was more on mathematics and Chinese. In addition, the English that I had learned was British English, not American English, and they had considerable differences. On the first day of school, I personally experienced all the classic jokes from asking for a "rubber" instead of an eraser to a "washing closet" instead of a bathroom. As you can probably imagine, my classmates' reactions ranged from utter embarrassment to uncontrolled laughter and mockery. Perhaps the most painful reality check for me was the first time I was called on by my teacher.

In Hong Kong students stand up to answer the teacher when called on. Culturally, it is the only acceptable way to show respect. Naturally, I stood up immediately to respond to my teacher. To this day, I still remember the shock on my teacher's face, and how much my classmates exploded into laughter and made fun of me. I wanted so badly to run away and cry, but I told myself to swallow my tears. For the first time, my smile was not genuine — I felt like I only had myself to fight for me. That moment was indelibly humiliating for me and marked the shattering of the hopes and dreams that I had of my new life in America, as well as my loss of innocence.

### Growing Challenges

Things only got worse when I went to middle school. Instead of being in the "regular" classes like the "normal" kids, I was assigned to the English Language Development (ELD) program. Basically, the ELD students had separate core classes from everyone else, and we joined the rest of the school for the elective courses. Though the ELD program was put together with good intentions to help integrate foreign students, it actually fostered bullying and ostracism. There were times when my ELD classmates and I would be shoved against the wall and cursed at for no particular reason. A close guy friend of mine even was dragged out to the field and beaten up. I was determined to get out of the ELD program as soon as possible — and I did. I put all my heart and soul into excelling in my academics and demonstrating to the school that I needed no additional "assistance."

Not long into freshman year in high school, I tested out of ELD and was fully integrated into the mainstream curriculum. I did not want others to categorize me as an FOB ("fresh off the boat," a derogatory term referring to foreign students). Thus, I tried as hard as I could to talk, dress, eat, and live the same as those who were born here. In my school, all the cool kids listened to rap, hip-hop, and R&B, so, I did too. I was especially drawn to rap music because it spoke to the anger in my heart. I would study every lyric in a rap song so I could learn the language and rap to it.

## Infatuation

Aside from music, the other common topic of interest among my peers was boys. Of course, the usual high school dances and valentine-grams spur on the "crushes," and I soon realized several boys were attracted to me. As a troubled teenager craving love, affection and care, I soaked up all the attention that I could get. However, I only had my eye on one — we shall call him Anthony. Anthony was smart, good-looking, popular, funny, and he loved rap music as much as I did. My mother was very stern about not dating until sophomore year in high school, so we started dating officially as soon as freshman year ended.

My family liked Anthony, especially because his grades were as excellent as he was charming. Moreover, they were also relieved that I would finally stop demanding attention from them, and redirect my efforts to someone else. For a while, things were great. Many thought we were a great match; it seemed as though we had everything — we had 4.0 GPAs, we played sports, we participated in social and academic clubs, we did community service, we received numerous awards from our school and our city, and we went to all the social events together.

But we did not have God. So on the inside, we were lost. We were both rebellious and angry with our parents for different reasons. We had no role models or disciplers to tame our immaturity. We fueled each other's godlessness, anger, and unbridled immaturity, so it became a recipe for disaster. It was true that we spurred each other on in our academics and other extracurricular pursuits, but we also encouraged each other in unhealthy emotions, thoughts and attitudes.

Soon into our relationship, we became co-dependent of each other, and I became more angry and insecure than ever before. We started fighting all the time. While our problems were bigger than we could handle on our own, we did not know where else to turn. Even though we fought, we also believed that we only had each other. I expressed a lot of my anger and negative emotions in my art pieces, which included scenes of suicide and illustrations of ostracism. My choice of music also became darker and despairing, and I would often close myself off in my room while blasting angry music.

## College Life

As graduation approached, Anthony and I talked a lot about our relationship as well as our academic future. We both wanted to attend the *University of California, Los Angeles (UCLA)* for college. At the same time, we came to a mutual decision that it would not be healthy for us to continue our relationship after high school. In the end, we were both accepted to *UCLA*. As much as Anthony desired to go there, he graciously decided to attend his second choice to help us both move on in life. Even though Anthony and I ceased communications long ago, my respect for him remains, and I am grateful for his generosity.

Due to my bad experience in high school, I was very excited to start a new chapter of my life in college. My first year in college was the most blissful time of my life. Ignorantly blissful, that is. The weather was great, everyone was friendly and eager to make new friends, there was no parental control, and the dining and entertainment options were abundant. Though I majored in computer science and engineering, which required challenging courses and a lot of studying, it did not stop me from making social life a priority in college.

First, I joined the *UCLA* badminton club, which was an athletic passion that I developed since early high school. Second, I rushed a sorority. The truth was, I had no idea what sororities and fraternities were all about before college, let alone the connotations that are usually attached to them. During rush, I was attracted to the ideas of sisterhood, community, identity, and love. In their slideshows, they showed photo after photo of the sorority sisters sporting their beaming smiles and enjoying life together—picturesque fulfillment.

I faithfully attended all their rush events, and purposefully got to know almost all of the members. I had many one-on-one conversations with these girls, who shared their journeys in finding their identities and deep friendships through the sorority. The more I found out, the more I wanted what they had. When they extended their invitation for me to join, I wholeheartedly accepted and dove right into their culture. I thoroughly enjoyed the friendships and pride that came along the way.

Then, there was another aspect to being in a sorority: partying. I had never been to a party with alcohol until college, but I became addicted to it immediately. It became typical for me to stay up partying until two o'clock in the morning on a school night, and either sleep through my classes or miss them completely. I became a big drinker, many times throwing up in people's houses, cars, the dormitory halls, and on the streets. There was also a lot of close, sensuous dancing between the frat girls and boys. We would regularly have these parties called "exchanges," where a fraternity and a sorority got together in a house to eat, socialize, and dance together—collegiate party life.

*False Love*

It was in one of these exchanges where I met Victor. Victor was very attractive and charming, and I fell head-over-heels for him quickly. We soon became inseparable, and I thought I had found "the one." Determined to make the relationship even more special, I foolishly became intimate with him. It was true that we became closer than ever before. In fact, I felt so vulnerable to him that I was scared and insecure all the time. He, too, was wary of any attention that I received from other men. As our jealousy and insecurity multiplied, our fights escalated. The relationship became a two year roller-coaster filled with pain and tears, and finally ended in a fiasco with the intervention of others.

That relationship was the darkest, most shameful time of my life. I was so depressed for a time that I was prescribed antidepressants as well as therapy sessions for my condition. I was scared to tell others what I was going through, and I ended many friendships as a result. I even withdrew from my sorority because the relationship alone was too much to handle.

### Beautiful Feet

During this entire fiasco with Victor, Tiff was the only person to whom I entrusted the whole situation and around whom I felt completely safe. Tiff was my roommate assigned to me my freshman year. From the first day that we met, I felt as if I met my sister from another mother. We had many common interests, and we could (and did) talk about everything with one another. We shared some of my most memorable moments in life when we roomed together, but the paths that we each chose were dramatically different. When I decided to join the sorority in freshman year, she chose to be a part of the "Grace On Campus" (GOC), a ministry of Grace Community Church. Though we made different decisions and roomed with different people as sophomores, we remained very close. In fact, she loved me enough to speak hard truth to me and she also shared the gospel with me whenever God presented the opportunity.

For the first year, my heart was hardened against God's Word. Then, my heart began to soften toward His truth during the lowest point of my life. When my other friends forsook me, God used Tiff to be there for me. She graciously invited me to visit her home with her during the weekends, which was only an hour away from campus. It was a safe sanctuary for me, and

I even started desiring to attend her home church with her on those weekends.

*Broken*

After my relationship finally ended with Victor, I was so overwhelmed by everything that I withdrew from *UCLA* and went home for a quarter to take classes at a local community college instead. I thought I was going home to recover from all the trauma that I just went through, but God had something much greater in store for me. Before I went home, Tiff invited me to spend the weekend with her again at her home. That Saturday night I abruptly woke up in sweat from one of the most vivid dreams that I have ever had. Startled, I started crying, and I woke Tiff up to tell her that I dreamt of Jesus carrying His cross for me. In the dream, I was a bystander who somehow knew that the cross that Jesus was carrying was mine. It was heavy, and Jesus' sweat and blood was dripping down His brows. I wanted to do something, but I was frozen — all I could do was watch as Jesus took the pain for me.

In tears, I asked Tiff, "What should I do? I feel so guilty. It's not fair that He carried it for me."

Tiff embraced me lovingly, and cried with me. She urged me to stop crying over people who hurt me, and to "fall in love with someone perfect." She encouraged me to seriously seek a relationship with Jesus, and prayed for me before we fell asleep again. The following day, we went to her home church, and I was especially attentive to everything that I was observing and hearing. I felt a peace with the people there, who genuinely seemed to be kind and caring. Before I went home, Tiff handed me a Bible and told me to take it home with me to read. I thanked her but honestly did not think too much of it.

*True Love*

When I got home, I tried to carry on as much of a normal life as possible by attending my classes and not getting myself in trouble. I was still hurting emotionally, but this time something was different — my heart was yearning for God. Nothing short of supernatural could have explained my heart's change, but I literally felt like God was calling me to Him through everything. On one particular night, as I was struggling through an emotional episode, my eyes made contact with the Bible in my luggage that I had almost forgotten about. Curious, I picked it up to read it. As I flipped through the pages, an index card fell out with Tiff's handwriting, that read,

> *Trust in the Lord with all your heart, and lean not on your own understanding. In all your ways acknowledge Him, and He will set your path straight* (Proverbs 3:5-6).

That was the first time I had ever encountered that Scripture, and as I read, the words pierced my soul. Suddenly, my crying ceased, and I felt a rush of comfort and peace pouring into every fiber of my being. It made complete sense. All along, I was relying on my own self and my own understanding, which clearly got me into all sorts of trouble. Once a nominal Catholic, I had always known of God as the Creator and the one and only true God, but I never acknowledged Him personally in my life, let alone with all my heart. I was prideful to think that I knew what was best for my life, but the consequences of my decisions were evidences that I could not do it on my own. For the first time, I relaxed at the idea of not having to be in control. I cherished the new perspective that I was given, and I enjoyed a restful sleep that night.

As Sunday drew near, I had a spontaneous urge to attend church. I thought of all the sweet people whom I met and all the peace-provoking sermons that I heard when I attended services with Tiff, and I wanted to find a similar place near home. Without giving it too much more thought, I Googled "Chinese Christian Church in San Jose." I jotted down the first result that showed up on the list, and I showed up there bright and early by myself on Sunday morning. It turned out to be a very intimate church started by a few families, and at that time they did not have too many new visitors, let alone strangers who showed up uninvited.

Because of this, everyone was even more excited to greet me, and I felt so welcomed and loved that it seemed like home my very first time there. Not only did the members introduce themselves to me, they were intentional in building a genuine relationship with me and getting to know me. I was very open with them about my desire to seek God, and in turn, they invested right away in ministering to me and caring for me spiritually. By the end of the first day I already had some deep one-on-one conversations with a few of the members, as well as invitations not only return the next Sunday, but also to hang out with them outside of church.

### The Prodigal Returns

As I said goodbye that day, Auntie Pinnie, a well-respected older woman from the church, left me with a few booklets that she encouraged me to read at home. As God was faithfully working in my heart, I was excited about reading them and could not wait to savor them. That evening, as I eagerly looked through the titles of the booklets, one in particular jumped out at me: *The Prodigal Son.* "Oh!" I exclaimed, "I remember that story from religion class in elementary school days!"

Initially only drawn by its familiarity, I did not realize how much I would actually relate to the prodigal son. As I was reading the booklet, tears streamed down from my face as I finally recognized how much I was sinning against those who loved me, and most importantly, how I had been sinning against God. I *was* the prodigal son. I chose to overlook every blessing that was right in front of me and went out looking for what I thought would make me happy, make me feel loved. I brought all these problems upon myself, and I disappointed those who were the closest to me. I went out seeking for love, not knowing that Love was always there with me. God *is* Love (1 John 4:8). He was, is, and will always be there. He is the unfailing, constant, unconditional, perfect Love that I have been looking for all my life.

At the very end of that booklet, the author illustrated the gospel. It was clear as daylight to me that I was born a sinner, and I have no power on my own to defeat my sin nature. The consequences of my sins would lead me to eternal condemnation, but the loving Father provided a hope that would rescue me from my fate. He sent His one and only begotten Son, Jesus Christ, who is 100% man and 100% God, to earth. Jesus became my personal high priest by being tempted by all the same temptations that I face daily, yet He lived a sinless life (Hebrews 4:15). Most importantly, He willingly died on the cross for me, to be the perfect sacrifice that satisfied God's wrath over sins and redeemed me from my deserved eternal punishment. Not only that, He conquered death by rising to life again three days after His death on the cross.

The author then asked me to pray to repent of my sins and accept Jesus as my personal Savior, so that I can finally be free from all my past, present, and future sins and share in eternal joy with Him in Heaven! Hallelujah! YES, YES, YES!! I could not help myself and got down on my knees right away to say my prayer. "Yes, Lord, I am sorry! Yes, Lord, please take me back! Yes, Jesus, I am forever yours! I am forever loved!"

> *If you confess with your mouth that Jesus is Lord and believe in your heart that God raised him from the dead, you will be saved* (Romans 10:9).

After I said my confession and started genuinely believing in Jesus that night, there was no looking back for me. No longer would I have to dwell in my past sins and hurts — I am now a new creation!

> *Therefore, if anyone is in Christ, he is a new creation. The old has passed away; behold, the new has come* (2 Corinthians 5:17).

I am now God's chosen one, holy and beloved (Colossians 3:12). I know of the eternal hope that I have in Christ — I have a reservation in heaven!

> *Blessed be the God and Father of our Lord Jesus Christ! According to his great mercy, he has caused us to be born again to a living hope*

*through the resurrection of Jesus Christ from the dead, to an inheritance that is imperishable, undefiled, and unfading, kept in heaven for you* (1 Peter 1:3-4).

Not only that, this hope that I have is secured. Nothing and no one can ever take it away from me:

*For I am sure that neither death nor life, nor angels nor rulers, nor things present nor things to come, nor powers, nor height nor depth, nor anything else in all creation, will be able to separate us from the love of God in Christ Jesus our Lord* (Romans 8:38-39).

## New Life

Since I have surrendered my life to God over ten years ago, not only do I possess a hope for the future, but I have also been sanctified by both blessings and trials that God has allowed in my life. I am still very much a sinner, but by the grace of God, I am being made more like Him each day. No one likes going through trials, but I have learned that when I am a Christian, I can experience joy and contentment in all circumstances, and that God uses all things for good and for His glory. *"And I am sure of this, that he who began a good work in you will bring it to completion at the day of Jesus Christ"* (Philippians 1:6).

As the Lord changed my heart and convicted me of my sins, I have since asked my parents for forgiveness and have grown in my affection for them. In 2009, God blessed me to be married to my best friend, Mike, who is a fellow believer.

Unlike my relationships in the past, each of us shares an intimate relationship with Christ Jesus, which also gives us an inseparable bond with each other. Instead of believing in the lies of worldly romances and fantasies as I believed in my youth, we both agree that love is not just a feeling — it is a choice and a commitment. Thus, despite the trials in life and our own imperfections, we are growing to love each other more each day. Together, we serve in our church in various ways, and it is our hope that God would continue to use us to serve Him and His people. *"As for me and my house, we will serve the Lord"* (Joshua 24:15). In 2012, God blessed us even more abundantly by giving us our first daughter, Macaria Joy. As a mother, I have been ordained by God to lead my children to know and love Christ. It is a daunting responsibility, and I have been learning to rely more and more on the Lord and His grace each day to accomplish His mission. At the same time, I have grown in my understanding of love exponentially, and I have come to an even deeper appreciation of my own parents and the love of God. We are currently expecting our second child, and I praise the Lord each day for the blessings of marriage and children! (Psalm 127)

As I was reflecting on my past and writing this testimony, one of my favorite chapters in the Bible, Deuteronomy 8, came to mind. In the passage, God reminded His people of what evil and hardships He had delivered them from, and commanded them to remember Him and keep His commandments. It has been so long since I had last looked back to my life before Christ, because long gone are the days that I would selfishly sit and wallow in my sorrows. At the same time, it is good and humbling to remember exactly what my God had delivered me from — the multitudes of troubles that I had created for myself in this lifetime, and more importantly, an eternity of deserved condemnation. In contrast, I now see that He showers me daily with His love, grace, and mercy. I spent my past life looking for false love, but it was not until I died to myself and my ways that I finally found true, biblical love. I am no longer the same lost soul meandering — I am now God's child, a wife, and a mother. I am loved, now and forever.

# 6

# *From Horror to Holiness*

*"God shows His love for us in that while
we were still sinners, Christ died for us"
Romans 5:8*

**S**ome of my earliest memories are of being at church. My mother brought me to church when I was just a baby. I was one of the little ones in the church nursery crib. I grew up attending that little Baptist church in the small town of Milpitas, California.

I remember sitting in children's Sunday school, singing children's songs out of an oversized picture book with the words to the songs. There was one with a picture I loved. It was of Jesus standing on a doorstep, knocking on a door with no doorknob on the outside. The words encouraged us to open the door of our heart and to let Jesus in.

It wasn't until years later that I would learn that picture was based on Revelation 3:20, and that Jesus in that verse was knocking on the door of a church...not someone's heart. In fact, it was the lukewarm church at Laodicea whom Jesus had threatened to "spit out." Far from a winsome call to salvation, it was the last chance for a church, where Jesus had been left outside, to turn in repentance.

### Raised In Church

The church I was raised in taught what I now call "easy-believism," the belief that salvation results from any profession of faith that someone makes. It's the popular, shallow teaching that a person is saved by performing some perfunctory task, like repeating a canned prayer, raising a hand, walking an aisle or signing a piece of paper, even if that person does not have full comprehension of the biblical gospel and its implications. It is as simple of a formula as this: repeating the "Sinner's Prayer" = being saved forever. The "sinner's prayer" was recited almost like a magical spell from *Harry Potter* that results in salvation.

As a boy, I responded to one of the "altar calls" that always came at the end of a Sunday service. While "every head was bowed" and "every eye was closed" (I confess that I always peaked to see who went forward), our pastor would make an impassioned plea for people to come forward and "give your heart to Jesus." There was always soft and emotional music playing quietly from the church organ in the background.

I remember walking that aisle with tears streaming down my face. I was met by a man who took me aside, and asked if I wanted to "ask Jesus into my heart." I told him that I did. He instructed me to repeat a prayer after him, and then led me sentence-by-sentence through a sinner's prayer. I know that prayer included a request for Jesus to forgive my sins, but there was certainly no real emphasis on true repentance. The prayer's focus was on making my own decision for Christ.

### Pseudo Conversion

Once we finished, the man placed his hand on my shoulder and welcomed me into the Family of God. He assured me of my eternal salvation. Then he prayed for me.

I'm sure that man was very sincere. But this event posed a HUGE problem—that man believed I walked away saved, but in fact at that time I was NOT saved...despite walking the aisle and praying the prayer. God the Holy Spirit had not yet made me born again. I did not realize it at the time, but I would much later in life. All that happened that day was that I had spoken some words, and at my baptism all that happened was that I got wet.

I certainly believed intellectually, just as I had confessed to that man, that Jesus is God come in the flesh. I believed that Jesus lived a perfect life, and that He died for our sins to bring forgiveness to sinners like me. The problem was...I didn't really think my sins were all that bad. I certainly would not have believed them to be bad enough to make me worthy of going to hell.

That church taught that the greatest sin was to not "accept Jesus"—so to avoid the greatest sin, I "accepted Jesus." I did not want to go to hell. Well, I had certainly done that. I had "accepted" Jesus and done so publicly. But I did not really become regenerate at that time. I learned to trust in the prayer that I had recited that day. I learned to trust in the assurance of eternal salvation that the man in authority had given to me. Whenever sin in my life caused me to doubt my salvation, I returned to the memories of going through these motions that continued to give me assurance.

I was now a false convert. I was a "thorny-soil Christian" that Jesus had taught about (Matthew 13:7, 22). I was still very much in love with my own sins and with the things of the world. In His parable, Jesus warned about this kind of shallow and even pseudo conversion this way:

> *Others fell among the thorns, and the thorns came up and choked them out.... And the one on whom seed was sown among the thorns, this is the man who hears the word, and the worry of the world and the deceitfulness of wealth choke the word, and it becomes unfruitful.*

In junior high school my parents sent me to a Baptist Christian school where I was surrounded by a lot of other kids who were just like me. They came from Christian families and called themselves Christians, but I suspect now that many of them may have been false converts just like me. Their lives showed no more biblical evidences of a changed heart, or of being a new creature, than mine did. Yet many of us were blind to our condition. The school's curriculum, though Christian, was no more convicting than what I was hearing in the "easy-believism" church I attended. There was lots of talk about the love of God, and little mention of sin and repentance. That is the exact opposite of how the Apostles shared the gospel in the Book of Acts. From a careful study of Acts, it's apparent that the theme of repentance from sin was just as important as the love of God in the evangelistic preaching of the Apostles.

*Compromise Sets In*

From my youth, I had always been a fan of horror movies. I stayed up late watching scary movies on TV's "Creature Features." The Hollywood blockbuster horror film, "Halloween," came out in 1976 when I was ten, and inspired countless R-rated horror films that premiered in our local theater almost every week. Each film was filled with scenes of graphic violence and overtly immoral sex scenes. Being tall for my age, and having a local movie theater that didn't seem too worried about checking I.D.s, I saw them all. I began to fill my mind with dangerous evil influences that would prove to have immediate detrimental effects on my life. The mixture of adrenaline and steamy sexuality was like a drug to me. My parents had no idea what I was watching.

Around 1980, a Christian urban legend swept though our church. The story was about a number of people who had received Social Security checks from the government that could not be cashed by their local banks. The reason the checks were refused, supposedly, was because the checks bore an unusual printed instruction on the backside. Supposedly it stated that in order to cash the check the bearer must have the proper identifying mark on their hand or their forehead. This sounded a lot like the mark of the beast in Revelation 13. The story claimed that when the recipients of the checks contacted the government, the authorities admitted to having made a mistake. Someone had opened a wrong box of checks. These checks were not supposed to be used, they explained, until 1984 (still just a few years away). The story ended with the admonition that with Christ's return nearly here, Christians needed to get busy reaching out to friends and family about Jesus Christ...before it was too late.

My mother was somewhat skeptical about the hoax, but said she was encouraged by the possibility that Christ's return might really be near. She said she couldn't wait to see Jesus, but I was horrified by the thought. I did not want Jesus to return until I accomplished all my goals and fulfilled all my teenage desires. I wouldn't be graduating from high school until 1984. I had seen enough from movies and television shows (that I shouldn't have been watching), to know of pleasurable things that happened between men and women. I knew enough to know that I wanted to experience these things myself. Of course I wanted to go to heaven, but if this story was true and the Lord could return in the very near future, I would never have time to get married and know the physical pleasures of this life. My young mind worried about being taken to heaven without ever having an opportunity to "know" a woman. I pictured myself forever lamenting that I had missed out.

I began thinking about ways that I might remedy this situation. The clock was ticking after all. Perhaps I needed to abandon my plans to wait until I was married. At a time when biology and puberty were already creating confusing new urges and desires inside a young man, I was now contemplating turning my back on what I believed was the "right thing to do" out of sheer urgency and desire. "Surely God would understand," I told myself. "I know it's wrong, but surely He won't hold it against me."

*Works Righteousness*

I was still lost, and still held to the idea that I could merit heaven by being good. I thought God would overlook my sins because I had "accepted Jesus." I figured God would know I was basically a decent young man. "Surely my good deeds would outweigh my sins. I'm certainly not a bad guy. There were lots of people who are worse than me." In my mind I rationalized that God must somehow grade us on a curve.

It never occurred to me that when Jesus bore the sins of guilty sinners upon the cross, it demonstrated that His Father would not spare even His own Son. If Christ would bear the sins of others, even He would have to pay for those sins to the last blow of the whip, to the very last drop of blood, and even to the death. Yet I thought the same God who would not, and could not, spare His own Son, would simply overlook my own sins and let me into heaven because of my decision for Him. I had no understanding of the perfect holiness and perfect justice of God.

I continued going to church only until I grew old enough to exert my own will, and until my mom couldn't make me go anymore. I had actually wanted to stop going for a long time. What a burden church was! It seemed like it never stopped. Half of my weekend was gone every week, and it didn't seem fair. Even school took breaks and gave us a little time off, but not church. Every Sunday I had to go whether I liked it or not. My dad didn't go, other than on major holidays, and he said he was a Christian. "Why couldn't I just stay home like him?" I could think of a thousand things I'd rather do with my Sundays, and chasing girls was at the top of the list.

*Planet Hollywood*

I finished high school and went to college. I didn't do very well because I had other things beside class on my mind. I discovered a new found freedom that I had never known. And, there were girls...lots of them. Like a lion studies the gazelle, I studied them. I learned how to talk to them. I read books about them. I learned how to get what I wanted from them, all the while making them think it was their idea. It was all a big game to me.

I started my hobby of collecting during this time. Through a friend, I met a number of people who worked in Hollywood for the motion picture industry. I began collecting real movie props and costumes. This was before eBay, when the only way to collect this kind of memorabilia was to be in privileged circles. People I met were dazzled by the rare props I owned, marveling at how I had ever managed to lay my hands on them. My house was beginning to look like a *Planet Hollywood* restaurant, and I loved the way people reacted to my collection. In fact, I loved my things and I served them. Somewhere along the way, I stopped owning them and they started owning me. I identified myself with these things. I had become an idolater to the first degree.

A girl I was dating introduced me to some people who were going to build a Halloween haunted house inside an old shopping mall. This was right up my alley. I loved horror movies, and I was already dabbling in special effects make-up. I really loved blood and guts, and I set up my own "Creature Shop," where I could create props and bodies for our shows. Soon we were buying supplies, and lots of them, like liquid latex in fifty-five gallon barrels.

I learned very quickly, and wound up in upper management, building professional "haunted attractions" for over sixteen years. It became a lucrative second job for me. I was in charge of building large-scale live attractions at theme parks and even for a Las Vegas strip casino.

The owner of the haunted attraction company was a man of Jewish decent, and I was the professing "Christian" guy who was always pushing to make our attractions even gorier, more horrifying, and more disturbing. We studied people to learn what worked really well and what didn't. I would stand at the exit of our attractions and listen carefully to what our customers said to each other as they came out. We were paid to create an intense, artificially-engineered emotional experience for our customers, and we were good at it.

To do our job well, eleven months out of the year we had to eat, drink, and breathe all things dark, murderous, and evil. We would take a break in December and then get busy working on our next attractions come January.

Oh, how I sullied the name of Christ back then. I publicly claimed to be a Christian whenever it served my purposes to do so, yet my life was no different than those of my unsaved friends and co-workers. What flowed out of my mouth and the relationships I was having would prove to anyone paying attention that I was a hypocrite. It amazes me that none of the actual Christians who knew me ever came to me to say, "James, you say you are a Christian, but your lifestyle says something different. Can I share some verses with you out of the book of First John?" But that never happened.

I had no time for God or His Word. The only time I ever opened the Bible was to use it to make a point by quoting some verse out of context, but I didn't actually read it. The truth is, I actually found the Bible to be confusing and hard to follow back then and I certainly didn't understand it properly. Instead, I used its verses to offer evidences for the existence of UFOs, and other paranormal phenomena. My shadow never darkened the door of any church.

*Conviction Sets In*

I got married in January of 2002. Looking back, Diane and I had more in common than we knew. We were both false converts. We both professed to be Christians, yet we both lacked any of the biblical fruits of salvation that you should expect to see in the life of someone whose heart has truly been changed by God. We had been friends since the mid-1980s and Diane knew me very well, so in a very short period of time I involved her in all of my favorite sins.

It was around five years later that God began to do a work in me. The sins that I loved were beginning to become a burden I had trouble bearing. I had developed an addiction to internet pornography over the last ten years, and it had become like a giant weight on my shoulders. Pornography is like a drug. In the beginning, it takes very little to have the desired effect, but as time goes on it takes more and more graphic images and more extreme subject matters to satisfy one's lusts. It's insatiable. Though the world wouldn't care what I was entertaining myself with, I found myself ashamed of what I was looking at and of the fantasies I was having in secret. My heart was growing darker and I knew it.

I had finally had enough. It is my belief that God gave me victory over this and a few other areas of sin in my life just before He saved me. It was June of 2007, though I don't remember the exact day that the most important thing that has ever happened to me occurred. It was a very stressful time for me at work, and I had commented to Diane that my neck was very sore and stiff.

As the hour grew late, Diane got up from the couch and told me it was time to come to bed. "I'll be right there," I said as she went into the bedroom. But, it was probably an hour and a half later before I finally turned off the computer and came to bed.

I walked into our bedroom to find the lights were still on. My wife had fallen asleep waiting for me. She was propped up against some pillows with her head slumped uncomfortably to one side. Lying across her lap was our large electric massager. I realized immediately that her beckon for me to come to bed was part of a plan to surprise me with a massage for my sore neck. Here she had sat waiting for her husband to come until she had fallen asleep. I felt like a world-class heel. I thought to myself, "How stupid and unthankful am I?" This woman loved me and wanted to do something kind for me, yet I was absorbed with other meaningless things. I was overcome with feelings of love for my wife, and with terrible feelings of guilt for my thoughtlessness.

I dreaded having to wake her up to get her into bed. I carefully picked up the massager and put it away. To my surprise, she rolled over and repositioned herself without waking. I made sure she was comfortable and turned out the nightstand light.

*Talking to God*

I climbed into bed as carefully as I could so as not wake her. I laid on my back staring up at the shadowy patterns on the ceiling. I was doing some serious soul searching. I had never been one to pray much, unless I wanted something, but I closed my eyes and I prayed.

I thanked God for Diane who loved me so much. I told Him I was sorry for not being a better husband. It was clear to me that God had blessed me with my wife, my family, my home, and my job, so I thanked Him for all He had provided. I wept quietly in the dark, not wanting to disturb my wife. I told God that I could see that He had done nothing but bless me over and over again throughout my life, and that I hadn't been thankful. I told Him that I recognized that my life was an offense to Him. I could see that He had responded to my sins against Him by blessing me again and again.

I was broken-hearted and low in spirit. I begged Him to forgive me, though I knew He had no reason to. I told Him I didn't want to sin against Him anymore, though I had no idea how I could ever stop. I begged Him to help me. I pleaded for His forgiveness (Psalm 32:5). I was afraid I didn't even know all the ways I was sinning against Him, so I asked Him to show me my sins and to help me stop committing those sins.

I had no idea at the time how powerful God's answer to that prayer would be. I told God that I wanted to serve Him. Suddenly, in the middle of my prayer to God, I was immediately shocked to have a family we knew slam into the front of my mind. It honestly didn't feel like it was a thought of my own. I prayed, "Lord, I know they have some issues, and I don't know what I could do for them. But if you want me to reach out to this family, could You please give me a sign or something?"

I honestly don't know what kind of sign I expected. I remember thinking maybe I would see a newspaper headline or something that would provide a confirmation somehow. The second I had prayed it, I immediately remembered my mom telling me that we weren't supposed to ask for signs (Matthew 12:39). We weren't supposed to test God. As I was thinking those thoughts I was overwhelmed by God's love for me in a way I had never experienced before—being born again seemed even tangible at the time. God had so radically changed me from the inside that I could almost feel it. When it happened I understood it to be a sensation of intense burning love that God had for me in Christ. It was so strong as to be extremely beautiful and almost unbearable at the same time. It positively took my breath away.

What was happening to me?! The sensation reminded me of walking to elementary school when I was still a boy. I had a tremendous crush, probably my very first, on a cute little girl named Emily. It was the early 1970s, and I remember she had a bee-hive type of hairstyle, that was unlike anything I had even seen on a girl my age. I had such a powerful boyhood crush on her that I remember that walk to school being absolutely torturous. I had a burning sensation in by chest as I thought about seeing her again.

Now, here I was as an adult experiencing a sensation of longing love that was so powerful it was nearly intolerable. It was similar to the sensation I'd felt as a boy, yet many orders of magnitude stronger. I'm glad that I was laying down when it came over me, as I believe it would have taken me off of my feet. I gasped and laughed out loud before realizing I might wake Diane. I was awe struck. The sensation subsided and shrunk back to the center of my chest and I silently prayed. In that moment I knew God had changed me. I believed that the Creator God of the universe had just reached out and touched me in a way that I would never forget. I knew that nothing would ever be the same again.

I don't know how long I stayed awake praying that night, but I know it was a long time before I finally fell asleep exhausted. When I got up the next morning, the events of the night before kept running through my mind as I got ready for work.

*A New Day*

I must not have been acting normally, because Diane stood next to me at the counter as I was finishing getting ready. She asked, "What's going on with you?"

I realized there was no way I could tell her about it then. I said, "I can't explain it now. I've got to leave for work in less than ten minutes. After work I'll take you out for dinner and tell you all about it. Don't worry, it's nothing bad."

We met after work at a restaurant called *Spoons*, and I proceeded to tell her the story you have just read. I had underestimated the emotions I would have recounting what happened. I cried. Diane cried. And people at other tables likely wondered what in the world was wrong with us.

I didn't realize at the time that I was actually telling her about how God saved me that night. Remember, I believed I was already a Christian. I thought I had "re-dedicated my life to God," or some such thing. It was only later that I came to realize that I had never actually been saved before that night.

It's worth mentioning that no one had recently come to me and shared the gospel with me. The only gospel I knew was what I had received thirty-plus years earlier at that little Baptist church. The seed of the gospel had remained in my heart for all those years. The Holy Spirit caused that decades-old seed to burst into new growth the night He finally brought me to true repentance and saving faith. Thank God for His glorious gospel!

*Now I make known to you, brethren, the gospel which I preached to you, which also you received, in which also you stand, by which also you are saved, if you hold fast the word which I preached*

*to you, unless you believed in vain. For I delivered*
*to you as of first importance what I also received,*
*that Christ died for our sins according to the*
*Scriptures (1 Corinthians 15:1-3).*

Amazingly, God saved Diane sometime within that same week! Both of our lives were forever changed and we have grown in the Lord together as a couple. I know many people who were saved by God, while their spouses remained unbelievers. I know how hard a thing that is. I thank God that He made both of us born again, and at the same time.

This time, salvation instantly changed me. There was real fruit in my life. By God's providence, my wife and I had carefully bubble-wrapped and boxed up all of my treasured movie-prop collection, and placed them in storage. Our plan was to stage our home and place it on the market to sell. That meant it needed to be stripped of all but the most basic furnishings. I was sitting in my chair one evening when my mind drifted to some of the objects that I had so loved as to make idols of them. I was shocked when I realized that the warm fuzzy sensation that I had always felt was not there. I thought about one item after another...and nothing. I realized that if all those things went up in flames, I'd be out lots of money, but I'd be okay with it. I was confused. It was as though someone had flipped some kind of switch inside me, turning off my love for those things. I didn't understand. I had no idea that my love for those things was sinful, but suddenly it was just gone. I admit that I mourned the loss of that love for about three days.

It took time for me to recognize the great mercy that God had shown me. I had prayed asking Him to help me stop sinning, even in areas of sin that I wasn't aware of. Trust me when I say that no amount of money could have caused me to stop loving those things. God had simply removed from me what would have been one of the hardest sins for me to give up. He had granted me victory over a massive area of sin in my life that I had yet to even recognize as sin. Like a skilled surgeon with a scalpel, He had removed it from me. Once I realized this truth, I rejoiced and praised Him. How I wish He would have removed from me other areas of temptation that I struggle against in the same way. God had demonstrated His kindness toward me once more. My idols were now just things. Their power over me was no more (1 Thessalonians 1:9).

In the days and weeks that followed we did reach out to our friends who had come to mind on that night that I was saved, and we found they were dealing with some problems that were much larger than we had ever known. By God's grace Diane and I were able to help them through some of their troubles.

*Growing In Grace*

We became convicted that we needed to find a good church—and soon. I didn't know much, but somehow I knew we needed to find a church that clearly taught the Word of God. I wanted to know God and His Word. We found a church with good teaching, and brothers and sisters who made us feel right at home.

It was only a short time before I became strongly convicted that I needed to start sharing my faith with others. The only problem was that I had no idea how to articulate the gospel to someone else. A pastor in our church gave me a book called *The Way of the Master* by Ray Comfort. It contained a copy of a message on CD called "Hell's Best Kept Secret." That book and CD taught me how to biblically share the gospel. Soon I was sharing the gospel with anyone who would listen to me. Even the folks who sat next to me at the oyster-bar of our local seafood restaurant were in danger of getting saved. I came to realize that I had a gift for sharing the gospel. It was easy for me and flowed very naturally out of my heart from the very beginning. Many Christians struggle with knowing how to transition everyday conversations into conversations about Jesus Christ, but since being saved that has always come naturally for me.

By sharing of the gospel, I saw God save a friend that I worked with, and then use him and myself to save his wife. How kind of God to show me the fruits of my labors so early on. I was on fire. The power of the gospel was amazing!

> *For I am not ashamed of the gospel, for it is the power of God for salvation for everyone who believes (Romans 1:16).*

I grew more and more convicted that I needed to go to the streets like the men in the Scriptures to publicly proclaim the gospel, but I was afraid. It's one thing to strike up a one-on-one conversation and share the gospel, yet it seemed to be quite another to stand up on a box and just start preaching. But I earnestly desired to do it. I even thought that I needed to do it. I just could not figure out how I was going to do it on my own. I longed for a brother to counsel me. I needed someone to stand at my side and help me. It is difficult to explain how hard it is to "step up on the box" for the first time. It was one of the biggest challenges I have ever attempted. My legs seemed too weak to stand. It was a spiritual battle raging inside of me.

I had heard about a street preaching school called the "Ambassador's Academy" that was part of Ray Comfort's *Living Waters* ministry. I made my reservations and booked a flight to Southern California.

It was there at the "Third Street Promenade"—a large outdoor mall in Santa Monica—that I first lifted up my voice to preach Christ in the open air. It was there I faced my first heckler. It was there my life was changed again. It was there I first realized that I had been called as an evangelist (Ephesians 4:11).

Whenever I see people congregated together, I long to stand up and proclaim Jesus Christ the righteous One, and Him crucified and risen from the dead on the third day. He is the light of the world (John 8:12). He is the forgiveness of sin (Luke 5:20). He is life eternal to those deserving only hell (John 3:36). It is my honor and my greatest pleasure to bring others to Him. I was once His enemy, and now because of what He has done in me, I am His forever. He is worthy of all that I have to offer.

I was blessed to discover a biblical evangelism group in my area. I began serving the Lord at the side of other brothers and sisters that the Lord had given a heart for the lost from a number of local churches. I was blessed to lead brothers and sisters in my own church in evangelistic efforts around our town.

I am not a good person, and I never have been. I am a bad man deserving of nothing by an eternity in hell. It has never gotten easier for me to confess that. I am a bad man who has been saved by a very good God; a God who loves perfectly the very people He should despise. How can we not tell others about the God who died that we might live?

# 7

# *The Trek for Truth*

*"The heavens are telling of the
glory of God; and their expanse is
declaring the work of His hands"*
*Psalm 19:1*

*M*y intention was a quick brush of my teeth in the dorm
bathroom, not a life-altering conversation. Unanticipated
moments like these, the significance not understood until much
later, are often wrapped around an inconspicuous brush of the
teeth or visit to the water cooler.

*The Journey Begins*

So it was, as I left my dorm room at the University of Colorado
at Boulder, the resident advisor, but still ever so influenced by
others' advice at the tender age of nineteen. The walls were brown
and drab, as was the carpet. But Dave was not. Dave was from
England and sounded erudite to my young ears, with his slightly

balding head, he had a few years on the rest of us. Before I could squeeze the CREST out of its tube, he caught me in the hallway. Our chat turned to spiritual matters. I remember nothing of our conversation except one thing: his question. One never before encountered during my Christian upbringing. "If Jesus was God, Paige, why didn't He come right out and say that?"

Silence.

"He never said that? He never said He was God?" I gawked.

Dave's wry smile, seeing me stumped, ended our conversation as he allowed me to finish my errand and went on his way.

*Raised In the Faith*

I had been raised to believe that Paul's directive to the Ephesians to *"no longer be children, tossed here and there by waves"* meant that doubts or expressed reservations about Christianity was rebellion. Thus, no tough questions were pondered around our dinners of paprika-sprinkled chicken, frozen green beans, baked potatoes and powdered milk. Never did we engage in debates about the authenticity of Scripture as we wound our way up into those sun-drenched Rocky Mountains with our Wheat Thins and cheddar cheese on a Sunday afternoon.

There was no lack of sweet family memories of reading the Bible, singing hymns, enjoying church together and reaching out to neighbors and friends with our faith. We would toss the big red pillows onto the floor and sit in a circle with Mom and Dad nightly. Out would come the *Children's Bible* with the fanciful artwork as we took turns selecting stories for Dad to read. Images of the Red Sea parting and of Noah's family floating in their ark would lull me to sleep after we had sung a few songs and prayed together. Dad's comforting, "Good morning, good night! Don't let the bed bugs bite. Adios. I love you!" as he turned out the light, made it easy for me to see my heavenly Father as a fun, loving, compassionate Dad. And, Mom's Bible-reading at breakfast sent us off to school on the right path. And most importantly, my parents planted the seed of the gospel in my young mind. The question remained as to when that seed actually sprouted and came to fruition in my life.

From the time I could read, the advice of my parents and Sunday school teachers was taken seriously: I prayed and read my *Living Bible* so that I'd know God and how He wanted me to live. But those sweet memories and consistent discipleship did not address the tough questions I would later face in college when I would be challenged by aggressive atheists and agnostics. In high school, those were people I knew only at arm's length, with little thought given as to why they embraced those beliefs.

My relationships had been focused on peers with a shared faith and our commitment to our savior Jesus. Those who saw the eternal in the everyday, who eschewed the parties, the sex, and the marijuana, who respected their parents' curfew, and needed to get home lest they be tired tomorrow—these were my kind of people.

Buddhist? Muslim? Hindu? There were virtually none to be found in my Colorado Springs high school, situated close to the distinctly American *Air Force Academy*. During elementary school I lived in a Muslim country for a year and visited Israel, but, during my pre-college years, very little thought was given to other religions. My friends were Mike, the Catholic with the doctor Dad; Tim, the straight-laced Christian brother of the crazy kid with the Mohawk; Tracy, destined to be the doting mom of a Chihuahua and always concerned that we had jackets should it get cold; and, Dave, the secret Eagle Scout who was always busy on Wednesday nights, but would tell no one why—the son of proud Presbyterians and very concerned about reputation. Even Julie, the freest of them all and my soul sister, kept herself squeaky clean as she loudly sang show tunes and donned her colorful scarves under the nose of her Dad, commander of the Medical Corps at the *Air Force Academy.*

Surrounded by this clean-cut crowd, my faith appeared rock solid, immovable and shining hot, a poker in the fire. Thus, Mom and Dad gave me freedom to choose my university. Not so with my younger sister, surely destined for bad things given bad choices she made in her teens. Off to a Christian college with you, sweet sister. My older sister had followed the way of the cross by choice; *Moody Bible Institute* for her. Off she went to the inner city of Chicago considering the life of full-time ministry.

"You'll do fine, Paige," confidently applauded my parents, when I chose a school known for its excellent journalism program, gorgeous campus and, for me—ever conscientious about stretching my dollar—in-state tuition.

## Rising Doubts

Now I found myself conversing with Dave in the hallway, early in my sophomore year, with one foot in each of two cultures at CU Boulder. With one foot, I sought Christian fellowship, but found it hollow and unsatisfying and, at times, even utterly unwelcoming and uncomfortable. How I detested those sizeable gatherings of *Campus Crusade for Christ* in the brightly-lit, theater-style lecture hall seating 400. "Mob Christianity" was new to me, but "mob anything" was anathema to me. Clearly, that was not my scene. The Navigators—they were a bit too nerdy and square for my desires for the beautiful, elegant and free. Not to be overlooked was my Church of Christ resident advisor from the prior year, whose goal had been baptism of all for salvation, whether previously dunked or not. Not a great start for budding friendships that might influence me for Christ.

Meanwhile, with the other foot, I was dipping my toes into the seductions that CU offered. Saturday nights might find me at a fraternity keg-party with a high school running buddy who did not share my faith, but was becoming an ever-closer friend. On these adventures, with new and old dorm friends, I would enjoy a beer or two, but generally stayed sober to observe the foreign scene and, at times, walk my stumbling friends home. There were the infatuations for this attractive guy, or that one, and dalliances that showed my naïveté. And at the infamous "Boulder Mall Crawl," on a star-studded Halloween, I observed mushrooms, the drug of choice on that night, passing from one person to the next.

*Real Questions*

Neither world felt right. I was not at home as the Christian groupie, the Christian conservative, or the partying college girl. There was some in-between place that had me in its grip. I was neither, so I found myself wondering who I was. I began asking the ultimate life questions like never before: What was real? What was true? What was important? What was to be pursued?

Into this in-between place, came Dave's stifling question early in my sophomore year. But this was not the first life-altering moment in my college experience. This was not the moment when my two-footed, dual-world existence began.

Let's rewind to the fall of my freshman year. Late one night, I prayed with *Campus Crusade* during a twelve-hour prayer vigil. That chilly night I was paired up with a handsome junior guy with whom I shared a blanket as we walked around the campus. His looks captured my attention more than praying did and I was more excited about him than I was about being spiritual, even though we were supposed to be praying for the students in the school of business.

The prayer warriors, myself included, not feeling very warlike, moved into a meeting room and continued, kneeling on the carpet in a large circle. As the evening progressed, I opened my eyes, looked around and wondered: "What am I doing here? What if this is all untrue? Is there a God who hears our prayers? Is this prayer vigil a ruse that is keeping me from the carousing that my roommate and dorm neighbors are surely enjoying?"

Looking at the strangers surrounding me on earnestly-bent knee, I was struck with a strong sense of my heart turning to stone. Through Ezekiel, God promised the Israelites that He would give them a new heart and put a new spirit within them. He would remove their heart of stone and give them a heart of flesh (Ezekiel 36:26). Yet, here I was experiencing the opposite. Suddenly, I didn't belong. Slowly, I got up and slipped out of the brightly-lit room; no one noticing; no one ever asking where I had gone on that lonely night. Sheer numbers made my exit anonymous, lost in the vastness of this college scene.

## The Tipping Point

Into the darkness of a quiet campus, punctuated by laughs from a dorm room full of intoxicated freshmen, it was as if I was stepping out of a space capsule onto the surface of the moon.

It felt new. "Did I just stop being a Christian? Is this the new me? What if I was to go through life alone, without God? What if the Friend I had known all these years was a figment of my imagination?" I had never before had the experience of being on the "outside" of the world of Christianity, looking in. But, that's where I suddenly found myself...I had leapt over the fence to the "other side."

One might suspect that this was the beginning of the story of a young woman who turned to alcohol and drugs and sex after years of repression. No—not at all. I was not happy to be faced with so many doubts about my faith. Up to that point, God had always been a positive, hopeful, comforting Friend. I felt taken care of and loved by Him, and by his Son. I did not welcome this intrusion of doubt into my spiritual world. But, I also could not deny that something unexpected had happened in my soul.

*Into the Maze*

That moment in September of 1986 ushered in an arduous journey that I spent wandering through a spiritual maze that did not allow me an exit until Easter of 2000...almost fourteen years later.

My Creator never stopped loving me even when I was confused. In His grace He sent me a gift. Robert Burgess, a fellow resident advisor, entered into my confused world and grounded me in a place that was neither snobbishly conservative, superficially cheerful, nor crassly obscene. Here, in this sweet Episcopal-turned-evangelical, I found a balanced and sober-minded senior-year engineering student. He settled the earthquake of doubt and the void of feeling like a castaway. Here it felt right, in his company, in his confidence, in his intelligence, in his ease with the world. He moved through life smoothly, with his laid-back California style, flip flops, shorts, beautiful tanned legs and sun-bleached hair. He met my expectations for "Mr. Right." There were to be troubles ahead and the road would be long, but, he did prove to be my "Mr. Forever." And God has used him mightily in my life to direct me, grow me, challenge me, and to teach me what the forgiveness from our Savior looks like when we're asked to apply it to our own lives. We have both had moments when we wished we had never met the other. But, God uses iron to sharpen iron (Proverbs 27:17), and opposites attract, and the attraction was strong then, and is now.

If you were to ask Robert about his life-altering moments, surely one of them would be the day that I announced my need to take a break from church—1995. We got married in the church where we made vows to our common God. Yet here I was, not asking permission, but telling him that I needed a break.

Wasn't all that behind us now? Hadn't I resolved the trouble in my soul during the five-and-a-half years that we dated? Hadn't I travelled enough? Hadn't I had enough life experience? Hadn't I worked through enough of life's challenges to be settled in my faith? Hadn't he waited long enough to be sure I was sure? Why now, nine years after that first moment at the prayer vigil, was I leaving the church?

But for me, the doubts had been veiled under the comforts of the Christian life. Robert's arms gave me solace. *All Souls Church* gave me friendship as an expat in London, where I lived during my first year out of college. The faith-based fellowship of "Overeaters Anonymous," where I struggled to make food an acquaintance rather than a best friend, showed me the importance of God as I worked through life's struggles. Two short-term missions (to Romania and Montreal) through *Operation Mobilization* gave me a sense of purpose. But, a quote from Paul Little's, *Know Why You Believe*, rang true for me: "One cannot indefinitely drive himself to do by willpower that of which he is not intellectually convinced. Witnessing, for example. He eventually suffers emotional collapse."

I had married a man who embraced biblical values, after having seen the contrast between the values and behaviors of unbelieving versus believing men. And once married, the camaraderie of fellow young-marrieds from *Peninsula Bible Church* had given us a new world to move in, a world of partnership, rather than self. A world of savory meals, late nights, shared dreams, nostalgic music, well-chosen wine, and a shared faith and grounding in the things of God. The world stood before us idealistic twenty year-olds. We would bravely face it together, enjoying the joys of married life and looking forward to all that God had in store.

*Still Searching*

But, in every spiritual encounter—whether a small group Bible Study, church on Sundays, or a social gathering with Christians—I was the one asking questions that bristled feathers. I'll never forget the anger I aroused in one of my not-easily-angered male friends, and, on another occasion, my brother-in-law, when I called God, "She." A need to reconcile feminism with the Bible was one of the many issues I grappled with.

When the soul is disquieted, it cannot be silenced forever. Given my expressive, honest and all-or-nothing approach to life, no veil could be thick enough to allow me to move in comfort in my all-Christian world with these lingering doubts indefinitely. The duality of my feelings was too much to bear.

As a member of the *Peninsula Bible Church* choir, I joined voices with others, singing God's praises. But another one of those "AHA!" moments was racing into our lives. As Christmas neared, so did calamity. I stood, well-dressed and smiling, hair freshly washed, face well made up, one among many in the rows of beautiful voices, singing:

*Silent night! Holy night! Son of God, Love's pure light. Radiant, beams from Thy Holy face, with the dawn of redeeming grace, Jesus, Lord at Thy birth, Jesus, Lord at Thy birth.*

Yet, I was listening to the words, really listening to the words, and what I experienced were the "heart-to-stone" feelings of years earlier. Do I really believe these words? Can I continue to stand up here, week after week, unsure if any of this is true? It's killing me. It's killing my soul to be in this conflicted place again. I wanted to believe. I wanted to! It was familiar and comfortable. But, I was skeptical about the truthfulness of any of it.

Despair. Darkness. Isolation. Freedom—freedom to be honest. Freedom to do what settled my soul. There were no parents to tell me I had to do this; had to go to church; had to believe. Had to ignore the waves of doubt crashing over me. Yes, there was a husband. But, I had chosen wisely, at least for this phase of life. I had chosen a man who believed, but was not overboard in his beliefs. He had come from a family of religious participation, but not religious extremism. And, so, I hoped he would bear my need for a religious time-out with grace.

*Time Out*

And he did, for the most part. What I now know, after twenty-plus years of marriage, that I didn't know then, was that Robert's smooth way of moving through life is also a veil—a veil over a soul that too had questions, secrets, and doubts. But since he does not live out loud as I do, this was not expressed. He acquiesced to my request, begrudgingly, but without protest. So we stopped going to church.

The following year or two after I stopped going to church, I contemplated my questions, told God of my doubts, asked Him for His help, but did not take the time to face the issues directly. I still led an upright life, even continuing to give ten percent of our income—but switching the focus of our giving from Christian organizations to secular "save the animals," "save the earth," and "feed the poor" non-profits.

I drifted. Life was busy, and good...so I thought.

There were the demands of the profitable public relations agency where I was a director, interfacing with the movers and shakers and their hard-working marketing executives. There were the business suits, fancy meals and pressing deadlines. There was the business travel, press tours to Boston, New York, and Las Vegas. Nice hotels; limousines; trade shows. And there was the money, so nice to see it coming in and accumulating, as we saved. It was nice to spend some of it relaxing during weekends away at bed and breakfasts, with wine-tasting, bike-riding and great food. Yes, travel, always the travel. Life was good and full and sweet.

And there were the friends, committed believing friends, despite the lapse in my faith. Friends who faithfully waited out my doubts: steadfast and wise Anna and Todd; honest and cheerful Dana and Steve; unwavering-in-their-faith and jubilant-in-parenthood, Diane and Todd.

And there was my family: worried and ever-prayerful Mom; steady Dad, who made me feel loved despite his disappointment. There was my older sister, who was glad to have me join her in the unbelieving ranks, glad to no longer be alone following her rejection of Christ as her faith proved too thin for encounters at *Moody*. And there was my younger sister, aware and caring, but busy with marriage and changes in her life.

### Around the World

And there was the travel again. Wanderlust; I had it. Travel was a passion, an obsession. It started in childhood. The most exciting and cherished year of my life was the one spent living in Egypt. We couldn't have been more surprised the night Dad paused in his perfect preparation of mashed potatoes and gravy to ask what we'd think of leaving our suburban Chicago life for a year living in Egypt. "Let's go!" So Dad agreed to a management consulting assignment with the Egyptian government's Water and Sewer Authority.

The smells, sights and sounds of Egypt stay with me. Piping hot pita bread, fresh out of the bee-hive oven, as I waited to take it home for breakfast in our ocean-side, penthouse apartment in Alexandria. There, we would fill the pita with honey as we watched ships come into harbor from our balcony and the delivery boys balancing crates on top of their heads, loaded with pita bread, as they weaved through traffic on bikes. There was the daily call to prayer from the mosques on each corner. I recall the wailing lament of hired female mourners at funeral tents set up to remember the departed. And in Cairo there were the bazaars in the winding, crowded alley-ways where salespeople hawked their brass pyramids, elegant smoke pipes and hieroglyph necklaces.

That year in Egypt engendered in me an appreciation for the incredible mysteries and stories to be unraveled as one travelled foreign lands. Seeing every country in the world seemed a perfectly reasonable aspiration. Dozens of European countries were already stamped into my passport as well as the nearby Caribbean Islands and border countries.

But Asia was calling me. During our engagement, Robert had agreed that travel did not have to stop once we got married. "A country a year," he promised.

"Even if it means we are apart at times?" I asked.

And so, it was agreed. In 1995, he had taken a break between jobs and travelled to Central America, studying Spanish, while I worked and visited him a few times. Then it was 1997, and my turn. I would travel to Southeast Asia and he would work and visit me twice.

I quit my job and eagerly anticipated the hours of alone time to be enjoyed while travelling. Time to write, explore, think, and, I promised myself, take seriously the faith questions which had gone unaddressed for too long. The backpack I carried was light with clothes but heavy with books. There were a variety of books, some spiritual ones but also ones on travel as well as classic novels I always wanted to read. There was one book of note in that heavy backpack called *Letters from a Skeptic: A Son Wrestles with His Father's Questions about Christianity*. My friends, Diane and Todd, gave it to me thinking that it might help me in my "spiritual quest." That book seemed a worthy starting line for my marathon exploration, so into the bag it went. Through Singapore, Malaysia, Indonesia and Thailand, the book was rarely touched. There were many distractions. New friends were made in the sweaty youth hostels of Singapore, the thatched roof huts and colorful waters of the South China Sea in the Tioman Islands, and amongst the mosques and quiet streets of Kota Bharu, Malaysia. The orangutans dancing in the trees outside my cabin in Sumatra and the dolphins dancing in the Gulf of Thailand had me transfixed, while I poured through my prized long novels.

Then Robert came to visit me in Thailand which distracted me even more from my studies as we swam among jelly fish in minty blue waters, ate fragrant shrimp under romantic lights at an island restaurant, and had an elephant ride to a remote village where some did unspeakable damage to themselves through opium use. And the morning of my thirtieth birthday dawned to the sound of pigs snorting under our raised bamboo house in a northern Thailand village where we met our sponsored Compassion child. But when Robert returned to his work in California, I acknowledged time's fleeting nature and determined to travel solo to ensure serious study and reflection.

*Drawing Near*

Surrounded by saffron-robed Buddhist monks in Laos, and quieted by the sight of gleaming gold temple roofs, I opened myself up to what God had for me in the pages of *Letters from a Skeptic*. I read as I sat at an outdoor café in Saigon, while masses of bicycling Vietnamese rode to work; I read as I floated down the river in Hue, eager to see ancient Vietnamese royal palaces. I read as I watched pink dolphins out the window of the hydrofoil between Macau and Hong Kong. As I ate from roadside food stands on the streets of southwestern China after a long bike ride...I read. I asked God to reveal Himself to me. I prayed for understanding.

Long ago I had tired of Christianity's "pat answers"—simplified and evasive responses that use Bible verses to explain questions at hand when often it's the Bible itself that is being questioned. Back up! I didn't trust the Bible as authoritative. So, answers from the Bible, at least at that point, did not do it for me. Thus, this book appealed to me. Edward Boyd freely and without guile expressed his mistrust of Christianity and asked specific questions to which his professor of theology son, promised to answer as thoroughly and as honestly as possible.

Enjoying the gentle sway of a train in Vietnam and watching the bucolic scenes whir by, I closed that book as I read its last page. I was silenced again. The book had given me the distinct sense that all of my questions were answerable. The human author alone could not quell my doubts, but, with a book like his and others I would find, my questions were answerable. I prayed,

> *Lord, I am moved by the evidence provided in* Letters from a Skeptic. *My mind still feels muddled and confused, and You know, God, that I cannot consider my destination reached until I have cleared the fog in my mind by finding answers. But, for the first time, it's conceivable that my doubts could be pacified through diligent study. So, God, while I cannot recommit my life to you yet, I thank you for revealing enough that You seem findable. Please, Lord, reveal Yourself to me completely and rightly. Let me find You*

*wherever You may be found. Let me leave no*
*stone unturned. I will continue this journey, and*
*be faithful to it, however arduous the process*
*may be.*

For a few days, I explored Hanoi, Vietnam as if in a dream. The sandwiches made of crisp French bread, the icons of communism, and the busy markets sought to divert me, but, I was resolved to determine, "What should be the next step?"

Processing my thoughts on paper seemed wise—I was a journalism major. Journaling had occupied hours of my time for many years. So, I determined to write down every question or doubt that troubled me. At first, I wrote question after question, with reckless abandon. No question was too silly, too far out, just as a "to do list" today helps relieve stress allowing me to focus on just one item at a time. The questions helped me start somewhere. Once it was complete, I determined to read *Letters from a Skeptic* again to record every answer that it provided to the questions I had written down.

After four months of a backpacking life, I returned home to my loving (and patient) husband and to the fast-paced, high-tech Silicon Valley. But I did not allow my search for a new job, or our move to San Francisco, prevent me from continuing my quest.

Having finished *Letters from a Skeptic*, the list of books I read and handled in the same manner grew and grew. Here are some of the books I read. Not all are recommended but they reveal the breadth of my reading and writing at the time:

- *Christian Apologetics*, Norman Geisler
- *Church History in Plain English*, Bruce Shelley

- *Created for Commitment*, A. Wetherell Johnson
- *Creation Spirituality*, Matthew Fox
- *CS Lewis and his World*, David Barratt
- *Eternity in Their Hearts*, Don Richardson
- *Evidence that Demands a Verdict*, Josh McDowell
- *Gnosis and Faith*, Riemer Roukema
- *Honest to God*, John Robinson
- *How to Believe*, Ralph Stockman
- *I and Thou*, Martin Buber
- *I'm Glad You Asked*, Kenneth Boa and Larry Moody
- *Know Why You Believe*, Paul Little
- *Letters from a Skeptic*, Gregory Boyd and Edward Boyd
- *Mere Christianity*, C. S. Lewis
- *New Testament Documents: Are They Reliable?*, F. F. Bruce
- *Orthodoxy*, G. K. Chesterton
- *Out of the Garden: Women Writers on the Bible*, Christina Buchmann and Celina Spiegel
- *Religions of the World*, Gerald Berry
- *Surprised by Joy*, C. S. Lewis
- *The Case for Christ*, Lee Strobel
- *The Closing of the American Mind*, Allan Bloom
- *The Feminine Face of God*, Anderson and Hopkins
- *The Hero's Journey*, Joseph Campbell
- *The Jesus I Never Knew*, Philip Yancey
- *The Quran*, Penguin Classics
- *The Pilgrim's Regress*, C. S. Lewis
- *The Universality of Jesus*, G. A. Johnston Ross
- *The Works of Josephus*, translated by William Whiston
- *Through Gates of Splendor*, Elisabeth Elliott

- *To Know: Guide to Women's Spirituality*, Jade
- *Who Moved the Stone*, Frank Morison
- *Why Believe in God*, Michael Goulder and John Hick
- *Why I Believe in a Personal God*, George Carey
- *World Religions, from Ancient History to the Present*, edited by Geoffrey Parrinder

Late at night, and, most especially during weekend retreats, I continued to read. Over the next few years, I visited a number of beautiful monasteries in California to focus on the work for concentrated periods of time. Soon, my journal became quite a tome. But I still felt jumbled. I longed for an understanding of how to complete my journey. Somehow, my need for orderly, complete answers wasn't satisfied.

Finally, during one of my retreats, a "logical progression" made up of nine questions crystallized in my mind. This thought process allowed me to organize my jumbled thoughts into what would be, once the questions were answered, a logical explanation and basis for my Christian faith.

Following are the nine questions that I ultimately had to answer, to my mental satisfaction, before I identified the faith of my life...ultimately, the Christian faith:

1) Is there a God?
2) If there is a God, then is He a personal God?
3) If He is a personal God, then He must have revealed Himself to me so that I know what kind of relationship He wants to have with me. How has God revealed Himself to me? (Evaluate the "revelations from God" found in the major world religions.)

4) If I plan to use the Bible as a source for God's "revelation," then why is the Bible a reliable book?

5) If I consider the Bible to be a reliable book, then what did God reveal to me through the Bible about how He wants me to relate to Him?

6) What does belief in God, the Bible and Jesus demand of me? What does God want of my life?

7) Specifically, what proof do we have, biblical or otherwise, that Jesus was/is God's Son, the Savior, the Christ, the Messiah?

8) Who do I say Jesus was?

9) Am I willing to embrace the Jesus of the Bible?

So, having formed a logical process for coming to peace with a faith, I acknowledged that I had never struggled with the existence of God. Creation was too powerful for that, as God, through Paul, foretold in Romans 1:20: *"For since the creation of the world His invisible attributes, His eternal power and divine nature, have been clearly seen, being understood through what has been made, so that they are without excuse."* But, I struggled with question number two: If there is a God, then is it a personal God?

*Coming To Jesus*

Nonetheless, I felt ready to attend church again—I had reached the point where I felt it would help me answer my questions, rather than prevent me from honestly searching. And so, in 1999, Robert and I found a church in the heart of San Francisco, *Cornerstone Church*. It was perfect for me, and Robert was willing to become part of any Bible-believing church that I was willing to attend. There, the atmosphere was new; it freed me to listen with open ears and see with fresh eyes. The fantastic music allowed my soul to soar to heavenly heights. The sermons were delivered in a style that quite gently, but unequivocally made the case for Jesus as the center of one's life.

The resolution to, "If there is a God, then is it a personal God?" came to me a few months after I began attending church again, but not within the walls of the church building but in the cathedral of nature created by God. This was my fourth "Aha!" moment.

My parents lived in Colorado. Robert and I enjoyed driving between California and Colorado—beautiful country! We especially loved Highway 50 through Nevada—called "the Loneliest Road in America" for a reason. During a drive back to California with Robert, my sister, and her husband, in 1999, I volunteered for a driving shift that allowed me to watch the sunrise over the deserts of Nevada. While at the steering wheel, thinking and praying, the sun began to rise, turning the dunes first a dark blue, then violet, pink, orange and finally a bright yellow. The light lit on me like the hand of God saying, "Yes, Paige! I am YOUR God. I am aware of your quest. I am present in the desert with you. I am here as your personal God and I want to have a personal relationship with you."

That winter, I was given the answer to my most challenging question. Yes, God was a personal God. And, therefore, the way I saw it, God must have revealed Himself to me somewhere in the religions of the world so that I could know what kind of relationship He wants to have with me.

Books on world religions, plus what I had seen on my travels, had easily convinced me that if God was a personal God, then

Jesus was the true revelation. There was not another religion that could withstand the scrutiny under which my faith fell. No other could offer the archeological evidence, historical veracity, countless manuscripts, fulfilled prophecies, or even compelling stories of changed lives. So, I knew that the next question, "How has God revealed himself to me?" clearly pointed to Christianity. I was standing at the edge of the precipice, acknowledging that a leap of faith was now required.

### Knowing Christ

That leap of faith was made easy in the context of our church's presentation of the Bible through drama. The Easter production in 2000 was a beautiful portrayal of the life of Christ, as seen through the eyes of Peter. During the play, when Jesus asked Peter, *"But who do you say that I am?"* I felt that Jesus was asking me that question. I had to say, quietly, in my heart, as did Peter, *"You are the Christ!"* (Matthew 16:16).

Thus ended my quest, during Easter of 2000. Through this honest search I came to a profound and solid understanding of my faith in my Creator and in His gift—Jesus, the Savior. Looking back, it's very possible that I was saved as a young child when I exercised that simple faith in the gospel. At the time I believed that I was a sinner; I could not stand before God because of my sin. Jesus' victory over sin and His death and resurrection secured my salvation. Because of Christ's blood, I could stand before God; my sins had been washed away. And, I was baptized to express my commitment publicly. However, my conversion and the sweet Christian family upbringing and consistent discipleship I received did not prepare me for the clash of worldviews I would face later in life, a battle that caused me at times to even doubt my faith. But Jesus proved faithful just as He promised. As His sheep I could never be snatched out of His or the Father's grip of saving love (John 10:27-29).

I do not want to stop growing in my faith. I have learned that by attacking a question of faith head on, the answers become clear. My studies, critical evaluation and writing are critical to reinforcing my faith whenever I have doubt, and to help me better articulate a defense of my faith, when asked. What's more, a still small voice has given me hope that perhaps, someday, my work will lead someone else into the place of comfort, intimacy and peace that I now claim as the most important thing in my life. Hopefully, this will aid another searching soul to be able to say, with confidence, "You are the Christ, the Messiah!"

*But sanctify Christ as Lord in your hearts, always being ready to make a defense to everyone who asks you to give an account for the hope that is in you, yet with gentleness and reverence (1 Peter 3:15)*

# 8

## *Suffering, then Glory*

*"Blessed are you when others revile you
and persecute you and utter all kinds of
evil against you falsely on My account"*
*Matthew 5:11*

*I* was born in Shanghai, China in 1967, the youngest of four
children. Born into a fourth generation Christian family, as a
young girl, I naturally assumed that Christians must give birth
to Christians. My mother's grandparents were one of the four
families in a village who had decided to follow Christ when
Hudson Taylor's China Inland Mission came to town in the
late 1800's. The gospel brought spiritual liberation, but also
practical liberation like social equality since the Bible teaches
man and woman are equally made in God's image. My grandma
therefore escaped the centuries-old Chinese practice of foot-
binding common among the women in that culture. To this day,
I blame my big feet on my grandmother.

*Piercing Questions*

One day, when I was seven, I had stopped by to play at a neighbor's home. Out of nowhere, the neighbor asked me if I was a Christian. I was dumbfounded by such a stupid question coming from an adult. Without a blink of an eye, I responded, "Of course! Now let me get on to my play time."

But she continued, "What does it mean to you to be a Christian if you are one?"

I paused and matter-of-factly replied, "I don't steal, I don't kill," giving her a list of all the "bad" things a seven-year-old can come up with while trying to get on with the priority of play time. This neighbor was a good family friend who helped my family survive Mao's Communist "Cultural Revolution" that spanned from 1966-1976. She was not satisfied with my curt answers and she was also persistent and so she continued to hound me by next asking, "Have you ever sinned?"

Highly annoyed, I quipped, "No! I'm a good girl." Insulted, I began thinking in black and white to myself, "What does she want from a perfectly good girl, whose biggest ambition in life at that point was to see her Christian parents get along with each other and to have a kind and loving home like this lady seemed to have?" Even at seven, I "knew" this was a noble cause and made it a mission of my life.

Just when I thought I was done with her final question, her mouth opened, yet again! "Have you ever lied, stolen from others, white lies, black lies, grey lies, saying things just to be polite when you don't really mean it?"

I thought, "That's what Chinese do when being offered something, we'll say 'no' three times before we say 'yes' out of politeness, what does she want from me? I'm a good girl, since when did proper manners become a sin?" Rolling my eyes in my head, she saw that I was at a loss for words.

Kindly she offered, "You don't have to answer those questions right now. But you should think about them when you go home. Have you ever invited Jesus into your heart?"

Confused, I paused and responded, "No".

*Gospel Truth*

She said, "We are all sinners; only the blood of Jesus on the cross can redeem us from our sin. To become a Christian, each person needs to be saved and, to come before Christ to ask Him to forgive our sin by the death of Jesus." Still lost in a train of thought as I was having a hard time processing all this new information, she went on, "I'm going to teach you to pray and ask Jesus to come into your heart and you can do it anywhere, anytime when you feel you are ready." I went home convicted, thought about everything she said, and decided to invite Jesus into my heart! That was forty years ago.

In Communist China, biblical Christianity was illegal. So every Sunday we would have an early secret family worship time in our house, after we carefully closed the door in the garden to the alley-way and the door to the house, locked the windows and closed the curtains. The whole house was sealed tight. Father would lead us in song and worship, full of joy and enthusiasm. Some of us would play the harmonica and others the accordion. We would march around the east side of our house as a little band singing hymns mom and dad just taught us...off key and off beat, but joyously nevertheless. Parents would signal us to hush when the four of us would get too loud when singing.

I was born during the heat of the Cultural Revolution, in the 1960's. Mom and Dad had hoped that my birth would be the end, or at least a break from their persecution, therefore they named me Elim. Elim is the name of an oasis in the desert mentioned at the end of Exodus chapter fifteen, where the Israelites were complaining about lack of water as they wandered in the Sinai Peninsula, trying to reach the land of "milk and honey" in the land of Canaan. And God led them to that oasis.

## Religious Persecution

The Communist revolutionaries interrogated my parents separately, seeking to extract illicit information in an attempt to turn them against each other. At that time they incarcerated my mom in an old British bank vault. They kept my three older siblings with my dad. And since I was still nursing, they decided to lock me up with my mom with three shifts of security guards keeping a watchful eye on us 24/7. My Christian mother was considered by the government to be the scum of society and an imminent threat, as she was spreading the good news about Jesus Christ, which they considered to be poisonous. They guarded her like precious crown jewels in a bank vault so that she could not run away with her nursing infant. They interrogated my mom throughout the day, fabricating stories about what my father had already confessed to them, attempting to force a confession out of her. They rationed one bowl of soup per meal, three times a day. It was just liquid, having no real content like meat or veggies. It was inhumane. They had no conscience about depriving a nursing mom of proper nutrition. They were bankrupt of basic human kindness. Ironically, the Communists boasted of how they were for the equality of all people, especially the working class. What a lie. They would mock my mom, telling her that God can perform miracles, so if she was hungry then she should go to Him for more. They would even harass and scare me and then tell my mom that if she only had denounced her faith and provided the names and contacts of other believers, then they would stop bothering me.

They tried to intimidate my mom through guilt telling her that she was the one needlessly bringing all these troubles on her kids and they questioned her true love for her kids and family. The truth was that my mom was the most fiercely devoted mother that I have known. They called her unwavering loyalty to her faith selfish stubbornness and accused her of how short-sighted she was by not giving in. They relentlessly blamed her faith as the cause for creating all kinds of troubles for her family, and the future of her kids would be affected because of her refusal to renounce her faith or give contacts of fellow believers.

My parents were also physically persecuted and tortured, along with being subjected to public humiliation. They were brought out in public to be made a spectacle for on-lookers, as they were spat upon and jeered while being displayed with a board hung on their necks with titles of their crimes, and slapped in the faces by the revolutionaries. Many times, mom was forced to watch as they beat my father with chains wrapped in rubber. The persecution got so severe my father lost his hearing, after his ear drums got broken from all the beating and slapping. His back was broken by several grueling beatings.

The physical torture began to take a toll on my father. They wanted him to denounce his faith in God and give away the contacts of his Christian network in the country. Many times, father had felt so hopeless and helpless, the moment of weakness caused him to begin doubting where His God was. One night after being beaten to a bloody pulp on his backside, he couldn't sleep on his back or sit. Laying on his stomach, he told mom to put all the best food available in the home for the last dinner for his family of six. He told her that he'd decided to wake up at 1:00 AM to turn on the gas to put an end to this endless physical, emotional, and spiritual torture. He said he saw no future for himself or his four children—they would suffer the same ill fate, why not end everything now?

> 'For My thoughts are not your thoughts, nor are your ways My ways,' declares the LORD. 'For as the heavens are higher than the earth, so are My ways higher than your ways, and My thoughts than your thoughts' (Isaiah 55:8-9).

### Our God Reigns

Our God is such a mighty God, so full of creativity and also intervenes with amazing providential personal care. God works in strange, miraculous ways. After father communicated his plan to end it all, mother ran to the neighbor after midnight so no one would see her. It was the same neighbor who had relentlessly convinced me of being a sinner. The two prayed together and begged God to somehow intervene. The alarm went off as planned at 1:00 AM, but father was so deep asleep that he didn't wake up till daylight had already broken in. He later kicked himself for having missed his opportunity to kill his family before they were killed by the Communists.

My parents were amazingly innovative. One time the commies told them that they were not allowed to have access to public water and that they should ask their God to provide water through a miracle if they needed it. So Mom and Dad dug a well in the yard and oh, how God provided some of the most refreshing, mineral-rich water I ever tasted! The neighbors would come begging for it in the summer when they wanted their watermelons cooled. To keep their rambunctious kids physically occupied with all that energy, father built a monkey-bar in our yard and kept us busy teaching us Chinese painting. He forced us to appreciate classical music with absolute quietness so we could become the next Mozart, or because he needed to take a nap in peace. He also had us get up early in the morning to learn stupid foreign languages so that when opportunity presented itself, we could escape to the Western world. On some Sundays, father would put all of us on a tricycle with self-made extensions borrowed from work along with some water and snacks and send us off to the park for the day. Despite all the inconveniences and hardships of being Christians in a hostile Communist country, as a little girl, I was sheltered by God through my strong, godly parents and life got managed.

Being the youngest of four kids, I had always been very dependent on my mother emotionally. When I did something wrong and wanted to avoid father's wrath, I would always run to my mom. Most of the time it worked unless father got to it before mother even had a chance. She is a super woman. Her passion for God, and her tenacity to pass the torch of faith to her kids has become a torch for me to pass down. One of the greatest gifts she gave is that this godly woman had taught me how to pray as a little girl even though it was against the law to teach your kids about faith and God. Years later I asked my mom why she risked teaching us how to pray. As though transcending into a different time, she paused for some moment, and said, "Many people, friends of ours, had decided not to bother with pass the torch of faith to their kids, but we risked our lives to do so. And we would do it again and again."

Pausing momentarily she then told me a short story: "It was a very firm vision your father and I had shared together that we must share the gospel with you four when we could. And it had become ever more clear when one time the commies came to fetch us in a jeep. Your older sister, Jireh, was four, your older twin brothers, Enoch and Isaac were three, you were not one yet, still nursing. They parked the jeep outside of our home; your father heard the commotion and had a feeling that it was not going to be good. Before we had any time to make a plan, the revolutionists had hopped over the wall and were already in our yard. They put your father in handcuffs and dragged him and me to the jeep. Your older brothers were playing with each other. You started crying, so Jireh went to get you; she held you tight trying to give you all the comfort she could muster as a four-year-old. She too cried, watching the revolutionists shove father and me into the jeep, tears quietly flowing off her cheeks. We didn't know when or if we would ever return to you kids again. That's when we vowed that if God allowed us to return to you, no matter how dangerous it was, we would teach you about our God so that no matter what might happen to us, you would always be able to go to the omnipotent God for help anytime, anywhere, under any circumstance."

And that's exactly what they did. They gave us the greatest gift, life after life.

## Escaping Communism

Under the religious oppression, many Christians, including my family, looked for all kinds of ways to escape to the free world.

My grandmother had moved to Hong Kong in the 1960's, shortly after her husband, a Lutheran pastor, was starved to death because of his Christian faith. The Communists forced him to stand ninety degrees for seven days straight. His persecutors mocked him, telling him that his almighty and merciful God can descend and rescue him. My grandma, the survivor, ended up going to college, a first for the family; and she even attended the first seminary for women in China.

My parents sought a visiting visa for over twenty years in an attempt to get out of China, but they were denied every time. So after twenty years of rejection they changed their strategy from trying to get a visa for the whole family to requesting a visa for just one person. It worked! The first visa granted was for my mother. After waiting for decades she finally received one granting her permission to leave China in 1980! Being separated from my mom was surreal; it didn't really sink in till the day we went to see mom off at the train station. I was one month away from turning thirteen.

Unbeknownst to me, my mom had been preparing me for this day of separation for quite some time. She routinely reminded me to turn to God anytime, anywhere. As I look back, I am awed by her wisdom and compassion during that time as she readied for the difficult transition, knowing how traumatic it would be for me. Her preparation then proved to have a life-long impact on me, even to this day. I'm very grateful for the time she took, the courage and strength she demonstrated, the gentleness she used to disciple me during a very short time frame and under very limited circumstances, while taking on such great risk amidst a politically unstable, anti-Christian environment.

She prepared me practically, but she also prepared me spiritually. Mother taught me how to have a daily devotion time. She said, "Whenever you miss me, read the Bible, because I will be reading the Bible. You can write to me and share with me the passage you've read. I will read them too. We will pray to the same God. When you pray and read the Bible, you will feel as though we were together. When you miss me, pray to God that He will reunite us soon. And guess what? He will answer your prayers. You can try God and see how faithful He is. I will pray for you as well."

None of her words made any sense to me because I'd never been separated from my mom, not even when they locked us up in the bank vault. And there were the times when I'd get up early at four in the morning just to be with my mom when she went to the stinky produce market where all the live chickens got slaughtered and the fish got killed during the holiday seasons. I loved everything about her; she's my hero. I always wanted to be just like her. When she was at work, and I'd be missing her, I'd go sniff at her clothes and felt comforted by that familiar creamy scent of hers. Like a lonely puppy, I'd get so excited and smother her when she got home from work. All four of us would line up at the front door around the time mom and dad would come home and greet them enthusiastically...mine was the most genuine for sure! My mother and I were inseparable. I couldn't comprehend what it meant to be separated from her.

*Separation*

But the day finally arrived. We went to the train station to see her off. Father helped to get her limited luggage settled. She waited as long as she could on the platform to be with us until the final call of departure got blasted in our ears. She moved to her seat and leaned out the window. I was still chatting up a storm about nothing as usual, laughing now and then as though nothing was happening. I remember her looking at me, more intently than normal, more than when I had played pranks on her and got into trouble for it. And then the train started to move slowly. That's when reality of our separation began to sink in.

My uncle always teased me of how I talked more than the aggregate of all five members in the family. Suddenly I stopped talking and stopped laughing, which was extremely unusual; I became speechless for once. As the train started to huff and puff, and picked up its speed, I no longer could hold it in. I burst into uncontrollable wailing, tears flooded my face. I stood on the platform, confused and wishing I could be in my mom's bosom one more time, smelling that familiar creamy scent and making it mine for good. When the train finally disappeared out of sight, my family motioned that it was time to leave. But I wasn't ready; I wanted to stand there as long as I could, as though by standing there I could bring my mom back to me. I lingered, but I felt embarrassed that I couldn't help tears from rolling down on my cheeks, or keep my runny nose from dripping non-stop. My father handed me three, four, five handkerchiefs after the last two got drenched.

On the way home, after accepting that I could not bring my beloved mama back, my next immediate and biggest concern was who'd be there to rescue me from self-inflicted naughty deeds. By the time we got home, I wanted to find a piece of mom. I remembered mom said to go to the Bible. I knew where my parents hid the one and only family Bible—under a thick mattress. I got it and remembered my mom said to start with the New Testament. I began reading the Bible on my own for the first time in my life, even though it was self-serving as I wanted to be connected to my mom somehow. Since my mom said I could go to God for anything, I also planned on counting on God to bail me out on these naughty deeds that I would get myself into. Even as a twelve-year-old, I found it difficult to maintain pure thoughts. Finding creative ways to provoke my older siblings had become a sport to me. It produced instant gratification, and at times, instant consequences, and now my mom was no longer there to bail me out.

As I carefully opened the Bible, and started reading, beyond my belief, I almost could feel that my mother was right next to me as though we were reading it together. I could feel my body leaning into her as she was helping me with those weird traditional Chinese characters that I hadn't learned in school under the simplified Chinese writing. Though my parents taught us the New Testament stories countless times, it seemed now as though I was reading them for the first time. It became addictive over time, as I longed to feel my mom's presence by going to the Bible just as she told me. It reminded me of her soft, gentle stroke, her kind comforting words, her protectiveness and extra grace on a helplessly naughty little girl. Oh how I missed her so terribly and I needed her protection so desperately. Now I had to learn to fend for myself.

### A Sovereign God

An important verse my mother had taught me before she left me to the wolves, my older siblings, was Romans 8:28: *"And we know that in all things God works for the good of those who love him, who have been called according to his purpose."* I couldn't see any good coming out of this separation. It always amazes me how creative our God is; how He can use all circumstances to accomplish His work. How sometimes His blessings are under disguise just to reach out to us. If my mom had never left me, I would always be hiding behind her skirt. When she was yanked out of my sight and life, I began to read the Bible on my own and very diligently, at least the first couple of weeks after she had left. The only solace I had found was reading the Bible and praying because that was when I could almost feel her presence, which was so important as a young and impressionable child.

So I hung my dear teenage life on it. I'd dig out the one and only family Bible from under the thick mattress and read. My prayer at the time was to be re-united with my mom soon despite the fact that I had been told repeatedly that it would take thirty to forty years to secure a visa to leave China just to visit a relative. Being only thirteen, the prospect of having to wait thirty years to see my mother felt like an eternity. If hell is eternal separation from God's love and presence, I thought I had a taste of that being separated from my mom for what seemed like forever.

Another important verse my mom taught me was Matthew 21:22, *"If you believe, you will receive whatever you ask for in prayer."* Guided by this verse, I began to pray every day, asking God if I could see my mom again even within the next year. I believed it would happen. Amazingly, by God's grace and mercy, I obtained a visa to leave China a year after mom left. I was so excited when I received the visa in the mail that a surge of energy charged through my body. I didn't know what to do to relieve such a strong sensation. I was so happy I felt I could die. One of my older brothers, Isaac, who had just turned seventeen, saw my excitement and thrill and thoughtfully advised that I run around the ally in loops to release that current of energy before I electrocuted myself. I took his advice but I didn't care about how silly it'd look to the neighbors, so I ran around the neighborhood in circles till I exhausted myself.

When father came home from work we told him of the good news. Streams of tears just rolled down his cheeks as he couldn't believe how quickly I was able to obtain the visa to leave China. We praised God for His miracles and thanked Him for his deliverance. During our family praise and prayers, I was secretly thanking God for His deliverance from my father as well, who was much more strict than my mom.

*Freedom!*

In the summer of 1981, I was just about to turn fourteen. I couldn't wait to get on that train to see my mom. After all the examinations, I was told that I needed to walk on a bridge to cross the border from China to Hong Kong. I looked at the bridge and thought to myself, "Really? That's the bridge to freedom? I will be able to worship God all I want? I can sing hymns without worrying about being followed and harassed?" My eyes focused on the other side of the bridge, as I was overwhelmed by uncertainties, such as "How am I going to adjust to the new environment? How am I going to make friends? How is our family going to make it as new immigrants? What if we are not so welcome in Hong Kong?" However, the thought of having the religious freedom we craved for so long and being able to worship without fear or a care, outweighed the anxieties of life's other uncertainties.

It was like yesterday, as I stepped on that bridge of freedom. Suddenly a heavy load lifted up from my shoulders. My steps were lighter as I crossed the bridge; understanding nothing about spiritual warfare, I know now that it was the air of satanic darkness that had just lifted from my shoulders. I began to speed up my footsteps, and started—with very faint volume initially—humming some familiar hymns my parents had taught me. Then I looked around to see if anyone was following me, taking notes of me. It didn't seem like anyone cared; everyone was almost running on the bridge, rushing to get from one place to another. I increased my speed bit by bit and looked around carefully to see what might be the effect. To my great disappointment, no one cared! Joy from the first taste of freedom so sweet and surreal, for a short moment, I bit my lips to see if I were in a dream. Freedom! How precious and empowering!

In the late 70's and early 80's, the political environment eased up a bit after the gang of four, lead by Chairman Mao's wife, had been overthrown in China. Father began to listen to a Christian radio station for hope and encouragement over short-wave. Having been comforted by the countless godly messages through Christian short-wave radio, father had made a pact with God, praying, "God, if You ever allow me to escape from Communist China, how I would wish I could have the chance to serve God through a short-wave radio ministry and bring hope and encouragement to those hopeless people just as I had been helped."

Right before mother was granted a visa to leave China, both my parents had been restored to their geological engineering profession. They worked in the same lab and father was given a prestigious position to lead the unit tasked with building levees—similar to those in Holland—to ensure Shanghai would be protected from floods. They were both talented and dedicated professionals.

Given very limited resources back then, they invented tools to measure the water level more effectively and accurately. They invented tools to measure drinking water quality, something they had to invent earlier from the well they had dug together to protect their family. They loved their country and serving their people using their expertise and talents. Both were well-respected at their work for their innovation, practical contributions, and fairness in treating their staff. They published inspiring articles that can be Googled even today. Though mom had left, the new leader of the unit recognized my parents' talents, so they promoted my father year after year to entice him to stay. He was a director by the time he was granted a visa to leave, having progressed from a lowly toilet-scrubber during the Cultural Revolution.

## Re-United

A year after I moved to Hong Kong from Shanghai, father joined us. Hong Kong was still a British colony in the 1980's. Trained as a geologist in the university in Beijing in the 1950's, and familiar with Russian the popular foreign language at the time, father's English was limited to the twenty-six letters of the alphabet. Imagine—he was my very first English teacher! I hated those ABC lesson times, so boring! As a British colony, most professional jobs required the ability to read and write in English. As a man eager to support his family financially, he could not find a comparable job in Hong Kong to utilize his geological training. He struggled and began to think about his nice post in Shanghai was, which would still be waiting for him as his boss promised. Mother just kept on praying, believing the impossible could become possible. Just as Romans 8:28 promised, *"And we know that in all things God works for the good of those who love him, who have been called according to his purpose."* And Isaiah 55:8-9, *"'For My thoughts are not your thoughts, nor are your ways My ways,' declares the LORD. 'For as the heavens are higher than the earth, so are My ways higher than your ways and My thoughts than your thoughts'."*

God was on the move again, this time for my father. One day after Sunday service, a brother introduced my father to his colleague, a sister in the Lord. After she introduced her profession to father, he instantly recognized her voice as one that was broadcast on the short-wave radio! She said she was one of the producers of the Christian short-wave radio programs on Transworld Radio, Far East Broadcasting Company, and Alliance Radio, who had blasted the gospel messages from all corners just outside of China, from places like Korea, Guam, and Taiwan. She went on to comment to my father, "Your command of Mandarin is so outstanding and you have a great voice. With your cultural background, you can understand what kind of messages are most needed by our suffering brothers and sisters in China. Have you ever considered getting involved in the radio ministry? We are really in need of someone like you, because there are not many Chinese believers in Hong Kong who can speak as good of Mandarin as you do, who has the cultural background, or they'd be interested in making money in the world. Would you please prayerfully consider it?"

Suddenly, as though an electric shock just went through father's spine, he froze, the Holy Spirit gently tapped him, and my father remembered his promise to God from several years back: "If God would ever allow me to escape Communist China, how I wish I could have the chance to serve God through a short-wave radio ministry and bring hope and encouragement to those hopeless people just as I had been helped." That's how father began his twenty years of service in the radio ministry and even got me to announce one of his most well loved programs, "The conversation from the heart, 心里话." with a large sum of a bribe...five dollars for a sixteen-year-old blossoming girl, who had suddenly discovered more ways to spend money than making money. After all, when a bubbly, outgoing girl had been cooped up for years in a drab solid color Mao suit, and was now liberated in the free world of Hong Kong, bombarded by fashion from the ugliest to the most sophisticated, one can understand the dilemma.

*Trials*

Life as an immigrant was very harsh in Hong Kong. We were mostly looked upon as the scum of the society, because we were dirt poor, didn't speak Cantonese (the official language in Hong Kong, which was more difficult to learn than Mandarin), and didn't know the culture. It seemed like we moved every other year, if not every year. Mother worked tirelessly and had managed to save up some money to buy a one room tin shed in the outskirts of Kowloon Peninsula. We moved from the storage room in an attic of a factory to our new home, the tin shed, a huge improvement in terms of our living condition. But shortly after we moved in the roof blew off from a strong typhoon. Rain poured in, wind howled, and we were all standing there, drenched, not knowing what to do or where to turn. I saw the terror and distress in my parents' eyes. Normally more talkative than all other five members of the family combined, at that moment I was too scared to make a sound. I watched silently, and then learned that some of our petty belongings got looted during the storm.

Though we felt we had lost everything in the typhoon, including the shed, God's unfailing loving-kindness and grace never ceased to amaze me. And the ways He providentially moved things around was so creative, beyond our wildest imaginations. He prompted a Christian brother to let us stay in one of his vacated condos until we were able to stand on our own again. My father was so overwhelmed by the loss we suffered during the typhoon that he was struck down by his recurring stomach ulcer. My mom, the unshakable pillar of faith in our family, was the only one now working while trying to help my father recover. I watched her pray incessantly as she believed God would answer her prayers and rescue us from all these troubles. In addition to falling ill, my father worried about our inability to pay the rent to this brother. It was a very nice condo, overlooking the misty mountains with a clear view in a densely populated metropolis. In fact, father didn't even want to move in initially because he knew we couldn't afford it and then insisted on moving out as soon as possible. My parents had offered to pay fair market value rent to the brother but he just refused any payment and reassured my parents that we could stay there as long as we needed to get our feet back on the ground.

*Amazing Grace*

Through the trials of life, self-imposed or inflicted by others, God's everlasting grace and mercy have accompanied me as

I've wandered through the desert for many years. He always provided an oasis to refresh me. I pray that I will have as much faith as my parents, and continue to believe in the power of prayer as much as my mother did. I pray that I can pass the torch of faith to my children as my parents had done to us so fearlessly and shamelessly, and they to their children. I pray that the ones in the free world will be grateful for the freedom they have, the price of such freedom, and cherish it and use it to preach the gospel courageously, and minister to those still in bondage for Christ.

# 9

# *True Riches In Christ*

*"For what does it profit a man to gain
the whole world, and forfeit his soul?"
Mark 8:36*

$A$ quick Google search of "define lost" results in the following definition: "unable to find one's way; not knowing one's whereabouts." It is a fairly clear definition to understand, that is unless you actually are lost. I was lost once, and the sad part about being lost is that more often than not you don't even realize that you're lost. There are so many things attempting to tell you what direction you should be going it feels like any direction is the right direction.

### *Starting Out Secular*

I was born an only child to a family with no real beliefs regarding anything typically categorized as religious. Life was relatively simple; study hard and get good grades, obey the law and stay out of trouble, the typical stuff parents tell their kids. My parents never mentioned their views on spiritual things and growing up I never gave it much thought. How did we come to be? If someone had asked me I would most likely have responded with some theory involving a Big Bang and some sort of primordial soup with a dash of probability leading to where we are today. The notion that we were created beings for the sole purpose to glorify our Creator was beyond me.

One of the things I remember vividly about my childhood was an overwhelming fear of death. It was probably a little early for an elementary school kid to be worrying about dying, but there were nights I laid in bed wondering what would happen to me if I died. What does it feel like? Where would I go? All I knew was it wasn't something I wanted. It's ironic how society has a fascination with vampires, creatures of the night with supposed immortality, when in fact it's the children of light who have true eternal life. As I grew wiser in the ways of the world I came to the conclusion that if life was finite I would simply have to make the most of it and live life to the fullest. But at the time I did not even know what that meant, for I was alienated from the Creator of life and I was hostile in mind, doing evil deeds without even realizing it. I was spiritually ignorant.

Somewhere along the way things began to complicate themselves. I was going through life checking off all the boxes of the things you're supposed to do; the things society expects of "successful" individuals. Outwardly you could say I was doing pretty well. I was a fresh graduate out of UCLA, one of the top universities in the world's most affluent nation with a shiny new car and poised to buy my first house in the Bay Area (one of the most expensive areas in America), all at the age of twenty-five. Sounds like a pretty good start to life. Right?

The problem with the world's view of success is that nothing is ever enough. Continually seeking more often leads to compromising on things, and pretty soon I found myself using the ends to justify the means. Everything I did was for me, myself, and I; there was nobody more important than me, but no matter what I did or what I had I "couldn't get no satisfaction." There's a reason why they say you can't buy happiness. Happiness isn't something you have, it's something you are. I tried seeking contentment in the things of this world and came away feeling empty. Scripture explains this clearly in 1 John 2:16-17:

> *For all that is in the world-the desires of the flesh and the desires of the eyes and pride of life-is not from the Father but is from the world. And the world is passing away along with its desires, but whoever does the will of God abides forever.*

However, without an understanding of the concept of sin I continued down my self-destructive path, all the while convincing myself that I was a "good" person because I wasn't overtly troubling society.

Jesus Himself taught on how difficult it is for the wealthy to enter the kingdom of God (Luke 18:24). However I believe sometimes He causes the sun to rise on both the evil and the good (Matt. 5:45) to demonstrate a need for Him. God's material blessings in this world alone aren't enough without His promise of salvation. God did not send His Son simply to bless the world with healing and miracles, but to seek the lost for the purpose of eternal salvation from sin for all those who would believe in Him (Luke 19:10).

## The Pursuit Begins

God has been patiently pursuing me since 1997 at the age of twelve, and even before that, when an incident caused my dad to suddenly have an interest in attending church. So he brought the whole family along. It was something new to me, and because it wasn't something I had chosen, I didn't have much interest in listening to the sermon. It didn't help that this was Chinese church where both English and Manadrin were spoken. I'm what you might call a "fake" Asian who never learned to speak Chinese, so the language barrier wasn't of much help. However, in my boredom I did manage to read through the first couple books of the Old Testament. The stories were interesting enough but I never considered them to be true history. Looking back, I think I would have been better off starting with the book of Matthew rather than Genesis, since I never got to hear the good news of the gospel. I experienced "church life" at an extremely superficial level, Sunday school felt more like an excuse to socialize rather than a chance to focus on truth. For better or worse, my dad got tired of this whole religion thing and eventually stopped going to church in less than a year.

I'd like to think that this experience is when the seeds of foundational biblical truths were first planted in my heart; the idea that God created the universe out of nothing, or the fact that the Fall of man was due to his disobedience to God's command, and the reality of God's historic promise to Abraham. But at the time, all this was merely trivia to me. Yet, God knew different and something bigger was beginning to take root in my soul. Over time God's Word would take root in my heart and begin to show itself. In the same way that Christ builds His Church one person at a time, He also draws His people to salvation one event in their life at a time.

*A Witness*

Most of the friends I have today came to know Christ during their time at college. I must be a late bloomer because I was still actively His enemy throughout my college years (Romans 3:18). Studying mechanical engineering didn't leave much opportunity for me to be contemplating the ultimate meaning of life and all its intricacies. Nevertheless, one of my most vivid memories of college life was when a friend of a friend sat down to simply chat with me and the question of whether or not I'd be interested in going to church with him came up. I refused the invitation, but I was impressed by his non-pushy nature. To this day I want to believe this was because of his understanding that if I were to come to know Jesus it would be on God's timing and not from his pestering or manipulation.

One of the instruments that God decided to use to rescue me was music. Music has always played a central part of my life. I grew up playing the piano and violin using the Suzuki method, which emphasized learning through listening so I've always loved paying attention to the lyrics of songs. I feel like the lyricist must have something to tell so it is my obligation as the listener to hear them out. I always was able to relate to the themes of the various pop songs on the radio; songs about pain and suffering, or the search for love, or the celebration of one's own achievements. It was as if there was always the right song for my current state of mind.

*Hillsong*

I had a friend who shared my love for music. We talked often about our favorite artists and songs. Sometime after college she introduced me to an Australian artist named Brooke Fraser. For some reason my friend did not tell me Fraser was part of a Christian worship group called *Hillsong United*. After finding her style of music appealing to my ears my friend threw in a, "Oh, by the way; she sings Christian songs as her day job and does secular music on the side," and asked if I'd be interested in some of those songs as well. I was guaranteed that her Christian songs were a lot better than her secular ones. For reasons unknown to all but God, I acquiesced and began listening to *Hillsong*.

I still remember the first song I heard from *Hillsong* called "Hosanna," which has the following lyrics:

*Heal my heart and make it clean;*
*open up my eyes to the things unseen;*
*show me how to love like you have loved me.*

These words had a profound impact on me when I first heard them and they really stuck with me because they were so different from anything that I had ever heard before. I had never considered that my heart needed healing or cleansing. What were these things that were unseen? Who is this that loves me? Or rather, who could love such a broken and incomplete individual such as myself? Trying to get ahead in this rat-race, known as "life in the Silicon Valley," had left me empty and without hope. I learned to rely on nobody but myself. It was a never-ending game of cat-and-mouse to stay ahead, all in some misguided notion of the pursuit of the "American Dream." I was like the Corinthians, puffed up with my knowledge and worldly success (1 Corinthians 8:1), but beneath the surface everything was rotting away. Without understanding love, true love that only God could demonstrate, I was merely a husk (1 Corinthians 13:2).

## Softened By the Spirit

My curiosity had been piqued and my heart finally softened. As I continued to listen to more of this Christian music I wanted to learn more about this Jesus person these people would sing about. Eventually my friend invited me to join her for a Sunday sermon and I decided to tag along to see what more I could learn. I still remember the message that day. The pastor was teaching on the subject of manna, the food God provided Israel during their forty years of wandering in the wilderness (Exodus 16).

Manna demonstrated God's providential care for His people, but at the same time it tested their obedience to His commands.

The Israelites were to gather enough manna for only a day and were not to store any for the next day because God would provide new manna each day, except for the Sabbath, Saturday (16:19). However, there were those that disobeyed and, as a consequence, found that the manna they had hoarded became infested with insects and started to rot.

> But they did not listen to Moses. Some left part of it till the morning, and it bred worms and stank. And Moses was angry with them (16:20).

I would later find out that this disobedience to God was known as "sin" and it was the cause of everything wrong with this world.

Manna was God's blessing on His people and it was meant to be shared because those that gathered much had nothing left over and those that gathered little had no lack either. Those who disobeyed and tried to keep more than they needed for themselves found that they were left with nothing in the end. God wanted to teach the Israelites to trust in Him and look solely to Him for their every need (Matthew 6:11). This message resonated within me, and convicted me, because I was doing everything contrary to what was being taught! I had been relying solely on myself and was consumed with a desire to store up treasures only for myself. Had I continued down the path I was on, I would have been left with nothing but rotten and worthless manna.

### Convicted

God was exposing my rebellious ways and this time I was finally ready to admit I was lost. I now had a name for all of my regrets—"sin." These were just the tip of the iceberg, merely just the times that I could remember when I had given in to the temptation of sin. My conscience could not bear the weight of all my sin. The burden led me to seek atonement, or relief, from my actions, but nothing I did on my own could clear that nagging feeling of guilt in the back of my head.

I needed an act of God, and act He did. He made the first move. He was the one to love me first, sending His own flesh and blood, Jesus, down to this fallen and broken world to live the perfect life so that He would become an acceptable sacrifice as a substitute for all of my sin. Human logic cannot explain why God would act in this manner and there is nothing that I did or can do to deserve any of the freedom and forgiveness that Christ gave me when He saved me (Titus 3:5). It is by God's overwhelming grace alone that my eternal salvation is ensured and my mind is blown away every time I'm reminded of this.

I'm still amazed how God saves by faith. *"By grace you have been saved by faith" (Ephesians 2:8)*. I'm an engineer by training, and faith as a methodology is contrary to everything I was taught about being an engineer. The scientific method demands empirical, hands-on proof and evidence to demonstrate fact—that which can be seen, and touched, and experienced by the senses. Nevertheless, God enables the spiritually blind to see and through Christ He has given me the faith to believe in the unseen, to know that His promises are real with greater confidence than even the most proven of scientific theories (Hebrews 11:1). For me, the study of science is no longer man trying to figure out the universe but man trying to get to know God better by understanding His creation.

It is by this faith that my actions are now guided. Scripture says, *"we walk by faith, not by sight" (2 Corinthians 5:7)*. Sin still finds ways to cause me to stumble, but by faith I can have confidence that Jesus has won the war on my behalf. If someone had told me ten years ago that I would be making claims like that I would have called them ridiculous. But it just goes to show how He transforms those He saves (2 Corinthians 3:18). It is a complete paradigm shift in the way I view all aspects of life. No longer do I ask myself, "What more do I want?" but rather, "How can I use what I have to bring further glory to His name?" It is simply astounding how much more fulfilling working for His kingdom is than laboring in futility trying to build my own.

## Treasures In Heaven

Jesus taught about laying up treasures in heaven rather than on earth (Matt. 6:19-24), and His conclusion was that we cannot serve two masters—we serve either God or money. This warning pierced my heart because it was exactly how I was living when I was lost. I was serving money and materialism.

The world preaches the message of immediate gratification. But the reality is that it is fleeting and shallow and leads to a continual search for the next thing that will bring even more gratification, which in the end breeds discontent. In contrast, Jesus' message speaks of genuine, everlasting gratification for the patient and faithful who seek Him (Luke 11:9). It is by design that we desire Jesus, we often simply fail to realize it. There is a reason why car ads market a brand's reliability; people want things to last. Sure, that sports car looks fun at first, but once the maintenance costs start piling up and the neighbor gets the newer, faster version, you begin to wonder if you might have been happier getting that reliable family sedan.

With this change in thinking comes new challenges, but at the same time brings an important constant. I once likened God to the ultimate universal algebraic Constant that can be used to solve any problem that comes my way. He is unchanging and eternal (James 1:17). Everything else in this life is temporary, fragile and passing away, so change is an inescapable truth. I understand that now as a Christian.

But that still does not diminish the fact that it's difficult to learn that the people you've called family for the past twenty some years will probably not be around to see you reach thirty. Finding out my father has liver cancer and that it has spread beyond the liver only to be told a few months later that my mother has advanced stage of lung cancer as well has been a challenging experience to say the least. The fact that both my parents have cancer would have broken me long ago if I didn't have the knowledge that the same God who loved me enough to die for my sins while I still was against Him was in control of all things. It's a great comfort to know that He is the one orchestrating all events including these trials we go through (Romans 8:28), and it is by faith alone that I know that He will see me through this chapter of my life.

*True Hope*

The fundamental shift from concentrating on temporary things to the promises of eternity with my Creator is what gives me the greatest hope.

> *So we do not lose heart. Though our outer self is wasting away, our inner self is being renewed day by day. For this light momentary affliction is preparing for us an eternal weight of glory beyond all comprehension, as we look not to the things that are seen but to the things that are unseen. For the things that are seen are transient, but the things that are unseen are eternal (2 Corinthians 4:16-18).*

No longer do I feel anxious about things such as pleasing people, but now I look to be a good steward of the gifts and blessings God has given me. I'm still a sinner living in a fallen world but at least I am no longer lost. God has provided the GPS for life in His Bible and now I have confidence in knowing my destination as well (Psalm 119:105; Proverbs 3:5-6). Through His Word He guides us and while the world continues to spew its erroneous ways, Scripture acts as a lens which we can use to magnify the truth.

One of my favorite stories in the Bible is the story of Jesus and the woman of Samaria that He met at a well (John 4). The story tells of Jesus' love for even the most outcast of society and illustrates His nature of always making the first move. The woman was a serial adulteress, leading a life filled with sin. She should have been stoned to death for her crimes (Leviticus 20:10). But instead, Jesus offered her salvation and total forgiveness! He told her that "Everyone who drinks of this water will be thirsty again, but whoever drinks of the water that I will give him will never be thirsty again" (4:13-14). I want the water that Jesus offers. I don't want to have to continually draw my own water whenever I get thirsty. I want to rely on the One who conquered death and created me and knows me better than anyone else. The world is a scary place. They say nothing in this world is certain except for death and taxes, but I've found one more thing and that is Jesus' promise of eternal life:

> For all the promises of God find their "Yes" in Him. That is why it is through Him that we utter our "Amen!" to God for His glory (2 Corinthians 1:20).

God uses only the truth of gospel to save, and different mediums to proclaim it—for me it was music. The power of music is so great because it speaks to the human condition. Since we all were created by the same one God, there are commonalities we can all relate to, which is why there is a song by Sovereign Grace Music that summarizes my testimony completely called "All I Have Is Christ":

> *I once was lost in darkest night*
> *Yet thought I knew the way*
> *The sin that promised joy and life*
> *Had led me to the grave...*
> *You bore the wrath reserved for me*
> *Now all I know is grace*

# 10

## *Living and Active*

*"In love He predestined us to
adoption as sons through Jesus
Christ to Himself, according to
the kind intention of His will"
Ephesians 1:5*

*"For by grace you have been saved through faith; and that not
of yourselves, it is the gift of God"* (Ephesians 2:8). This verse
epitomizes my transformation from death to life in the same
way that it defines the salvation of every believer. Coming to
faith was clearly all of God and none of me.

I was born during a blizzard in Boston, MA in March of
1994. My parents were living in Boston while my dad attended
business school and then moved to Nashville, TN three months
after I was born. My mom grew up in Nashville and my dad
attended college there (Go Vandy!), so the move was more of a
homecoming.

*Family Religion*

My parents grew up very differently. My mom had a stable and loving home, but my dad didn't. Born in Texas, my Dad moved around a lot which made an unstable home; church was not a part of his upbringing and faith in Christ was scarce in the family.

In contrast, my mom attended an Episcopalian church throughout her childhood and had a profession of faith in Jesus Christ. Church attendance wasn't a priority but the family did attend the two "most important" services of the year: Christmas and Easter. In the South it seems everyone claimed to be a Christian. It was a cultural thing. Your parents are Christians, so you're a Christian.

So I was three months old when we moved back to Nashville. My dad started a company, and my mom took care of me. Fifteen months later, my mom gave birth to my sister, Lydia. I was not a fan of this intruder into a world that was otherwise completely centered around me—a prime example of my innate sin nature (Romans 5:19).

Two years after my sister was born, my younger brother, John, entered the world. I cannot remember if I was more excited about my new brother or the cookie that I was given upon entering my mom's hospital room. Soon after John was born, our family of five moved into the house in which I lived until college. Life was pretty good. We were a family of significant resources, and we attended my mom's Episcopalian church—*St. Matthew's*. Initially, I did not like going to church; it meant itchy clothes, boring ceremonies, and being bullied in Sunday school.

I was bullied because I was short—*real* short. When I was younger, my height was something that defined me, part of my identity. I was always the shortest kid in my grade until sophomore year of high school. I was shorter than every guy and, most unfortunately, every girl. Although I was short, I was also strong for my size.

### Karate Kid

Age five is where my testimony really begins. I started *taekwondo*, and I liked it. It was fun, and I'm sure my mom appreciated this outlet for my energy. The first *dojang* (martial arts school) that I attended was great, but it closed, so we had to move. The next place was also fun, but the instructor moved to Florida; we had to move again. My mom decided that the third *taekwondo* studio was too rough, and that was that for *taekwondo*. My mom told me that it was time to pick a new sport.

Since I was strong, I flipped around a lot in our house, but neither of those were the reason that I picked gymnastics. I began gymnastics for the medals and ribbons I could win. I started lessons at *Sun Street Gymnastics* and attended twice before the instructors told my mom that I needed to join a boys' team program. *Sun Street* did not have a boys' program, so they directed me to my second home for the next twelve and a half years of my life: *King's School of Gymnastics*. That is where I first came to take the gospel of Christ seriously.

Gymnastics was a sport where my height (or lack thereof) was largely a good thing. It helped me, except on pommel horse. It made me strong. I remember almost always winning the chin-up contests at practice, and, in sixth grade, I set the school record with five hundred push-ups (actually they were half push-ups). Rings and parallel bars were my best events, but I usually did pretty well in the all-around. The best part of gymnastics though was not the gymnastics at all; it was my coach, Andrew.

### Coach Andrew

When I became friends with Andrew I was not saved. We went to church as a family until I was about ten years old. My mom stopped going after a lady at a church dinner told her that she was not a Christian if she did not believe in hell. I remember her discussing at Christmas Eve dinner how she did not believe that Jesus was the Son of God, how she did not believe He was anything supernatural, and how maybe that made her a Jew. My dad kept taking my siblings and me to church for a while, but soon he tired of the whole endeavor as well and so he stopped taking us after a few months.

Even though we no longer went to *St. Matthew's*, I considered myself a Christian. I remember reading a children's storybook Bible all the way through when I was younger, and I always said my prayers. My prayers consisted largely of a ritualistic incantation of the Lord's Prayer and a list of selfish petitions to God. I believed in God; I just didn't know Him personally.

In seventh grade, I was confirmed at *St. Matthew's Church.* Confirmation is when a boy or girl is recognized as an adult member in the Episcopalian church. In prep for Confirmation, I had a list of tasks to complete at home. Reading a Gospel was one of them, so I read through Matthew for the first time. After a retreat, I was confirmed into the church. But I did not have a grasp that the Bible was God's unchangeable, perfect Word. I did not truly know the Lord. I believed some of the Bible, but, mostly, I had a shallow understanding of Christianity.

It was about that time that I had the political discussion with Andrew that changed my destiny. We were talking politics at practice when the topic of gay marriage arose. After talking with my dad, I had decided that maybe gay marriage was alright. I mean, why not? If two people love one another, why not them get married regardless of their respective genders? Andrew disagreed. I still remember him saying, "Daniel, aren't you a Christian?"

I responded, "Yes." I knew where this was going.

He said, "Well, don't you know that the Bible says marriage is between a man and a woman?"

"Well, yes", I said. "But, I guess I don't believe that part of the Bible." Deep down, I knew the hypocrisy of that statement, but I said it anyways. I wanted it to be alright to only believe parts of the Bible even if it wasn't.

Then Andrew shocked me as he declared, "Daniel, the Bible is not a banquet. You cannot just pick and choose what you want to believe from it. It's an all-or-nothing thing." These words were life-changing for me. I was not saved at that point, but God began to use that simple principle—that the Bible is either one hundred percent truth or total garbage—to save my soul.

I remember responding to Andrew with something like, "Yeah...well...I guess...yeah, that's probably right." My stomach was churning a bit. Andrew had certainly read more of the Bible than me; he certainly knew more than me. So, I decided that I would accept what he said about the Bible, at least until I had read more.

## Biblical Conviction

Up to this point I had a "pick-and choose" theology that I inherited from my parents. We were told that we could believe whatever we wanted—truth is relative. That kind of thinking had a profound affect on me. Growing up I did not believe that "all Scripture is God-breathed" (2 Timothy 3:16). Even after I decided that the Bible was an all-or-nothing prospect, I still did not drop all of my unbiblical beliefs at once.

After that conversation with Andrew, as I entered high school, I began to take faith in Christ more seriously, but life still unfolded in a series of emotional peaks and valleys. God was working on me but I still don't even know whether I was saved in high school or college. All I know is that God has saved me from my spiritual death and raised me to spiritual life, and I praise Him for that (Ephesians 2:1-6)!

Reflecting on the emotional turmoil and sin of my old life, I cannot do much but just think, "Wow, praise God for saving me, for removing satanic blindness, and for calling me into the flock over which Jesus Christ superintends." As I look back on my life now, I realize and remember that I was deeply sad or stressed for most of my life before salvation. I was constantly depressed and fretting. I knew it too.

When I was younger, gymnastics, school, and kissing a girl were my biggest idols. I was a type-A perfectionist, to the extreme. I wanted to be the best in gymnastics, get the highest grades in school, and I wanted to kiss a girl by the age of thirteen because I thought that was the age by which any cool guy would have kissed a girl. Until I met the Lord, I cycled through many periods of depression and melancholy. Even after coming to faith, I went through a deep depression. But I came to realize that *all who call on the name of the Lord will be saved* (Romans 10:13) and that Christ truly frees.

*A New Church*

Soon after my conversation with Andrew, I began attending *St. Matthew's* again. That didn't last long. It seemed dead to me, so I began praying that God would lead me to a new church. Sure enough, I was invited to a youth event at *River's Way* by my friends, the Stevenson's. *River's Way* was more alive than my old church. The people there wanted to know God personally–they even clapped to the beat of some worship songs. That was a new experience for me.

My parents kindly chauffeured me to and from *River's Way*. The Stevensons would invite me to lunch after church regularly and I was blessed. I really liked *River's Way*. The people there were so kind. One such family was the Johnson family. They had five kids, and I thought that they were the friendliest, most joyful, Christ-loving people I had ever met. They attracted me immediately. I had met Mr. and Mrs. Johnson once before when my dad hosted them for a business dinner at our house. Upon seeing me at church, they immediately invited me to lunch, and from that moment on, I became like a son to them.

After several months, I began to integrate into the youth group more. Most of the guys and girls my age had been a part of the youth group since middle school, so that made the group a difficult one to truly break into. As a result, I gravitated toward the older people. Out of all these new relationships, the people whose influence impacted me the most were the Johnsons.

In retrospect, *River's Way Church* was not a strong Bible church. It was not committed to healthy, systematic doctrine. Nor was the simple message of God's grace in Christ taught faithfully. These two deficiencies stemmed from the church's overall low view of Scripture. But despite *River's Way's* deficiencies, the Johnson family held God's Word in high regard. And in God's providence this family had more influence on me than anyone else at that time. When I met the Johnsons I did not have a concept of sound doctrine. But, I knew from reading the Bible that Christ demanded nothing less than absolute obedience from those who follow Him: *"If you love me, you will keep my commandments"* (John 14:15). I knew that Jesus had said, *"He who loves father or mother more than Me is not worthy of me" (Matthew 10:37)*. I knew that being a believer meant laying down my life, taking up my cross, and following Christ (Matthew 16:24). The Johnsons understood this basic scriptural demand of absolute obedience to God's Word. They seemed to seek God and to love Him with their entire beings. The Johnsons reinforced in my life Christ's unerring demand for our entire beings, and for that, I am supremely thankful.

## Charismatic Christianity

The Johnsons were also charismatic. That became a problem for me over time. They did not believe in the sufficiency of Scripture, but believed in ongoing revelation. They encouraged me to seek revelation from God outside of Scripture. By the time I was a senior in high school, I sadly began trying to subjectively "listen" to God instead of standing firm on the promises of His Word in Scripture. I was also trying to prophesy and heal, but "listening" to God was by far the most destructive practice in my faith. The general rule was that as long as what you heard was not against the Bible, it could be from God. I was still very much insistent on obeying God's Word, but I began basing the Spirit's leading on whatever I *felt* He wanted me to do. This walking by "feeling" was all the more entrenched by a cultural over-emphasis on emotionalism in worship. I based how God felt towards me on how I felt. I reduced God to little more than an emotional fluctuation, instead of the always true, unchanging Lord that He is (Hebrews 13:8).

Growing up in a church with no theological framework, I learned my theology from God's Word and from the church culture around me, so it was eclectic at best. I believed in absolute free-will because I was taught that "God does not want robots to love Him, so He would not predestine people to be saved." Because of this unbiblical belief, I had no concept of grace. I did not understand that it is by God's gift of grace alone that I was saved (Ephesians 2:8). I thought that I had contributed some part in my salvation. As a result, I thought I could lose my salvation if I sinned too severely. This led to a terribly works-centered walk with the Lord, and terrible insecurity. It inculcated a legalistic approach to spirituality, much like the Pharisees. I wrongly believed my eternal security was based on my behavior. I believed I could lose my salvation, but also believed I could earn it back again with acts of obedience. So really, eternal life was not eternal but elusive and in-and-out based strictly on my behavior. I thought that God loved me, or at least liked me, more or less based upon my obedience. Praise God that He has given the Son with a perfect love. Perfect love has no gradation.

The greatest liability of my works-oriented, Charismatic faith was the emotionalism that I mentioned earlier. I believed God allowed me to feel more or less love for Him based on how pleased or displeased He was with me. I believed His love was conditional and subjective, not constant based on un-changing truth. I also thought that an emotional experience was the critical component of all worship, whether the worship was singing, reading the Word, or prayer. How I "felt" was the basis by which I evaluated how successful a time of worship was.

I remember going to a Thursday night "worship" (singing only) service in high school. The service, called "Sanctuary," had a rock band and was typified by hand-raising, many tears and various emotional experiences. I do believe that the Lord really touched my heart at that service. I felt like I was worshiping the Lord with my entire being, and I thought, "If this is what heaven is like, I can't wait. I could do this forever." There was no better feeling than worshiping the Lord with all that I had, laying all of myself before Him. I praise God for how great an affection I felt for Him there, for how sweet a spirit of worship He blessed me with. But, I regret that seeking an "experience" on an emotional "encounter with God" was the priority. I began basing my relationship with the Lord, especially after "Sanctuary," on how I felt instead of on His promises in Scripture. Soon after this experience, there was a turn in my relationship with the Lord that became the darkest year of my life.

Entering my senior year of high school my relationship with the Lord was based on how I felt. I was driven by my emotions. That is when my depression set in. My depression started with a question: "Do I believe in Christ just because it makes me feel good?" Soon my mind began to race. "Do I believe in Christ because He is truly the Savior of the world or because it is a really nice concept?" Doubt started flowing. Unfortunately, I did not wield the sword of the Spirit, the Word of God, to slay my doubts and the attack on my thinking (Ephesians 6:17). I wanted to have an unwavering, child-like faith in God and "feel" the love for God that everyone around me seemed to feel. All the people around me were always talking about the incredible emotional experiences they continued to have with God, and the great love they felt for Him. I just could not compete.

I wanted those experiences, and I manufactured some, but the doubts were still there. I tried to convince myself of God's truth through apologetics, through remembering old experiences, and through God's Word, but I did not take God at His Word alone. Scripture was not yet the foundation of my life, and as I type this, I am beginning to see why the Lord allowed a year and a half of the most intense internal pain and turmoil that I have ever known to plague me—He wanted me to trust Him. He wanted me to take Him at His Word. Praise God that He truly does work all things together for the good for those who have been called by Him for His purposes (Romans 8:28)!

### Doubt and Fear

Doubt, fear and depression continued after high school graduation. I knew that doubt was a sin, or at least opposed by Christ (John 20:27). And I knew that salvation comes through faith. So did that mean that I wasn't saved—if God is really there? I was very confused. I longed for eternal security but I was terrified by my doubts and the potential consequence of an eternity of hell. To make matters worse, I was still trying to listen to the Spirit of the God, Whose very existence I was doubting. I was spiritually schizophrenic.

I constantly felt like God was telling me to fast (food), and I knew that I had to be obedient to God, even if I was not totally sure that He was there. I felt a further compulsion to fast because the Johnsons and others around me told me that fasting was a spiritual discipline that must be practiced, like prayer, and that fasting causes one to draw near to God. I later learned from Scripture that food does not draw us closer to God: *"food does not bring us near to God; we are no worse if we do not eat, and no better if we do"* (1 Corinthians 8:8).

In ignorance I tried fasting to bolster my faith, but faith comes only by hearing God's Word (Romans 10:17). It was also during that summer that my charismatic friends tried to "deliver" me from the demons afflicting me. "Demons?" you might ask. My friends were major advocates of spiritual warfare and deliverance ministry. They incorrectly believed that Christ gave all believers the ability to cast out demons like the Apostles were able to do. From their influence, I attributed much of my depression and doubts to spiritual warfare and the work of Satan and demons.

One day I asked them to cast out any demons in me. They were happy to, and so I went over to their house one Sunday night for "deliverance." We went into their children's playroom, they spoke kindly and lovingly to me, telling me what they were going to do, and then we began. They started by taking turns "talking" to the "demons" inside of me. I was just supposed to let the demons talk by saying whatever came to my head. It felt kind of contrived, but I was so desperate to be rid of my doubt and depression that I bought in almost completely. But nothing really changed after my "deliverance." My depression and doubt were still ever-present burs in my spirit, but I tried to convince myself otherwise. I wish I had known before all of this that it is impossible for a believer to be possessed by a demon. Believers are hidden with Christ in God (Colossians 3:3), and there is no evil in God (1 John 1:4; 3:5). Of course, I did not know this until my life became more founded on the rock of God's Word

(Matthew 7:24). Praise God for His goodness because this is where my story takes a turn for the best!

## Collegiate Life

It was the end of the summer, and I was off to college for gymnastics. I was recovering from shoulder surgery a few months before so I was still very skinny and weak from the surgery. I knew that every guy on the team was better and stronger than me, even when I had been healthy. My nerves were on edge about gymnastics, and I was fretting even more about all of the atheists and agnostics that I expected to meet who would try to destroy my already brittle faith. God was so graciously good to me during this time. He kept me just as He had kept me throughout the year and half of doubt and depression, and just as He keeps all who are His.

It was almost as though when I stepped on campus, the doubts began to fade. I can't exactly explain it or understand it other than to attribute it to God's sovereign grace on me. I left an environment that was affirming of faith, and entered an atmosphere largely hostile to Christ, yet God protected me. He promises that He will never allow us to be tempted more than we can bear, and He always provides a way out of that temptation (1 Corinthians 10:13). Not only did God fulfill this promise of His Word, but He went on to bless me at college beyond my wildest imagination.

The hardest part of my entire freshman experience was related to the gymnastics team. I was the smallest and weakest of the freshman—many of the upperclassmen thought that I would quit—and I thought I was the only Christian. While other freshmen were targeted with insults based upon the size of their mid-section, I was ridiculed for my faith in Christ. Praise God that I was counted worthy to suffer for the name of Christ. I only wish that I had stood more firmly in the faith.

One instance stands out as a time where I feared man instead of fearing God (Matthew 10:28). It was an experience that I regret and of which I am ashamed. It was at the "freshman dance." It was a choreographed dance that the freshman gymnasts were required to present in front of the entire gymnastics team. We guys were instructed to make the dance as raunchy as possible. I tried every way to get out of it. I even spoke to one of the captains about why I did not want to participate because of my faith. He granted me a reprieve from the dance but that was later manipulated to be a pardon only from participating in the explicit portions of the dance.

In the days leading up to the dance, I was constantly being told that I was distancing myself from the team and not trying to be part of the team. I did not want to do that. I wanted to be in the world but not of the world, and I was not sure where to draw the line. I thought there was a good possibility that it was not even right for me to even stand alongside the morally base actions that were choreographed. But I feared that I was wrong, alienating the teammates that I wanted to evangelize. I wasn't wrong, but my unsure conscience and (especially) my fear of how the team regarded me, convinced me to participate. During the dance, I mainly just stood with a blank face, attempting not to make eye contact. I danced some to parts of the non-explicit portions of the dance, but my very presence of participation was sinful because the song to which we danced was so vile.

Remember, the entire men's and women's gymnastics teams (almost thirty adults my age or older) were watching the dance and expecting *every* freshman to participate. After I did not dance, I received weird looks from many on the women's team, and a few of the older guys chastised me for "intentionally distancing" myself from the team. They said it was alright for me to not take part in certain portions of the dance, but I should have participated in the non-explicit portions. Though they were obviously in no way the arbiters of what was right and wrong, I was convinced of my alleged wrong-doing, and apologized. Had it not been for a conviction that the Lord wanted me to be a missionary to the gymnastics team, uniquely placed in a dark village of flips and iron crosses, I would have surely quit gymnastics.

## Cross Training

Gymnastics was not all bad. In fact, the Lord used a Christian teammate to trigger the greatest series of blessings in my entire life. One day after practice, my friend took me to a Christian fellowship group called *Cross Training*. Almost immediately, I fell in love with the group. Unlike my experience back home, the fellowship drew people who loved God's Word—it was more than just cultural. Many of the members there had a unique zeal for God's Word.

A couple of weeks after my first encounter with *Cross Training*, they hosted a freshman dinner. It was there that I first met Dr. "E"—a man of God used by the Lord to influence my life tremendously for Christ. By God's magnificent providence, Doc, a 47-year-old surgeon with no real affiliation to *Cross Training*, ended up hosting a bunch of college kids at his house for dinner, including me. Doc loved God's Word and began leading the *Cross Training* freshman guys small group a week after meeting us. Praise God that I was a freshman guy! This group was one of greatest blessings in my entire life. The guys in my small group became my best friends, my brothers in the truest sense. For the first time in my life I had male, Christian best friends who were actually my own age. I would die for any one of those dear brothers in a second, and they would do the same for me. Ours was and is a supernatural love.

The intimacy of our group was rooted deeply in a love for the Lord, which came from the knowledge of Scripture. For this, I can only praise God that He gave Doc to our group as a leader and guide. His reverence for Scripture was something I had never seen before. For him, God's Word was not just another part of the Christian life, but the foundation of everything. It was (and is) the rock on which our faith was built (Matthew 7:24).

## *The Sufficiency of Scripture*

Doc taught me a high view of Scripture. He said the Bible was God's very words to man, and he taught me that Christians can't bring any preconceptions to the Bible. God's Word means what it says, and God says what He means. The Bible is a more sure testimony than any experience, and completely sufficient for our faith. Doc's love for the Lord was testimony enough of the incomparable riches contained within the Bible, and his faith became contagious for our entire small group. Instead of receiving our praise, Doc continually directed us to the source of all knowledge about the Lord—Scripture. He said the Bible, and only the Bible, is how we come to know and love God in truth (2 Timothy 3:16-17).

As I stood more firmly on the promises of God's Word, those doubts that had so tormented me in the past began to disappear. By God's grace, I was taking Him at His Word (more), and He was blessing it. Scripture was giving me assurance and security. I still remember one of the most life-changing lessons that Doc ever taught me on the sufficiency of Scripture, using 2 Peter 1:16-21. In the passage, Peter describes his experience on the Mount of Transfiguration–when he heard God's voice and saw the very glory of Christ–and proceeds to remark that Scripture is a more sure testimony than that experience. This blew me away! Peter heard God's very own voice. He saw some of Christ's heavenly glory. He spent time with the spirits of Moses and Elijah, and yet he says that Scripture is a more sure testimony of God than these experiences! My view of Scripture was elevated after hearing that truth.

*Fasting*

Doc later said once that if you want to hear God audibly, read the Bible out loud. I heartily agree, and wish that I had understood the import of this statement when I was in high school. As freshman year continued, my faith grew and my doubts were being assuaged, but my spiritual life was still in a state of semi-constant tumult. Why? I still believed that being led by the Spirit meant being lead by my feelings. Fasting was the largest manifestation of this theological error. Though I would not have admitted it at the time, I hated fasting. Our bodies (or at least my body) were not meant to do four hours of gymnastics a day without any God-given food to fuel them. Praise God that even in my error, He sustained me.

Fasting finally came to a head for me on a team trip to Sweden over Spring Break. The weeks prior to this trip were a period of tremendous fear in my life. I felt that the Lord may have been calling me to a forty day fast. I was terrified of fasting for forty days but knew that I must obey the Lord at all costs. Right before the trip, I had stopped fasting, only to begin again on the trip because I felt like God may have been calling me to fast.

My coach caught wind, spoke with me, and even called my parents. Praise God that someone–I do not even remember who–helped me to understand that I would obey God by obeying my coach who wanted me to eat.

### Free-Will

While I had grown in the Lord up until Spring Break of my freshman year, I was still theologically weak. This was, in part, because I had not yet submitted my entire self to God and what He said plainly in His Word. This began to change at one of our Tuesday night small group meetings. Doc was teaching on the fundamentals of the Christian faith, and we came to one of the most contentious topics: "Free-will vs. election." I expected him to immediately establish his belief in free-will, only to be dumbfounded when he did just the opposite. Doc said that election is clearly taught in the Bible, and thus, people are elected to salvation. Initially I was not convinced. I saw the many Scriptures that supported the doctrine, but I also thought that there was some basis for ultimate free-will based upon verses like 1 Timothy 2:4.

I went back and forth between believing in election and free-will. But, more than anything, my own pride inhibited me from fully receiving the glorious doctrine of God's sovereign election. The form of free will to which I subscribed went something like this: because God is outside of time, He saw who would choose Him from the beginning and then predestined those who would choose Him. Of course, I now know that this is an unbiblical doctrine, but I clung to it because of my pride.

My pride was two-fold. I took pride in "choosing" God, and I took pride in helping to save others. Deep down, I wanted to take some credit for my salvation. I wanted to have loved God more than other people. I wanted to have, by my own will, submitted to Christ when others would not. I wanted to be superior to those who did not choose salvation. I wanted to give myself some praise for my salvation. It was and is shameful.

Regarding evangelism, I recognized the clear command God gives all Christians to evangelize the lost, and I felt it was largely neglected by the Christians around me. There were people perishing all around, and God gave a clear command to tell them about the gospel, and yet Christians were largely disobedient. I didn't want to be one of them. Part of that was certainly a desire to be obedient and to see men saved. Part of that was to feed my pride. I desired a large tally of people whom I had lead to Christ. Praise God that He used my partially pure pursuit of evangelism for His glory!

In addition to sharing Christ with my family and team, I started a Bible study for non-believers my freshman year. Some of my classmates heard the Word, and I was able to share the gospel with at least one friend in the study. It is now the summer after my freshman year. I am still at school, working, training, and wrestling with the doctrine of election. I had learned and heartily accepted earlier in the year that it is only by grace that we overcome sin; we cannot live the Christian life without the constant aid of the Spirit. But I was still skeptical of the word "election." My hang-up was really with "double-predestination," which is unbiblical. I could not understand why God would force people to go to hell. Praise God, once more, for Doc. He had me to dinner many times that summer and lovingly showed me again and again why election is a truth of Scripture. I remember the night where God gave me a gift of grace, allowing me to lay down my pride and preconceptions of His Word.

*By His Grace*

From that point on my spiritual life flourished. My love for Christ and my relationship with God bloomed like never before. I cannot praise God enough for His grace in saving me and, ultimately, allowing me to submit more and more to the truth of His Word. I finally had so much of the joy and love that the Bible said should manifest in the life of every Christian. I began learning so much about the Lord, and I believe these were all God's blessings for not trying to manipulate His Scripture to mean something other than what it does. If you feel like your life with the Lord is stagnant, if you feel like you are not learning from the Word as you would like, check to see if you are coming to God in His Word, ready to submit to whatever He says.

The greatest changes in my life and walk with the Lord were related to how I regarded His Word. I came to faith after my fateful, political conversation with Andrew where he told me that the Bible is not a buffet. It is all or nothing, true or worthless. Then, I felt like I almost came to know the Lord again. I came to know Him with the intimacy that I believe His Word illustrates and demands when I came to understand better the reality of God's ultimate sovereignty. I decided to take God at His Word. And I came to know Him with the intimacy that He designed and that He demanded. All of this, my testimony, was by His grace alone.

# 11

## Father to the Fatherless

*"Blessed be the God and Father of our
Lord Jesus Christ, the Father of mercies
and God of all comfort, who comforts
us in all our affliction so that we will
be able to comfort those who are in any
affliction with the comfort with which
we ourselves are comforted by God"
2 Corinthians 1:3-4*

*I* was born into a nominal Roman Catholic family. Although we did have some fervent relatives, even priests, who could stand proud in the fact that my great uncle, the Very Rev. Oscar Huber, gave President John. F. Kennedy the Last Rites. Ironically my mother despised the religion ever since her childhood, so after I was baptized as an infant, my spiritual training was quite delayed, and our home life was predominantly secular.

*Broken*

My parents divorced when I was about two after which my mom had numerous short-term marriages to men of questionable character. Some of them abused my mom and even became an imminent threat to me as a young girl in light of their addiction to alcohol and seductive tendencies. Those repulsive experiences tainted my young, developing judgments about men. I began to think of them as distant, impersonal and transient since they played a minimal and disinterested part in my life, and had no definable role. My own father was in the Air Force and lived all over the U.S. and remarried, so there was minimal contact. I had no emotionally healthy or loving father figure I could trust.

My mother was a strong, independent, and capable woman who excelled in various fields of employment as the years passed. Though she always said she wanted a daughter, I looked like my father which constantly brought back painful memories for her and put a bit of a wedge in our relationship. Her child-rearing style was authoritarian, so I obeyed more out of fear rather than respect or love. We had some fond moments but being a single, working mother with two children brought constant pressure and stress to the home.

Because my mother worked so much, I took on adult household skills and responsibilities while other girls were playing with their dollies. My mother took pride in independence and self-sufficiency and touted their virtues to us kids. Though I loved the independence, I also yearned to be a normal kid who could depend upon my mother without feeling shame and failure if responsibilities became overwhelming.

This premature independent spirit had its drawbacks. When I was nine my teacher wrote a crushing comment on my report card saying I was "bossy" at times in the schoolyard. I was so surprised and ashamed because I felt betrayed by a teacher who I had liked yet who had never mentioned this to me before. I thought being "bossy" was quite ugly and shameful, and though further report cards documented much improvement, this was the first warning of a particularly distasteful character trait.

## Catechism

It was at this time that my mother suddenly decided that my brother and I were so "bad" we needed to be sent to church to begin catechism. There wasn't anything my brother or I could remember that specifically instigated this event, but our sentence was to serve time at *St. Gregory's Catholic Church*. Even though my mother didn't like Roman Catholicism, I don't think she knew where else to send us. Initially the classes were frightening and shaming because of my lack of spiritual knowledge compared to the other students, but gradually catechism and church opened up an entirely new intriguing world. I was spiritually sensitive and loved all I had learned, soon receiving my First Communion and a year or so later my Confirmation—two of the seven sacraments. I believed what I was taught wholeheartedly and developed a very sensitive conscience of right and wrong. However, with several moves and family upheavals, church attendance slowed to a stop.

In junior high someone gave me *Twixt Twelve and Twenty*, a book written by Pat Boone to help teens mature in many practical areas. I loved reading about the beautiful young lady

I could become so I read the book over and over. The author wrote as a loving father with such warmth and kindness, which I was hungering for, even though I feared men and could only relate to them superficially. At the time I thought, "Why care? They would just leave, and when they were in the family, there was just trouble." Additionally, my mother's attention shifted almost solely to her new husband, leaving me feeling out in the cold. I was awed by this author who seemed so "safe" and who talked about God in ways that others didn't outside of church.

My mother then married an alcoholic which resulted in a great uproar and abuse in the family. I became my mother's protector by preventing frequent arguments. When things got heated, I'd do what I could to create a distraction seeking to calm things down for a while. Once I grabbed a butter knife and threatened my step-father with death if he didn't quit pushing my mother around. I was serious. God seemed to have been forgotten and far, far away.

Later, I was sent to live with different families at various times because of dissension with my mother. I returned only to find her recovering from being stabbed almost to death by an alcoholic step-father. They soon divorced and I felt great guilt and responsibility for not being there to help save her from his attack. In all this, I had no prayers or thoughts of God. I had a love for my mother, yet on the other hand I felt great anger and resentment towards her. In my eyes, all the troubles between us were her fault due to her apparent lack of compassion and quick temper. I played the martyr and had lots of pity parties. It didn't seem to matter that I had a temper, too, and just didn't know how to be quiet or stop arguing.

*Growing Up Fast*

I did well in school, which was my one place of peace. At age fifteen I started my first job in the restaurant business. I soon started accumulating home goods as I planned to move out when I turned eighteen. Though I liked having a job and making money, it was my first, real experience in dealing with the public. That ugly side of me poked out again. Though I was a hard worker, responsible and wanted to impress the boss, I was also impatient, proud, and somewhat rude with the customers. It was difficult to restrain these attitudes which surfaced more at work than in my social relationships.

At sixteen I became sexually active as I succumbed to the desire for independence, the approval of friends, gratification of hormones, the influence of easy-to-get booze, and a fear of rejection if I said, "No." I knew I was doing wrong but I was too weak to stop myself. My priority was to find acceptance. The truths of Pat Boone's book became more of a fading memory. In my senior year my brother and I assumed even more unhealthy independence when we lived in a small apartment in northern California while my mother found employment and lived in southern California. Despite being busy with school and work, all the unhealthy extracurricular activities led to my pregnancy. It was the one time when I finally thought of God and prayed, "Oh, God, please don't let me be pregnant!" on my knees beside my bed, though I already knew the answer in my heart. Initially I refused to speak with the baby's father because of humiliation and hatred I felt towards both him and myself for our predicament. Without any advice I decided to release our baby for adoption. I wasn't aware of any pregnancy centers, and I believed abortion was murder. The father and I didn't have true love or commitment and I could not raise a child alone. Also, I did not want to subject my child to a life without a father. The baby's father readily agreed to adoption, a readiness that hurt me despite the reasons for my own decision. I took it as a rejection—not enough care to fight for me or his baby, so the adoption decision was confirmed.

When my mother became aware of the pregnancy, she was surprisingly supportive and didn't want me to marry either. However, she soon insisted upon a paternity suit to help finance my tuition at a business school while pregnant. In court all the immoral details were humiliatingly revealed before the father's parents who were total strangers. Thankfully my mother wasn't there to hear it all, as she was at work. My only other prayers during my pregnancy were that my baby would first be a Roman Catholic, and secondly that God wouldn't let her be fat like I thought I was (wrongly so). No other prayers, just fear for my future after I delivered.

There was one person who was exceptionally kind during the adoption process—the attorney in charge of the adoption. He was sympathetic and the only one who asked me to really consider whether adoption was best. He suggested some physical harm might possibly happen to me, and I may not be able to have any more children. More denial, "Oh, no, not me!" Little did I know how prophetic his words would were. Amazingly, I graduated from high school in the midst of all this (despite cutting about a third of my senior classes). I actually loved being pregnant, but I stuck to my adoption plan and released our baby for adoption with sorrow that was tempered by the assurance that she was going to a family with both a mother and a father who wanted her and would love her. It was a closed adoption, so I could never see her. My mother wasn't present during my delivery—too busy at work. It made me sad but also resentful. I interpreted her absence as rejection.

## On My Own

After giving birth a friend of my mother helped me obtain a job in San Francisco for the PT & T Co. as a marketing representative. I made new friends, was living on my own and, sadly, returned to immorality. *"Like a dog that returns to his vomit is a fool who repeats his folly" (Proverbs 26:11).* Within six months of delivery I started to have chronic pelvic symptoms, and within one year I had to have a total abdominal hysterectomy for a disseminated pelvic infection. I knew it was God's judgment upon me for unrepentant sexual conduct— my attorney's prophecy realized. Though my guilt was heavy, I continued to live a life of immorality with various men. I believed that physical intimacy was what men primarily wanted from women but desperately hoped that cynical belief wasn't really true. I was always seeking a man who loved me for myself, but I was quite afraid of intimacy, feeling certain no one could love the real me. Yet at the same time I feared rejection. It was a "lose-lose" proposition.

I soon suffered severe financial hardship. The routine of getting up, going to work, and then going to bed was depressing. Was that all there was to life? I became desperate. Spontaneously I ran to the church to pray. I quickly drove that night to a familiar Roman Catholic Church, tried to pull open the doors, but they were all locked. I yanked and tugged, sobbing, and couldn't believe it, since I had grown up in a time when the church doors were always open. Somehow I was longing for the only thing religious that I was familiar with—a reverent, dark silence; the marble altar and big, gold crucifix; the pew kneelers; and the scent of burning candles seemed to be the proper place to talk to God—a holy place. I sadly drove away and not long afterwards realized that I didn't really know what was true religiously after all, so I decided I was agnostic.

## Nursing

With a great stroke of kindness my mother offered to send me to nursing school using grants and loans. I loved the profession, did exceptionally well, graduated and started a job in a San Francisco teaching hospital as a medical-surgical nurse. It was during these times that I realized that I greatly longed for the approval of others, what the Bible calls the sin of the "fear of man." I became a perfectionist at work. Any mistakes I made on the job were hidden whenever possible if they threatened my image before others (though not at the risk of hurting people). Outer appearance and actions were all important to me; I took pride in being a people pleaser.

Soon all the emotions relating to my past home-life and the loss of my baby caught up with me. Depression and crying were frequent despite a happy public face. I sought secular psychiatric counsel. The biggest help was being able to vent. I left when I ran out of tears.

I tried to bury depression with the busyness of life— *Cosmopolitan Magazine*, learning new skills at work, joining in exciting sports with friends (like skiing) and traveling, my world was broadening. With the high stress level at work (now an intermediate intensive care RN), I took frequent vacations, thanks to a good salary, yet I was burdened with the guilt about the true me—a hodge-podge of fun and niceness, but peppered with self-righteousness, a quick, rather cynical, sarcastic tongue, a critical spirit, and wanting the last word (or eye-roll). My temper was easily provoked, typified by grumbling and name-calling under my breath while slamming things around when I thought nobody who mattered was near. Justifying myself was easy despite being aware of my emotional problems. I had high standards and could never understand why people just didn't do what they were supposed to do, especially at work. Craving attention, I could gather it by being a bit of a comic, especially since I found it easy to inject my chit-chat with a good shot of exaggeration for that perfect laugh. I never thought of it as lying. Being the martyr brought more attention due to people's desire to help. I felt quite ashamed by these weaknesses and immaturity. It was difficult to look people in the eye.

Family-life remained fragmented. My mother and I had long periods of distance from one another starting in my mid-twenties all the way into my late thirties. My father and I had only rare, stilted telephone conversations, and my brother lived hours away. Since my teens, my only goal in life was to get married and have a happy family. I foolishly married at age twenty-eight despite a stormy engagement. Planning the wedding, we ran into a barrier when the Catholic Church refused to marry us since my fiancé wasn't Roman Catholic. I did not attend church, but I did want my white wedding to be blessed by God. So I crossed the street to the beautiful Protestant church nestled in the lush redwoods. The pastor married us and for a brief shining moment my future husband and I became closer because of a bit of spiritual guidance. However, there was no gospel presentation, no biblical challenge to our immoral lifestyle and after one traumatic year of mutual distrust, explosive arguments, and physical abuse, I divorced him.

With the divorce, I felt amazing relief, freedom, and safety. Dating resumed; life continued more peacefully but with personal perfectionism and legalism increasing at work where I was then an ER nurse. My co-workers and I enjoyed one another socially, but few looked forward to working with me. The pace and challenges of the job, which were initially exciting, became increasingly more stressful and were causing added pressure with the responsibility. I was tense, anxious and was always thinking about the future. I was getting older now, in my thirties, and needed alternate life plans to ensure security in my life.

The amazing opportunity came for me to purchase a duplex along with a co-worker. This was a wonderful time of nesting, decorating, and learning about homeownership in all its differing aspects. My co-owner would have a significant influence in opening new doors into my personal family life apart from just helping supply a residence.

## The Search for Truth

I had become confused about truth, not just in the religious realm, but in all aspects of life. I initially thought truth could be discovered in the sciences and humanities but found they couldn't be trusted; everyone seemed to have a different opinion about everything. Who was right? What was right? I especially needed to know truth as it applied to love in personal relationships because I was a woman so needy for it. Mature love seemed unattainable, if not a lie. So far it had meant being at the mercy of my emotions with few happy times spoiled by self-centered desires, episodic abuse, fear, and feeling emotionally smothered or controlled. To find truth in all its fullness, I concluded I had to go to the source, God alone. My early religious training had taught me at least a few honest facts that had penetrated: there was a true God; He made and knew all things, and He had the highest moral code of right and wrong.

I had tried to read the Bible, but our *Douay Version* mired me down in the "begots." It was then that I received a suicide call in the ER from a young woman. We talked for a while, and she asked me why she shouldn't kill herself. I paused slightly thinking that if I had expounded upon reasons from my student psych manual, it would obviously have sounded canned and insincere. Also, if I told her I thought she might go to hell for committing a mortal sin, then I'd be in trouble for proclaiming my personal religious opinion. Another important reason for that pause was because I was depressed myself. I had no absolute authority assured in my heart from which I could speak to this patient. I don't know what she interpreted in that pause but she said, "That's all right. You've been very nice, but I'm going to do it anyway," and abruptly hung up. I never knew what happened to her, but I watched for any suicide attempts coming in the rest of my shift, and there were none.

That failure led to a more definite search for truth. Besides, wasn't a nurse supposed to be well-rounded by being able to address the physical, emotional, and spiritual aspects of health? I decided to read about all the major religions of the world and then determine where truth laid its elusive head. I'd start with the Bible again but was deterred a bit thinking about my last attempt.

Meanwhile, during the "Color Me Beautiful" era I got caught up in the art of color in make-up and clothing for enhancing one's appearance. I attended training and became a color and cosmetic consultant in addition to nursing. However, frustrated with the superficial, I soon realized it was the inside of people that needed changing, not simply the outer appearance—and that primarily meant me! Though this artistry had its place, I knew God thought it was hypocrisy if taken too far in an attempt to cover the ugly inner person with a colorfully painted, pretty mask.

Though I had divorced, I wanted to know if in God's eye's I had the right for re-marriage. Driving home from skiing one evening, I turned on the radio and found a radio station with a call-in, Bible question-and-answer program where the host was instructing a caller about that subject. What impressed me more than his answer was the way he calmly handled the extremely abusive caller who didn't agree with his views. I wanted to have that calmness he demonstrated while talking with a difficult person. As the months passed, I would occasionally come across that station again and listen to the show. I was interested in what God's thoughts were, and only the Bible was used for replies, not the opinions of others. Later I would again find that station, and I started to learn more about the gospel and the Christian faith.

Coinciding with this occasional radio teaching, I thought I could get closer to God by digging out my tarnished rosary my grandmother gave me, and putting it to use. I polished it and reviewed how to say the rosary. I lit a candle, draped my head with a long chiffon scarf, and then knelt beside my bed to regularly pray each night with those sterling silver beads. All the preparations made me feel peaceful, feminine, and godly, but did it bring me closer to God? Before I knew it, I was face down on the bedspread snoring before three Hail Mary's passed from my lips. At the same time I was hopping down the Wayne Dyer path of philosophy, and was also involved in a new hopeful romantic relationship. I felt I had found unconditional love. However, I realized I needed to know how to love maturely, to know what true love really was, and more importantly, to have the wisdom and power to be able to do it. "Why couldn't I love like the rest of the world? What was wrong with me?"

## Re-United

As an ER registered nurse (RN) I'd often care for teen girls following various suicide attempts that often resulted from feeling rejected or unloved. It became clear to me that my daughter, who was in the same age bracket by now, might feel that same depression from feeling rejected by her natural parents. I didn't want her to commit suicide thinking I hadn't loved her. I wanted the best for her. I decided I should write her a short letter of explanation, but I did not want to come between her and her adoptive parents. Finding her would be like looking for a needle in a haystack. It became legal for patients to have access to their medical records. With that, I went to the hospital where I delivered my daughter, reviewed my chart, and found the adoptive parents' names and address. Through God's providence, I found her within three months.

Everything just fell into my lap even though I had not yet considered God to have been the sovereign coordinator of it all. I notified my daughter's natural father so that he could initiate a relationship with her if he desired which he soon did. Little did I know initially that her adoptive mother was dying of cancer in an extended-care facility just miles from where I lived. My daughter was eighteen then and attending junior college in northern California. I learned she had been told early on that she was adopted and was secure in her relationship with her adopted parents. Sadly, her adoptive father had died when she was fifteen, and within six months of our reunion, her adoptive mother had died also. When I had initially called her, she thought that I was a nurse calling to let her know her mother had died. No, I was a nurse calling to tell her that her mother was alive. We began a loving relationship that has continued until now.

Work relationships were still rather rocky though some good did result from these troubles. Responsibility weighed heavily on my shoulders because of the nature of my job, fear of failure, and the load of my sins, though I didn't call them that yet. One day while making an extremely difficult, emergent nursing decision, I almost froze with fear. After the call I realized why. I had already felt responsible for my mother's near-death; I didn't want to be responsible for another's. I later sought help from a workplace counselor and through him was able to understand myself better, become encouraged, and not be so harsh. I also realized my false guilt about my mother and that my work responsibilities weren't to be solely on my own shoulders.

### Humbled

On my thirty-ninth birthday in the fall of 1986, I received an anonymous, hateful birthday card and suspected that it came from someone at work. After ruminating about that card one evening, with overwhelming sorrow and anger, I had a melt-down temper tantrum face-down on my living room floor. I pounded the carpet with my fists, flooded the rug with tears, and called out to God for help. "What do I have to do?!" I tried to be the kind and good person I wanted to be, but I was a general failure. I tried counseling, self-help books, talked with friends, but it was all for nothing! I kept bawling while my dog wondered what in the world was going on. I was so loud I think the neighbors heard me in turmoil.

Not long after, I came across a Billy Graham crusade on TV as I was channel surfing. Curious, I listened to him preach. He cut right to the gospel and I was pierced by the Holy Spirit on the spot, and I believed everything he said. Convicted, I fell to my knees crying, confessing, and praying to receive Christ. I sent for the crusade's new believer handbook and completed all its basic little Bible studies. Soon after that, I found an unclaimed Bible at work, *The Way*, and began to devour it.

About the same time I had visited my brother and sister-in-law. My sister-in-law had been attending Bible Study Fellowship and she answered many questions I had about Catholicism and the Bible. They then took me to a special Easter service called, "Then Came Sunday," at their "Protestant" church. It was foreign to me—the huge railroad-tie cross up front, and a new kind of music, so moving. The words filled my heart as I stared in awe at that cross. The Holy Spirit was drawing me closer to Jesus.

I took some commentaries home that my sister-in-law gave me and began reading *The Way* from the beginning. At first I thought, "What am I supposed to do? Sacrifice? I guess I could go to the pet shop and get a few pigeons," but thank God, He held me back, and I just kept reading. As I kept reading the Bible and the commentaries I realized that God was starting to answer my questions about life right there. I consumed the truth.

Within two weeks I had finished reading the Bible, because I did nothing else but go to work and then run home to read. The dishes piled high, the dog hardly got walked, and I stayed up half the night. There was no need to search further into other religions to seek the truths I sought. I committed myself to God and His Word, though I still had so many questions and a limited understanding about Jesus and salvation.

I started attending a local Catholic church and read *The Way*, even during Mass. I didn't yet understand about Jesus dying for the forgiveness of *all* my sins, past present *and* future. I was still trying to perfect myself in the flesh. One Sunday the priest preached from John chapter one explaining how Jesus came to teach us and show us the Father. I had a sudden "Aha!" from the Holy Spirit. I was starting to understand more about Christ and was absolutely thrilled. I craved more biblical instruction than what this church offered, however, and I soon found a new church, Roman Catholic also, which seemed more progressive and lively.

During this time I had my first experience in a Christian book store. I was hunting for a book that could advise me on remarriage. I was shocked at the number of books just on Christianity. But soldiering on, I chose *The Great Divorce*. Little did I know that this book would hardly address my concerns! Regardless, I was entranced and often surprised by what C. S Lewis had to say. I returned to the bookstore and I purchased my first study Bible. I became so excited and tried to share my new discoveries with people at work, who did not seem as excited.

Work relationships improved over the next year, and I was filled with wonder and fear when one day I quietly prayed for the return of a heart rhythm and life to a young man in full cardio-pulmonary arrest who was undergoing resuscitation. I suddenly saw, "blip! blip! blip!" on the cardiac monitor and heard the docs call out, "He's got a rhythm!" They stabilized him for transfer to ICU, and I walked away in awe after experiencing such an amazing immediate answer to prayer about such a critical situation.

Not long after this, I had a traumatic experience that I'd never forget. Someone I knew decided to have an abortion, and though I tried to dissuade her, even offering to raise her baby, I was ineffective. Despite believing it was murder, I accompanied her during the abortion, because she was totally alone. I didn't want her to be in that state during something this important, even if I didn't agree with it. I remembered feeling alone too often in my own life, especially after the birth of my baby. After the abortion I watched them wheel the treatment cart away, and suddenly in distress and confusion, I turned to rush after them thinking the infant (two-three months gestation) should be baptized. However, I didn't have enough courage to call out to stop them. The mother then sat up on her treatment table and said, "I'll *never* do this again," which doubled my sorrow. I cried my heart out all that day driving home and for many days afterwards. It was just as if I was the one who had the abortion. That murder, combined with my weakness, overwhelmed me.

## True Repentance

I left the Catholic Church at that time for various reasons. I also ended my relationship with my boyfriend, as we were unequally yoked. I wanted Christ now and saw the hypocrisy in the physical impurity of our relationship. At the same time I had become physically involved with another. I had been deceiving myself and was still living my life according to my emotions. However, in my growing Christian walk I was horrified at my stumbling and cut off that relationship, not to fall again. I counted the cost of following Christ, especially in regard to my past weaknesses in immorality, and resolved to remain pure, even if it meant remaining lonely and celibate—following Christ was worth more than anything or anyone.

I soon found another Christian radio station with Bible teaching. One day one of the pastors extended an invitation to come to his church which wasn't far away I knew I needed to find a faithful, Bible-teaching church. So, off I went to check it out. However, I suddenly became alarmed when I saw their sign that said it was a "Baptist" church. As a former Catholic, I had heard in the past that Baptists did strange and wild things, and I feared going in. I cautiously did, however, was warmly welcomed, and found that the church, of course, was nothing like I feared. The scriptural teaching was strong and always seemed to hit me where I lived and to answer questions I had about my new faith. I soon joined the church, made new friends and was growing in the Lord.

God started to help me take baby steps in controlling my temper. When at work, if frustrated and angry, instead of grumbling under my breath with bad language, I quickly jumped into saying the Disciples' Prayer as fast as I could, even repeating it if needed. My emotions were initially too intense for me to be able to say my own prayer, so I cried out to God for help and prayed what first came to mind.

I had heard another gospel sermon and was uncertain if initially after hearing Billy Graham, that I had "done it right" on my part. I really wanted to be a Christian wholeheartedly. So, I prayed again on May 5, 1987, to receive Christ as Lord and Savior. I wanted to be "born again" again!

My new church had another surprise for me. Up high in the front was a huge "dunking" baptismal that mildly shocked me. I was only familiar with infant baptism. What I had feared became something of great joy, for on 6/21/87, I was baptized. My baptism almost felt like a wedding day it was so special to me. Seeing my brother's smiling nod as I went down into the water made it even more memorable. Afterwards I celebrated with friends and some family.

## Trials

In mid-1987 I developed a sudden onset of disc degeneration and osteoarthritis of the spine which resulted in chronic pain that has continued until now. I experienced low back, hip and thigh pain and was unable to work, and was placed on disability for fifteen months. No longer would I be able to work in an ER or bedside nurse setting. During my disability I was required to lie down much of the time. This allowed me much time to listen to good Bible teaching on the radio from strong teachers. Listening to God's Word helped me escape from the pain.

God always provided for me throughout my disability in amazing ways. An MRI bill was mysteriously paid by another. I was unable to do my yard work during this time, and one day I was crying out to the Lord about my yard looking so terribly unkempt. What was I going to do? I couldn't afford a gardener. Suddenly I heard a loud whirring motor sound that seemed to be right outside my front window. Peeking out, I saw my neighbor, Clarence, mowing my lawn. After mowing, he went on to edge it, too. Not only did he surprise me with this wonderful service that day, but regularly until I restarted work and was able to hire a gardener. I found that Clarence was a Christian, and he later said that all he knew was that he saw the mowing needed to be done, so he did it. I was so indescribably grateful to both God and Clarence, because the yard care was such a big job. That God sent him at the moment of my heart-felt prayer showed His watching eyes and caring hand. This gave me a growing sense of security when in the midst of my unemployment and debilitating health challenge.

While puttering in my backyard one day I was thinking of my job as a nurse, a position from which I had always obtained my personal worth and security. The ER, the specializations, the nursing and teaching skills all vanished overnight. I had taken pride in my skills, but now I didn't even know who I was since I had always defined myself by the significance of my job. It hurt to be humbled, yet I was starting to learn how to define myself through Christ. However, when I came towards the end of my disability benefits with no job in sight, fear overtook me. "What will I do? How will I support myself?" What kind of work was even possible for me to do? I prayed over and over in anxiety rather than quiet trust. I tried to remember how God had kept me so far, but in that giant battle between fear and faith, it seemed like fear was winning.

## God Provides

At some point after reading about Abraham offering Isaac, I tightly clung to the truth that one of the names of the LORD is Jehovah-Jireh, "the LORD Will Provide." The Holy Spirit deeply impressed upon me that God was my Provider just like

Abraham's. So I picked up the classifieds, saw an ad for a Poison Information Specialist at a nearby hospital in their poison control center, applied, and was essentially hired on the spot. My thankfulness was overwhelming, and faith in my Provider swelled. At the poison control center we handled calls about all types of exposures, including overdoses.

During one of these emergent calls, I continued to talk with the patient over the phone while waiting for the ambulance arrival. After addressing her physical needs, God opened the door for us to have a short spiritual discussion. I tried to encourage her in Christ, but how much help I was, I don't know. This I do know. If she had asked why she shouldn't have tried to commit suicide, by God's doing I was ready with some sure and truthful answers.

It was only because of Jesus that I had the desire and courage to reach out to my mother and be reconciled. If it had not been for Him, I would most likely not have sought any relationship with her at all. God has been faithful to help us as we have had our ups and downs, but the greatest gift was the LORD showing me where I needed to change by having more compassion, humility, forgiveness, and especially patience. Countless times He has worked in both my mother's heart and mine to forgive and seek peace. Christ is teaching me how to level our see-saw relationship though that is a constant challenge.

God showed great mercy in directing me to *Community Pregnancy Center (CPC)* through a friend and where I was counseled about my part in the abortion. Though a degree of sorrow remains, it doesn't overtake my life, and I have been able to embrace God's forgiveness. Steps were taken to explain to the abortion center how the abortion affected me, and there has been forgiveness, especially considering my part in the tragedy. I later became a *CPC* counselor for a time, something both exhilarating and frustrating. While volunteering for them, I felt the strong desire to use Scripture to write an abbreviated story in biblical verse about the abortion, its judgments, and healing. I searched avidly for just the right verse and came up with about fifteen that described the major events. I felt that if any stranger was to pick up the story, he would be able to determine basically what had happened along with its consequences. It took quite a bit of time studying before I could resolve that what I wanted to do next was right and wholly true. With the help of Christian counselor at the local cemetery, I set a memorial stone in place, and had the abortion date inscribed, the name I had given the baby (Grace), and underneath that, the phrase, "Alive with Christ." I hope to have this same truth engraved when I depart to heaven. I then tucked a laminated copy of my scriptural story under the plaque. All provided me considerable comfort and peace.

I continue to lead Precept home Bible studies, teaching children's Sunday school and help with other areas of service in the church.

To our blessed Father alone be the glory for all His mercy and grace poured out upon me for salvation, to grow in Him, and *"to will and to work according to His good pleasure" (Philippians 2:13)*. I'm often reminded that time is short, and I want to make the most of my time left here on earth as a representative for Christ.

# 12

## *Knowing God*

*"And this is eternal life, that they may
know You, the only true God, and
Jesus Christ Whom You have sent"
John 17:3*

*I* still can't believe that He saved me. I still can't believe that
He's using me.

I was a sinner from the beginning, and deep down I knew
it. I was born in Quezon City in the Philippines, in 1984. I had
three siblings and our family was well off. Raised in the Roman
Catholic religion, I was always aware, even as a young boy, that
God existed. I clearly remember frequently looking out into the
surrounding mountain range from my parents' bedroom and
contemplating how the God who created this world extended
beyond that mountain range, and how mind-blowing it was that
He had neither beginning nor end.

## Natural Revelation

Though my parents never really talked to me about the nature of God, I was aware of His eternality, of His power, of His sovereignty, of His "bigness." And, to be honest, it scared me. I knew that such a powerful God was watching me and contemplated my every move and thought, and that I was nothing compared to Him. Because of our family's religious background, I attended Mass every Sunday, and prayed in front of carven images of Mary and the saints—often with a rosary in my hand.

I was always fully aware of the righteousness of God—even as a young child, my mind was independent from that of my parents, and I did whatever I could to do to earn the favor of God so He would grant me a ticket to heaven. I knew of a heaven and a hell—that those whom God approved went to the former, and those whom He did not went to the latter. So as an elementary child I did whatever I felt would impress God and earn my way to heaven. It's amazing that, even at this age, a works-based approach to salvation was already ingrained in me. Maybe I was precocious; every night during those elementary-school years, I would think about the day when I would stand before this God and give an account of every action, word, and thought that I did and had. Such pondering often led me to tears and sleeplessness, though I never told anyone about it.

When I was in first grade, I became aware of the tension that was developing between my extended family and my Uncle Gines, who was saved and became a follower of Christ. It became more of a reality when I was scolded while visiting my grandmother in the hospital for flippantly telling my sisters that praying to Mary was wrong—something my brother and I had been told by Uncle Gines. For a while, I decided to listen to my parents and purposely viewed my uncle as a religious "heretic" and whose beliefs were dangerous to me—often covering my ears and opening my own little picture Bible to "protect" myself when he would discuss certain theological issues with my brother during family dinners.

*Hearing Truth*

But one day, during that same year in first grade, I decided to make a trip up to his room. While the rest of the family was busy chatting over the dinner table in my grandmother's mansion, I quietly slipped my eight-year old self up to Uncle Gines' room, where I knew he had retreated. He invited me in, and sat me down. That night, from opposite ends of his massive couch, I asked him all the questions that my mind had been pondering over the previous few months— mainly why he was a "born-again Christian" and why he didn't pray to Mary or the saints, and what exactly he thought was the meaning of life. Needless to say, he answered my questions truthfully. Even though I was told countless times that he was of the "wrong religion," I believed everything Uncle Gines told me that night. I wasn't saved that evening, but something did "click." Not too long after that, my family moved to Hawaii.

During the years that followed, and behind my parents' back, I stopped praying to Mary and the saints. It was also during those years that my older brother, Vincent, came to know Christ (also through Uncle Gines' evangelistic efforts), and had several conversations with me concerning the truth of the Bible. Though I believed his words like I did Uncle Gines', and though our parents treated us with equal love and dignity, I was bothered by the fact that my brother seemed to have something in him that I didn't.

He would tell me about the times when he would read the Bible and discover an amazing revelation, and I would think to myself, "Why is it that when my brother reads the Bible, he seems to discover joyful things... but when I read it, I don't get impacted in the same way?" It wasn't so much that I was jealous of Vincent; I just felt condemned by my conscience. I felt that, though we both were created by God, Vincent had a relationship with God that I didn't. It only served to condemn me, for deep down I realized that if I stood before God, I would have no defense given for all of my sins. I distinctly remember a time in fourth grade when, due to such introspection, I locked myself into my room and wept for an hour straight because I felt that this powerful God—who my uncle and brother seemed to love so dearly—would end up sending me to hell. While crying, I wrote a letter to God in which I asked Him not to send me to hell. I sealed the letter in a yellow envelope, and stuck it behind one of the picture frames in my room so that my parents wouldn't know that I was struggling with such thoughts. I still have that letter with me today.

## The Full Gospel

As I matured into my later elementary school years, Vincent shared the full gospel with me. He didn't do it in one sitting—at least I don't think he did. He shared the gospel in its entirety over a period of time, and I never doubted his words to be true. "Of course Jesus died for our sins," I would think. But deep down, I for some reason doubted that He would forgive me of all of my sins. I suppose I wanted to forgive myself, and I wanted to feel good about myself. I couldn't get to the point of fully confessing that I was a condemned sinner deserving of hell. I was too proud and afraid to admit that. Still yet, when it came down to choosing between the religious views of my parents and those of my brother, I chose to follow the latter. I called myself a Protestant—mainly because I knew that I didn't want to be known as a Catholic.

In 1997, before entering junior high, my parents divorced, and I moved to Los Angeles with my mother and two sisters. The smooth life I had known previously shattered, and I was away from my brother for the first time (he stayed in Hawaii to finish his senior year). With all of the tension that resulted from our family situation, I didn't know where to turn for comfort, so I turned to excelling in school, which at the time felt like my only source of joy and identity. I decided to place all of my efforts and all of my pride into my success as a student. For the next six years, up until I graduated from high school, I developed into a young man ravenous for worldly success, marked by competitive ambition. I put all of my efforts into getting good grades, shunned my family, and did everything I could to win the approval and esteem of others. At the same time, I attempted to begin a church life for whatever reason.

As a sophomore in high school, after my family moved to Las Vegas, I decided to officially stop attending the Catholic Church against my mother's wishes. It started on a Saturday evening, when I told my mother that I was heading out to *Barnes & Noble* to read, with which she had no problem. I did go to *Barnes & Noble* that evening—but not until after attending a Saturday night worship service at an evangelical church near our house. A few months later, I began to attend *Warm Springs*

*Baptist Church* in Las Vegas, and eventually involved myself in the church's musical praise team. I also started to attend a small Bible study with my Uncle Gines (he and his family had also moved to Las Vegas) and a few church friends twice my age.

I took personal pride in my decision to leave the Catholic Church and join a Christian fellowship, and proclaimed myself to be a Christian to all because of the new body of teaching that I intellectually affirmed. My motives at the time were partially selfish. On the one hand, I really did believe what the Bible said to be true. But on the other hand, I was driven by a rebellious desire to be different from the rest of my family. In reality, I had one foot in the church, and another in the world, but neither of those feet were running towards Jesus.

If anything, church was merely a place for me to clarify in my mind what things were permissible and what things were forbidden. And I did everything I could to be of the world while at the same time maintaining moral externals that would seem to be permissible by biblical standards. It was clear that I was not living to please God. I merely kept these biblical morals because I thought that they would keep me out of hell. So I still had a works-righteousness mindset.

## Hypocrisy

Everything else that I could do that would serve myself, I did. It was a shameful life that I lived in trying to fool people and God that I was a Christian, when the only person I was fooling was me. Did I really know Jesus as my personal Savior? If the time I was unable to provide an answer to my church's praise-team leader about when I had accepted Christ as my Savior was to serve as evidence, apparently I did not know

Jesus. Such hypocrisy was all-the-more apparent to my non-Christian friends and classmates before whom I claimed to be a Christian. I recall one online conversation that I had with my Hindi classmate and best friend at the time:

"Hey, I have a question," my friend asked. "You're not a Christian, are you?"

"Of course I am!" I said, a little shocked.

"Oh, ok, I just wanted to make sure," he responded.

"Why do you ask?" I inquired.

"Well..." he typed, "I don't know much about Christianity. But from what I've seen in you, well, you're pretty bad."

He wasn't the only person to say that. All of my friends were aware of my hypocrisy. Though I was a self-proclaimed Christian who had made a vow to abstain from pre-marital sex, they heard me talk obscenely about women. Though I had told them my stance about alcohol and how I didn't believe in getting drunk, they watched me waste hundreds of dollars on alcohol during our senior class trip to Cancun because it was "legal." After seeing such things, another friend—an atheist—to told me forthrightly during Chemistry class:

"Why do you call yourself a Christian? You're going to hell anyway! You're a hypocrite!"

So there I was, as a college-bound student, running straight for worldly success carrying around a Christian nametag. I was a hypocritical, self-proclaimed devoted Christian sprinting straight to hell.

## True Belief

It still brings me to my knees to think about the night God saved me. The events that took place that night are still fresh in my memory. It was a Thursday night, on September 25, 2003, while walking back to my dorm room before the first day of college, that God stopped me in my tracks and rescued me. I had been in San Diego for almost two weeks, having spent a weekend with *InterVarsity Christian Fellowship* and most of the school's welcome week, attending free barbecues and dessert nights held by other fellowships I had considered joining.

That night, that Thursday night, before walking back to my dorm, I found myself talking and praying on one of the library walk blocks with a fellow incoming freshman and childhood friend. Having just left an *InterVarsity* large group meeting, we found ourselves praying, asking God to take control of our college careers, and to make our time at UCSD a time for Him. In all honesty, although it was my idea to pray, I only did so because I thought it would sound spiritual. Did I really know what I was talking about? No—well, at least, not till a few minutes later. As we separated to go back to our dorms, I was suddenly convicted of a sin that I was always too afraid to admit, that I never wanted to confess—I did not love God!

I looked up to God, while walking across Mandeville Auditorium, at around 11:00 pm, and admitted to Him that I had never loved Him. I admitted that I might have not even been a Christian at the time. I realized, at that moment, that not once in my life did I truly love God, and I knew that this was enough for all of my external actions to be counted as futile. I realized my state before Him, as a lost sinner who did not know where to go.

I sat down on one of the chairs in front of the auditorium, and asked God to forgive me for having my back turned to Him for nineteen years, and told Him that I now needed Him. I confessed my need for Jesus' work on the cross to save me, and told Him that night that I wanted to give the rest of my life to Him. It was the same prayer I had prayed only a few moments earlier, but this time out of a broken, fearful heart that was looking to Christ for the first time as the only way to salvation. I had already heard the gospel message before, but that night was the first time when I truly embraced Christ as my Savior, fully admitting that I was unable to save myself. I understood for the first time that night that I was a sinner, and took joy in the fact that the punishment for my sins had been paid for, and that now I was going to heaven. It was no longer just a theory, but a personal reality. I had always understood it with my head, but that night I finally understood it with my heart. I remember praying, "God, for nineteen years, I have been running away from You. But You were patient with me, in waiting for me to repent and genuinely call upon You. Now, my life is Yours. And now that I'm Yours, no one can ever snatch me out of Your hands."

It wasn't until a few weeks later, when my small group leader at the time asked me to prepare a testimony for the group, that I realized that it was on that Thursday night when I was saved by God and was named a Christian for the first time. Granted, the first few weeks were puzzling to me, since I knew that I felt different but was not sure why. All I knew was that I loved God genuinely for the first time, and was all of a sudden willing to live for Him and not for myself. But while writing the testimony, I asked myself the following: "If I had gotten into a car accident during my drive down to San Diego from Las Vegas (where I attended high school), would I have gone to heaven?" I concluded that the answer was no. It was during that time as I wrote my testimony that I realized September 25, 2003 was not just a date when I decided to be more passionate to live for God. Rather, it was the date when God saved me, and gave me a new heart that could finally look to Him as Savior, embrace Him for that, love Him for who He is, and commit to living for Him.

*Struggles*

The following year, however, wasn't quite the year that I had imagined my first as a genuine believer to be. Though I initially enjoyed the activities of my new Christian lifestyle—I had involved myself with an on-campus fellowship and was busy running around from one Bible study to large group events—it didn't take long for the emotional scars from my past, along with my idolatrous insecurities, to resurface. During the beginning of my sophomore year, I began to struggle with depression. Till this day, I'm not exactly sure what it was that ultimately triggered it (the heart is, after all, deceitful: Jeremiah 17:9). What I do know is that, in my immaturity, I responded sinfully to my emotions. I responded to all of the anxiety and insecurity through self-mutilation and several panic attacks. I followed the advice of my staff leaders and began to see a psychologist, who diagnosed me with manic depression and "dissociative trance disorder" (I believe that his diagnosis was incorrect, but that's for another story).

Though I went to counseling sessions regularly and was prescribed anti-depressant medication by a psychiatrist, my condition only worsened and the self-mutilation increased in frequency. My on-campus fellowship leaders, charismatic Christians who were deeply concerned about my worsening state, eventually tried to cast demons out of me during a Bible study—claiming to have exorcised four demons in the process.

But they were wrong; they did not cast any demons out of me. Only a few days later, I was hospitalized for trying to jump off a small bridge next to the campus library. After I was released, my mother and brother drove down to my dorm room to pay me a visit. Seeing the condition that I was in brought my brother to tears (it was one of only three times that I've witnessed him cry). That was in December of 2004.

## Knowing God

Entering Christmas break, I realized that I was at a precarious point; I would either change or continue to spiral downward. Afraid that I would end up committing suicide, I committed myself to read six books during that three-week vacation. One of those books happened to be *Knowing God* by J.I. Packer. As I read the book and all of its Scripture references, I was for the first time exposed to the attributes of God as revealed in the Scriptures. I was overwhelmed. In the midst of my depression, I began to see God for who He is and not for who I wanted Him to be—He is a holy, righteous, sovereign, wrathful, gracious, jealous, loving, good, majestic God who works all things for His glory alone. It was then that I began to realize that I was ultimately created not for my own glory, but for the glory of this magnificent God I was reading about. For the first time, I began to see that I was designed not to live for myself, but for Him who died and rose again on my behalf.

Though I had been engaged in Christian activities for over a year up to this point, that Christmas vacation marked the first time I truly understood the deeper essence of what it meant to be a Christian. For the first time, I understood the purpose of my existence: to bring glory and honor to my Creator and Savior in all of who I am and in everything I do. This was the reason for which I was justified; this was the reason for which I would be sanctified. A few months later, I was baptized. A year later, after seeing the kind of transformation that God wrought in me, and having been infused with a passion to see His power effect others in the same way, I entered into vocational ministry.

## Ministry

God has faithfully continued growing me through trials and struggles, blessing me with joys, and providing me with brothers and sisters who have over the years sharpened me, provided me with true fellowship, and built me up in Him. In 2006, I enrolled at *The Master's Seminary* and graduated in 2011. I've served as a youth pastor, college and associate pastor, elder, and now as a pastoral assistant of Christian Education at *Grace Bible Fellowship*. I am also a biblical counselor in training.

Being in vocational ministry has brought about a tremendous amount of trials that have brought me to breaking points. But it's all worth it. And in light of all that I've done, I am still amazed that Christ Jesus has chosen to put me into service for Him. That He would choose a man like me—who had been so blasphemous and dishonoring toward Him and His gospel during my teenage years and who behaved so immaturely during my first year as a believer—to preach His Word, disciple His saints, and minister on His behalf has never ceased to amaze me.

Even more recently, God has blessed me with the opportunity to shepherd my own family—my beautiful wife, Kathy; my wonderful son, Jayden; and a precious daughter, Emma. What a privilege it has been to be called to love them, disciple them, and lead them for the glory of my Savior. It truly is a noble calling to lead a wife and child to God, but is there a more privileged task than this? It is unbelievable that He considered me faithful and entrusted a family and a ministry to my care, after all that I had done. Is there any greater joy than knowing that the very Creator who runs the blood through my veins is shaping me to become more and more like Jesus Christ?

Before college, I was trapped in sin with my back turned towards God. Now I am currently struggling hard against sin and the sins of others, and walking with Jesus. I suppose that I've never forgotten the things that I did against Him. But I've also never forgotten the grace that He showed me.

I still can't believe that He saved me. I still can't believe that He's using me.

*It is a trustworthy statement, deserving full acceptance,*
*that Christ Jesus came into the world to save sinners,*
*among whom I am the foremost.*
*Yet for this reason I found mercy, so*
*that in me as the foremost,*
*Jesus Christ might demonstrate His*
*perfect patience as an example*
*for those who would believe in Him for eternal life.*
1 Timothy 1:15-16

# 13

## *Mustard Seed Faith*

*"Truly I say to you, if you have faith
the size of a mustard seed, you will
say to this mountain, 'Move from
here to there,' and it will move; and
nothing will be impossible to you"
Matthew 17:20*

Jeremiah 1:5 reads, *"Before I formed you in the womb I knew you...."* From eternity past, before time began, the Lord knew me personally just as He knew Jeremiah the prophet. My existence, and all it has entailed, is a testimony of His lovingkindess and grace.

When I look back on my life, there are many things that I remember vividly; my first day of high school, my first solo drive with my license, watching my parents drive away on my first day of college. My life has held many beautiful moments and reflecting on them brings me a great deal of joy. Inevitably, as I grow older there are fewer experiences from my earliest

222 MUSTARD SEED FAITH

childhood years that I can still recall with great detail. Fortunately, my parents are able to supplement the times that are less clear in my mind and fill in the gaps when necessary.

*Mom's Perspective*

Of all the memories that require parental assistance, none is more significant than the day I chose to follow Jesus Christ as my personal Lord and Savior. For the sake of accuracy, I have asked my mother to describe to the best of her memory the details of the most important decision I have ever made:

> As a mother you pray persistently that your children will grow in the faith that you hold dear. Our family belongs to Jesus and our relationship with Him is everything. We believe that to know Jesus personally you must accept Him as the one and only Son of God, recognize and repent of your sin, and believe that Jesus came to the earth He created to save you from sin. He was crucified on a cross and conquered death through His resurrection in order to offer us eternal life and a wonderful relationship with Him as Lord.
>
> Austin grew up singing about Jesus, memorizing Bible verses and asking a million questions. His curious mind was always putting together new pieces as the Lord revealed new truths to him. One day we were driving down Shea Boulevard on our way to church when Austin asked this question; "Mommy, do you mean that if I don't ask Jesus into my heart for my naughty

things that I will go to the fiery sea and never get to have Jesus as my friend?"

I answered, "Yes, that is true."

As I continued to drive, he started to pray; "Dear Jesus, I ask You to forgive all my naughty things and accept You into my heart so I can live with You forever."

I had always envisioned what this moment would look like. I had pictured Austin asking me before bed and kneeling together as a family to pray, or having him repeat a prayer after me. It is always fun to dream, but God achieves everything in His perfect timing and often gives us a more perfect moment than we could have ever imagined. I will never forget Austin's moment at three years old when the truth hit him, and he entered into a relationship with Jesus! There was too much traffic to stop the car, and so we continued down the road as the angels and I celebrated the eternal salvation of my precious little boy.

Some people may find it hard to believe that the greatest moment of my life is one that I can hardly remember. While I may not recall the events of that special day, everything I need to have confidence in the security of my eternal future exists in God's Word. In First Samuel 16:7, God says, *"God sees not as man sees, for man looks at the outward appearance, but the LORD looks at the heart."* On that blessed day the Lord saw the heart of a three-year-old boy and through an act of grace forever claimed it for Himself.

*Simple Faith*

Many may also find it hard to believe that I became a believer at such a young age—three years old! But Jesus did say, *"Unless you...become like children, you will not enter the kingdom of heaven" (Matthew 18:3).* God wants child-like faith from His people. Also, the Bible says that all that is required is mustard seed faith (Matthew 17:20), or small faith—a tiny portion of genuine faith that God could grow over time. And that is what God gave me when I was young. The ability to believe in Him was actually a gift that came from Him (Ephesians 2:8) as a result of hearing the gospel and His Word (Romans 10:17).

As I look back there are even clear evidences of spiritual fruit in my life that testify to the integrity of my young, immature "mustard seed" faith. When I was four years old, I asked the pastor of my church if I could sing a solo of my favorite Christmas song at church on Sunday in celebration of the birth of Christ. With my mother standing next to me for support, I took the microphone from the pastor and sang the entire first verse of, "Hark the Herald Angels Sing," as loud as I possibly could—in front of a full congregation of saints. At a young age I was diagnosed with many food allergies, one of which was tomatoes, which can be difficult in a culture where the majority of kids grow up eating Ketchup. As a result I became incredibly found of mustard, and at five years old proclaimed to my grandmother, "I love mustard. It's what they make faith out of, you know?" At six years old I was playing on the swing set with my mother when a man happened to pass by the playground. I took the opportunity to ask the man if he loved Jesus with all his heart, mind, soul and strength. When he said that he didn't, I quickly told him that if he didn't love Jesus and ask Him to forgive all his naughty things that he would have to spend forever in the fiery sea. The man was initially shocked, and then became angry and walked away.

Perhaps one of the most memorable moments for me was when I was in fourth grade. I had an "episode" occur between my favorite elementary school teacher and me. During a science lecture, this teacher explained how the world was created through evolution and that humans evolved from apes.

I knew that she was a professing Jew, and I shouted out in distress, "But you are Jewish, and the Bible says that God created the world and made man in His own image! Don't you believe what the Bible says?"

This caught her off guard, and in her flustered state she replied, "Don't make fun of what I believe."

At the sound of the last bell I ran as fast as I could across the playground to tell my mother everything that happened. It was blasphemous to me that someone could profess allegiance to the God of Israel while at the same time reject what the Old Testament clearly taught about creation. As a ten-year-old I thought that was a clear mockery of God's Word.

As a twenty-six year-old who loves Jesus, I can never remember a time when I doubted my faith in the gospel, the reality of Christ, or His love for me. My faith has only grown stronger with each passing year. I have lived a short life, full of trials like most people, but my salvation and love for Jesus has never been in doubt. In times of deliberate sin I remember experiencing severe conviction by the Holy Spirit. These were all manifestations of fruit that God was working in a real way through His Spirit who lived in me since I believed in the gospel.

*Trials*

The years passed and I continued to grow in the knowledge of the Lord and the truths of His Word. As a family, we experienced seasons of abundant blessings and joy, as well as times filled with immense hardships and trials. Perhaps the most difficult to endure was our battle with alcoholism. Those who have walked through a similar situation understand the unique challenges associated with substance abuse. Alcoholism, like any addiction, can cause deep pain, confusion, disunity, and can plant seeds of bitterness in your heart.

When I turned ten, I became more aware of the effects that alcohol had on our daily lives. I began to experience a great deal of pain as my heart struggled to rectify the brokenness that I felt. In an act of desperation, I went before the throne of my Heavenly Father to cry for help in my season of distress. God was faithful to hear my prayer and answer my plea through the goodness of His Word. Isaiah 53:4-5 in the Old Testament gives a prophecy of the coming Messiah that was later fulfilled by Jesus in full: *"Surely our griefs He Himself bore, and our sorrows He carried...the chastening of our well-being fell upon Him, and by His scourging we are healed."* God cared so deeply for us that He was willing to suffer and die for our griefs and sorrows in addition to the entirety of our sins. That kind of sacrificial love is worthy of all that our finite lives have to offer.

After a trying five year period, my parent's marriage ended in divorce when I was fifteen. If you or somebody you know comes from a broken home, you have seen or experienced the ramifications that follow in the wake of such an event. My mother, my younger brother Hunter and I held tightly to each other as we moved forward with the responsibilities of life. We had very little money and a great deal of debt that made living in the wealthy town of Scottsdale, Arizona extremely difficult.

While friends of mine were receiving cars for their sixteenth birthdays, we were sharing the one pair of jeans we owned between the three of us. In addition to club baseball and schoolwork, I got a part-time job as a janitor at our church to help bring in additional income. Although I often wrestled with entitlement and was discontent with our financial state, I recall many memories from that season of life with great affection. We did not have much, but we had each other. Simple movie nights and long drives in the car late at night with the music blaring brought us closer together and gave us a sense of hope that someday things would feel normal again.

*Cancer*

Six months after the divorce we discovered that our dream of normality was further off than expected when my grandmother was diagnosed with stage five inflammatory breast cancer. Due to our proximity to the hospital and the immediate need for aggressive treatment, my grandparents moved into our small house. My mother graciously gave up her bedroom during their stay, and spent six months sleeping on an uncomfortable couch while her mother fought for her life. Together we walked alongside my grandmother during her treatment knowing that the possibility of losing the battle with cancer was an everyday reality.

Over time I grew increasingly exhausted from all that life had thrown our way. It seemed that the amount of hardships we had to endure was incredibly unfair. Life was hard. Once again I went before the Lord in order that I might find rest for my weary soul. As a musician, I have always found great comfort in the Psalms of David and their ability to minister to the current state of my heart. Psalm 27:13-14 says, *"I would have despaired unless I had believed that I would see the goodness of the Lord in the land of the living. Wait for the Lord; be strong and let your heart take courage; yes, wait for the Lord."*

After an emotionally draining fight with cancer, my grandmother finished her final round of chemotherapy and was declared cancer free! I will never forget the incredible example of courage my grandmother displayed during that season of her life. Few people could have endured the amount of pain and suffering brought on by the severity of her cancer. And yet, in the weakest months of her life, she possessed the full radiance of the composure and grace that anchored her personality. I witnessed first-hand that in the face of great suffering, one's ability to endure is directly related to their capacity for hope. My grandmother's hope was rooted in the security of her relationship with Jesus Christ, and the promise of eternal life with Him gave her supernatural strength to withstand each hardship.

*A New Family*

As she began to regain her strength, my grandparents were able to move back to their home in Strawberry, Arizona. Life slowed down to a much more manageable pace. Before entering my senior year of high school, my mother met and married a wonderful man with two sons and we moved in to our new house just before the school year. My brother and I were greatly blessed by the addition of two brothers, especially when it came time for the Thanksgiving Day family football game. I have heard many horror stories about the complications of blended family life. We have had some challenges along the way, but the great majority of our time together has been a tremendous blessing to all of us.

## Music

During my senior year of high school I started to get really involved in music. My history with music up to that point had been an interesting one. I began taking piano lessons when I was seven. I thought it sounded like a great idea until I found out all the practicing and responsibility it required. I was not a very disciplined pianist, and I once ran away from home to avoid going to a lesson (to the chagrin of my grandfather). I disliked practicing, and only wanted to play music composed by Scott Joplin, the popular ragtime composer. However, my mother had wisely discerned a musical gift in me when I was young, and after many years I began to develop a passion for playing.

Over the course of my last year in high school I played a battle of the bands competition with my new brother, Robert, I was constantly writing and performing original songs, and even won "Best Musician" for our "senior class mosts." As college deadlines approached, I began to weigh my passion for music with logic about the best possible career choice. I heard stories about musicians who lived gig to gig and often experienced seasons without a reliable source of income. It was upon acceptance to my parents *alma mater, Point Loma Nazarene University (PLNU),* that I decided to make the "safe" choice and major in business for the well being of my future family. I registered for my freshman year, and headed off in a car with my parents for San Diego, CA.

When I arrived at *PLNU*, and stood at the check-in table surveying the ocean view that would be mine for the next four years, I had an unmistakable change of heart. I felt convicted for my decision to pick a major based on future financial stability instead of choosing to be courageous and further develop the gifts God entrusted to me. So on my first day at *PLNU* I changed my major from business to music. Thankfully, there was room for me in the B.A. program, a spot for me in the Concert Choir, and the opportunity to learn the language of music from experienced professors. Upon changing my major I found out that all music majors needed to have an instrument they studied privately in order to complete their degree. It may sound like common sense, but I was surprised and instantly anxious. I declared piano as my instrument and once again came face to face with the rigors of private lessons.

I was not qualified to be a pianist in a college level music program. I worked hard to adapt to the increased demand of practicing, but I lacked the fundamental skill-set to play the required music. It was during this semester, as I lost hours of sleep each night, that I discovered singing could be an area of emphasis. I had never thought of my voice as an instrument, but I signed up and switched almost immediately. For those who don't know me, I was born with a song in my heart. I sing all the time. Singing is definitely one of the strongest gifts that the Lord blessed me with, and it was a perfect fit for me academically. Under the guidance of a wonderful voice teacher, my ability to express myself through song grew significantly over the remainder of my career at *PLNU*.

My undergraduate experience at *PLNU* held four of the best years of my life. I met my two best friends on the first day of school, and our relationships continue to grow to this day. I played volleyball at Mission Beach, took surfing class, and went running on trails that overlooked the ocean. No matter where I live, San Diego will always feel like home.

I was also able to grow spiritually during my time at *PLNU*. Like any Christian college, there were people with different ideas regarding Theology and Doctrine, but the majority was anchored by a true passion for God. While there were times that I was encouraged by the ministry *PLNU* offered to students, it was still crucial to use discernment founded on biblical truths. No Christian school will ever be perfect, because we are all sinners and perfection does not exist in this lifetime. But God promises that you will seek Him and find Him when you search for Him with all your heart (Jeremiah 29:13).

After countless hours of singing and performing, it was time to start thinking about the future. I was fortunate enough to audition for *The University of Southern California (USC)* in the final semester of my senior year, and was accepted on top scholarship into the "Thornton School of Music." After a summer spent in Aspen, Colorado with the Aspen Music Festival, I packed up my car and drove off to LA to start a masters degree in vocal arts.

## Isolated

When I arrived in LA, the realities of my new home became evident immediately. No longer was I in a Christian environment that cultivated and cared for my spiritual growth, but a secular culture that thrived on immorality. I attended church by myself for an entire year. I spent many nights sitting alone in a practice room until the early hours of morning to avoid the outrageous parties of the roommates I had been randomly assigned. I ate the majority of my meals without the company of friends I used to cherish. I have never felt so isolated in my entire life. I spent countless hours before the Lord in prayer, often without words to express the depth of the pain I was feeling.

Seasons of isolation are some of the most excruciating times in the life of a believer. However, God gives us comfort through the examples written in His Word. Before Elijah would be called a man of God (1 Kings 17:24), the Lord needed to refine him through an intense period of isolation. It was at the Brook Cherith that Elijah entered into a rigorous time of spiritual training (1 Kings 17:3-6). God needed to strip Elijah of anything unnecessary to his calling and replace it with more of His presence. My entire first year at *USC* was my own personal season at the Brook Cherith. God provided for my basic needs, and everything else was stripped away so that I would learn to depend completely on Him.

*Answered Prayer*

That summer after my first year, as I prayed for a new place to live and a Christian community to join, I reconnected with an old high school friend who attended *USC*. He mentioned that AGO, the Christian fraternity he was a member of while in school, needed help with the rent and was looking for boarders. I was able to get connected with the housing manager and secured a room for the coming year. I had no previous experience with the Greek system and was nervous about what the coming year might hold. After a summer of singing opera in San Francisco, I gathered my things and headed to the house to move in for the school year not knowing what to expect.

Looking back, I can say without hesitation that the decision to live in the AGO house was one of the best I have ever made. I had finally found the Christian community I had been searching for. There were organized activities every night of the week, a group of people to go to church with, and most importantly people to share fellowship with during meals. AGO life was good, and I embraced every aspect of it.

## Desires of the Heart

It was at this time that I began to have another change of heart. I had spent the past years grooming myself for a career in opera. During my time at *USC*, I enjoyed a great deal of success in the singing community inside and outside of school. I performed with many great singers who have gone on to do incredible things. I still had a passion and love for the music, but my desire to pursue opera as a career was beginning to diminish.

The fall of my second year I tackled the greatest operatic challenge of my life. *USC* Opera had joined forces with "Visions and Voices," the university's Arts and Humanities Initiative, to put on the west coast premier of Lee Hoiby's adaptation of *The Tempest*. I was selected to sing Prospero, one of Shakespeare's greatest characters and the main protagonist of the opera. This role required countless hours of preparation and study. I began to feel overwhelmed at my inability to properly identify with a character way beyond my years. Thankfully, the show's run went very well and I felt great about my performances. However, in the end something became very clear to me. My passion for opera was no match for the joy I experienced when spending time with brothers and sisters in Christ that I had met throughout the year. Later that spring, as I prepared for my final opera with *USC* and my graduate recital, I reflected on this realization in my journal as I prayed for future direction:

*March 25, 2013*

> *Lord, prepare me to embrace a call to ministry sooner than I originally thought, and may I trust You to provide for my needs and bless me with the desires of my heart. Help me to surrender all and embrace a joyful life as a servant for Christ. "Twill be my joy through the ages to sing of His love for me."*

When I graduated from *USC*, I moved up to the Bay Area for a temporary summer job—working as a counselor for a kids' summer camp. It had nothing to do with my major at *PLNU* or at *USC*. But it was the only job I could find at the time. I had no idea what I would do afterwards, or if I would be involved with opera ever again. Through a mutual friend, I was able to find a place to live with a Christian family of six. The husband of the family was a pastor-teacher at a local church, and so I began to attend church with them on Sundays. Throughout the course of the summer I grew very close to the family, especially to their two teenage sons. We made many memories and enjoyed sharing life together.

### Church Ministry

After my summer job ended, I applied for a full-time job with the company I had worked for. I felt as though the company was a great fit for my skills and they spoke very highly of me. It seemed certain that working with them was the next step in my career. I easily passed the first three rounds of interviews and was offered a spot in the final round. The night before the final interview, I was sitting with Pastor Cliff on the couch catching up on the latest sports news. Our casual conversation took a very serious turn when he mentioned the potential of a part-time internship for me with his church. Not sure what to do, I went before the Lord in prayer and asked that He only open one door and close all the others. After a great final interview, I got a call later that week saying that they decided to go with another option. I felt this was the Lord's guidance for the next season of my life, and after a formal process I accepted a part-time internship with *Grace Bible Fellowship of Silicon Valley* in the areas of youth and music.

I recently celebrated my one-year anniversary working for the church. When I was young I had a desire to work in vocational ministry, and over the past year the Lord has confirmed that desire through this exploratory internship. When you trust in the Lord to prepare your path, it is amazing to see just how true God is to His Word (Proverbs 3:5-6). He has kept His promises and extended innumerable amounts of lovingkindness and grace to me throughout the years.

## Joy In Christ

Ever since accepting Jesus into my life, I have known an incredible joy. Yet, I have experienced great trials too. Life as a follower of Christ is not always easy; in fact, the majority of the time it is much more difficult than not. A true follower of Christ is hated by the world for not being of it (John 15:18-19).

The gospel of Jesus Christ is life-changing in the best ways, and yet wildly offensive to all who encounter it. It shatters what we think of ourselves and exposes the depravity of who we really are apart from Him. We are weak, lacking and selfish (Romans 3:23). Christ is strong, sufficient, and gracious. Many will hear the call and yet few will respond (Matthew 7:13-14).

If you are reading this and have heard the Lord's call in your heart, I want to encourage you to pursue Him with all you possess. When you give your life to Christ, you are not guaranteed the comforts of the flesh that the world around us so eagerly seeks. However, when you place your trust in Him, He will be faithful to reveal His goodness to you in this life and it will serve as a foreshadowing of the eternal glory that is to come for all who believe.

> *These things I have spoken to you, so that in Me you may have peace. In the world you have tribulation, but take courage; I have overcome the world (John 16:33).*

# 14

## *A Mighty Fortress*

*"But God, being rich in mercy,
because of His great love with
which He loved us, even when we
were dead in our transgressions,
made us alive together with Christ
(by grace you have been saved)"*
*Ephesians 2*

$A$s I start my testimony, I'm overwhelmed with gratitude
for the opportunity to share of my Lord's faithfulness. He has
placed favor upon me, though I've repeatedly, and in a multitude
of ways, sinned against Him. Indeed His grace is worth sharing!
I boast not in any of my accomplishments or victories over
sin. Rather, I desire to impress upon you the love, grace, and
power of the Lord. My story, glory, and praise is in the God
of the universe—the Father, who has forgiven me, Christ, my
Redeemer, and the Holy Spirit, my Guide and Counselor. His
love is my story and life! May you, dear reader, rejoice as I

recount of His mighty power, some of the individuals He has sovereignly placed in my life, and His powerful life changing Word, the Bible.

It is not by chance that you are reading this true account. My thoughts and prayers have been for those who will read this. As I write, I imagine my aunts, uncles, cousins, parents, children, husband, friends, ladies whom I've had the privilege of discipling, my spiritual mentors, individuals who come for various reasons within the walls of our home, my precious church family, my beloved pastors and those I've never had the privilege to meet face to face. May you be encouraged to pursue Christ wherever life may find you.

Because I have faced trials of various kinds, lived in many different circumstances, and have been tempted with a host of sin, I suspect you might be able to relate with me on one level or another.

*My Heritage*

On October 18th, 1976, Anastasia and Joseph Obojtek welcomed me, their only child, into the world. I was born in Akron, Ohio. God had finally granted my parents the desire of their hearts for a child. They had been through three disappointing miscarriages. Though I wasn't the boy my father had always envisioned, he and mom fell in love with me at first sight and loved me deeply throughout my life. Mom and Dad, along with many family members, had prayed that they would have a child and indeed God granted them their desire.

Before my first birthday, my mother and father made a decision that would affect all of us greatly, for the rest of our lives. They got divorced. In rural Ohio, during the 1970's, divorce was rare. My mom was the first and only one in her lineage to pursue a separation.

Prior to marriage, my father was a member of a motorcycle group. He traveled throughout the country, leading an extremely pleasure-seeking life. Troubled and searching for joy and peace, his journey led him into a life-style filled with drugs, sex, and alcohol. He was influenced by the immorality of the sixties that was rampant in America. He was a living victim of the biblical truth that says, "Bad company corrupts good morals" (1 Corinthians 15: 33). His compromised life-style had life-long consequences.

The fruits of hanging around dangerous bikers spilled over into our life once in a life-threatening way. One ordinary day, while I was just a baby, a stranger barged into our home and violently violated our lives. This dangerous intruder tried to harm my mom and sought to take revenge on my father. This extremely sickly-looking man had just been released from prison and was a member of a violent motorcycle gang.

However, this is not the end of his story or mine. We have a gracious God who pursues us even when we shake our fists angrily at Him running the other direction.

## My Childhood

My parents and grandparents were committed to raising me as best as they possibly could. Being their beloved only child, I was the center of much attention. God used my grandmothers greatly to form and fashion me into the person I am today.

After my parents got divorced, our lives changed significantly. Before the devastating divorce, I was enjoying the blessings of a stable, two-parent home. My mother was a homemaker and completely free from the burden of outside employment with dad as the sole bread-winner. I still can remember our humble home and the precious moments from early childhood. Now all that would change.

As a toddler, I began attending "Aurora Day Care," leaving my home each day prior to the break of dawn. My mom, needing to provide for us, could no longer stay at home with me so she found employment at a factory. She faithfully endured unimaginable trials to make ends meet.

At the age of three, I endured a very difficult trial, which God used for good in my life. As we were preparing to go for dinner, my mom looked out the window to witness her baby girl being thrown into the air as a truck speeding down our street collided into me. I remember being thrown into the air and onto the ground and then riding in the ambulance on the way to the ER. I vividly remember just wanting my mama. I cried out for her and found significant comfort in her presence. The doctors told my parents that I likely would be brain-damaged and paralyzed for life. My brain CAT scan was a blur and my left hip was fractured. For over a month, I rested in traction, with my left leg raised up to reset my hip. The cast went around my midsection and down my left leg.

By God's grace, He brought good out of this difficulty (Romans 8:28). First of all, my mom and I were welcomed by my grandmother to move in with her. From that point on, I was under my precious wise grandmother's full-time care. She was the most nurturing, stable vehicle of grace one could ever desire. Having lived through the depression, Grandma Bovino nurtured me and raised me in wise living. She consistently cared for mom and I and we brought joy and purpose to her in the last chapter of her life. Only under a watchful, providential eye could God arrange such grace towards me. My mom was awarded a settlement for the accident which she wisely invested and later used to fund my college and other opportunities beyond what we would have been able to had this incident not occurred.

Although my parents divorced, they both continued to have an important and hands-on influence in my life. After the divorce I lived with my mom and grandma during the week and I got to spend time with my father on weekends. So my dad and I continued to have a close relationship.

Sometime during my late elementary years my father's life dramatically changed. What he was so desperately searching for was found. Thanks to his faithful sister he heard the gospel, and over time he repented of his sin and started a relationship with Christ. Though he had been raised in the Catholic Church hearing messages based on Scripture, prior to this point He did not have a personal relationship with His Creator. My parents were both Catholic when they got married and baptized me in the Catholic Church when I was born. So we had religion but did not have true spirituality in Christ at that point.

After my dad got saved, even as a child, I noticed a significant difference in him—he became a different person! He wasn't the same pleasure-seeking father I knew my entire life. Instead, he had peace with God. He said God had removed his desire for drinking and smoking and replaced it with a heart to love Him and others. This made me curious.

### A New Creation

I vividly remember when dad took me into his room with his Bible and a gospel tract. He spoke of God's holiness and righteous character. He spoke of how we, His creation, are separated from Him due to our sin. He told me that I was a sinner along with everyone else. This I knew for sure. The wages, or consequences, for sin is death. I remember him asking me if I wanted to live with my Creator forever. Truly I did, but I knew I was a sinner.

I would lie about being sick because I didn't want to go to church prior to this time. Often, as a child my ugly temper would rise up and get the best of me and I would give into sin, and feel remorse afterward. Dad told me that everybody is a sinner but that Christ paid the penalty for sin on the cross (1 Corinthians 15:3). This reminded me of times at Mass when I heard that Jesus said, "My God why have you forsaken me?" I did not understand why Jesus would say that if He was perfect. My father explained that with this comment, Jesus was willingly offering Himself as the perfect substitute and sacrifice on behalf of sinners to pay the penalty for the sins of those who would believe in Him.

Dad asked me if I wanted to repent of my sins and trust Christ as my Savior. The Lord drew me to Himself and I was sure that I wanted to be His child. My favorite Bible passage is Ephesians 2:8-9, which best summarizes my salvation experience.

> *For by grace you have been saved through faith. And this is not your own doing; it is the gift of God, not a result of works, so that no one may boast. For we are his workmanship, created in Christ Jesus for good works, which God*

*prepared beforehand, that we should walk in
them (Ephesians 2:8-10).*

From that day on I was able to understand the Scriptures. My
father became part of a biblical church where I had the privilege
to hear the Scriptures explained and experience real Christian
community. At that time I also got baptized in obedience to
Jesus' command for all believers to publicly identify with the
Church through baptism. What an amazing opportunity and
preserving effect the Church and God's people have had upon
my life!

My dad was always looking for opportunities to serve the
Lord and he took me along with him. Dad started out helping
in the mailing room at the church and along I went to assist. He
had a heart for the needy and was eager to share his testimony.
I fondly remember going with him into the inner city to pick
up people for church on Sunday that were shut-ins or poverty-
stricken, or children that had parents that did not attend church.
He trained me to share my faith as he took me into hospitals
asking if people needed prayer as he carried his Bible and shared
with them the good news of the gospel of Jesus Christ. Being
fond of music, he served the church in that area as well. He
helped in many of our church concerts. I was blessed to have a
father who loved the Church, people, and above all, Christ.

In middle school, I had the privilege of being part of a
wonderful youth group. What an impact Matt and Katy Stevens,
our youth group leaders, had upon our impressionable lives. I
was asked to be a co-leader and we all grew in the knowledge of
the Lord Jesus Christ during those precious formative years. To
this day, I still specifically recall some of the messages I learned

during that season of life and as well as the fun we experienced in our church group. Another blessed memory was being in "Young Life," a national outreach ministry geared toward teens.

I'll never forget participating annually in the "Alive Summer Conferences" with my father and youth group. Christian bands played worshipful songs which were such a joy. Josh McDowell came and spoke. One message that made an indelible impact on me was about purity and the sanctity of marriage. Of course this message was counter cultural. Before my dear Lord, I cried out most earnestly to preserve my purity and to grant me a marriage that would please Him. I wanted to break the cycle of divorce that occurred between my parents as well as my paternal grandparents. Josh McDowell's book, *Why Wait*, protected me from much temptation. I still have a picture of that book on the very day my dad gave it to me as a birthday gift.

Even though I was a believer, the high school years posed a great challenge to my young faith. Though victorious on some fronts, the forces of evil pursued me and I often gave in to sin that so easily entangles. One of my greatest temptations came to me in the form of the excitement and pleasure-seeking lifestyle of the party scene.

The church of my high school years became weak and so I also became weak. That dear, precious church of ours went through some difficulty which resulted in a church split. For a significant portion of my high school years I did not have biblical teaching consistently that provided practical grace and protection. My church became a shell of what it once was. Proverbs 29:18 states, *"Where there is no prophetic vision the people cast off restraint but blessed is he who keeps the Law."* Prophetic vision refers to the revealed Word of God which is Scripture. With a shortage of biblical truth I cast off some restraints and became vulnerable. In addition, I also started hanging out with the wrong crowd. I never abandoned my faith, and I even continued to read my Bible, but little by little, I gave in more and more to the influences of unbelieving peers around me. Scripture speaks to this danger about unbelievers. Paul warned the Corinthians to be guarded in terms of who they associate with: *"Do not be deceived: 'Bad company corrupts good morals'"* (1 Corinthians 15:33). As a result, I struggled tremendously in my walk with the Lord during this difficult time and, though He pursued me still, I sought my joy and peace in the sinful allurements of this world.

The Lord is faithful to bring His Word to convict and confirm each of His children when we struggle. When we fall, He picks us up. As I cried out to Him in repeated repentance and guilt, Proverbs 23:29-35 became well worn verses in my Bible:

> *Who has woe? Who has sorrow? Who has strife? Who has complaining? Who has wounds without cause? Who has redness of eyes?*
>
> *Those who tarry long over wine; those who go to try mixed wine.*
>
> *Do not look at wine when it is red, when it sparkles in the cup and goes down smoothly. In the end it bites like a serpent and stings like an adder.*
>
> *Your eyes will see strange things, and your heart utter perverse things. You will be like one who lies down in the midst of the sea, like one who lies on the top of a mast.*

*"They struck me," you will say, "but I was not
hurt; they beat me, but I did not feel it. When
shall I awake? I must have another drink."*

It was during my first semester of college that I would forever
say goodbye to overindulging in alcohol and find freedom from
such bondage. At *Miami University* I was blessed with a Bible-
believing church which faithfully preached the Word of God
and had a thriving campus ministry called, "Campus Crusade
for Christ." Watching peers diligently living out their faith with
obedient lives convicted me and spurred me on tremendously.
The Lord faithfully brought me Christian growth through
discipleship, Bible studies, noon praise, prime time, evangelism
classes, and much more.

## Dating and Ross

God convicted me about the sacredness of marriage in
a unique way the latter part of my freshman year in college.
During high school and college I had heard various believers
say that they were going to refrain from dating for one year to
focus on their relationship with Christ. This idea intrigued me.
At that time my view of men and dating was unbiblical. I became
convicted so I began to focus my attention on my relationship
with Christ before pursuing another serious relationship. I
contemplated and prayed for several months before making
a vow to set aside dating for a year. For me it was a serious
commitment. Instead of using my time getting involved with
men intimately, Christ led me to use that time to deepen my
walk with Him. I turned down plenty of dating opportunities

at that time and instead stayed in my dorm room to study the Scripture and pray.

Several months after making that commitment I met Ross Bradley, who would become my husband. We met at Bible study at *Parkside Church* in Chagrin Falls, Ohio. I was eighteen years old. Ross and I were surrounded by hundreds of college students and singles who were wholeheartedly pursuing Christ. This church was led by Alistair Begg and many other godly elders, and soon we found ourselves at home under the care of Rick and Nancy Hoppe who discipled us. Rick and Nancy thought Ross and me were compatible so Nancy asked me if I would consider Ross. I was still in my year of "no-dating," but I had the opportunity to get to know Ross in a group setting. We clicked. We enjoyed sharing with each other what God was teaching us and wanted to grow together in our faith, encouraging and spurring one another on to godliness, love, and good deeds.

## The Blessing of Family

After my no-dating commitment passed, Ross called me up on the first day asking me if I would prayerfully consider courting. We had both been praying toward this end with hopes for marriage. I said "yes" and less than a year later Ross proposed. Eight months later, on May 30, 1998, we married, at ages twenty-one and twenty-six!

God graciously provided amazing, life-altering premarital counseling for us. We met with John Street and he walked us through many biblical texts and books to prepare us for the joys and trials we would face for years to come. To this day we often remember truths we learned like the rules of communication from Ephesians 4, biblical financial stewardship, and the roles of women and men. Indeed God has blessed and transformed us through godly mentors who dedicated their lives to His service.

God has blessed us with two children though after the birth of each of them I struggled with my health. I had postpartum eclampsia with dangerously high blood pressure and I needed to be hospitalized. By God's grace He preserved my life and I am so thankful to have the opportunity to be a mother and wife.

What anticipation is ours as we eagerly await all He has for us in this current season of life where He has placed us. He has rescued me by His grace and continues to change and conform me into His image through His constant means of grace—worship, the Word, and His people.

*The Lord has done great things for us and we are filled with joy! (Psalm 126:3)*

# 15

# *A Sweet Work of Sovereignty*

*"And we know that God causes all
things to work together for good to
those who love God, to those who are
called according to His purpose"
Romans 8:28*

*I*t wasn't until well after I was born again at age nineteen that I started to recognize how God had prepared me for salvation long before I actually repented from my sins and embraced Jesus Christ. There are delightful hints of sovereignty throughout my childhood and into my young adult life that testify to God's tender and patient care for my soul. Yet, to appreciate these hints of divine providence it is necessary to start at the beginning.

*Growing Up Catholic*

I was born in Billings, Montana and grew up in a practicing Roman Catholic family. We went regularly to Sunday Mass and were faithful to attend all the holiday services. My parents participated in various Bible studies and retreats, and they made sure my three sisters and I were all baptized as infants. Even our education was Catholic. From kindergarten through high school my parents made sure that all four of their children would be taught and trained in the same manner they had been several years prior—in the local Catholic school system. I even started my college education with two years in a Catholic university, but we will talk about that more in a moment.

Although my introduction to the gospel occurred outside of the Catholic Church, I am grateful to God for using my upbringing to solidify some important theological truths in my mind and heart in preparation to hear the good news of God's grace in Christ. As a result of my education and experience in the Church, I believed in God and Jesus and the Holy Spirit; I believed that Jesus died on a cross and rose from the dead; and I believed in heaven and hell.

I even had an interest in the priesthood at an early age. I didn't like the Church's requirement for celibacy—I liked girls and wanted to get married—but I admired those who had seemingly dedicated themselves to serving God and helping others. Perhaps I could be exempt from years of tradition—or become a catalyst for change—and be the first married priest? Well, that wasn't going to happen any time soon, and, frankly, I had other competing interests like making a lot of money and becoming a famous musician that pushed these budding desires for the priesthood out of the realm of serious consideration.

As I made my way through grade school and high school, however, I found myself becoming less interested in religion on one hand, and more interested in it on the other. Mass was excruciatingly boring, and serving God was not an option if it meant that I had to give up what I wanted to do with my life. As I transitioned into my first year of high school, my life started to take a turn.

## Confrontation

When I was in eighth grade, my oldest sister, Kathy, confronted my parents and me claiming she had recently been "saved." (By this point all three sisters were out of the house and were either married or living on their own, so I was the only child at home.) Whatever "saved" meant, we weren't sure. One thing we were sure of, though, was the dramatic change in my sister's life—it was undeniable. She had swiftly, but certainly, turned from a life characterized by cursing, anger, disregard for Jesus, and disdain for church, to now seeking only to speak words of edification and taking strides to control her temper. She also told us she loved Jesus, loved going to church, and enjoyed studying the Bible. What? This could not be the same sister with whom I grew up! Indeed, she wasn't. As I would learn later: she had become a new creation (2 Corinthians 5:17).

What hadn't changed in my sister, however, was her "in-your-face" kind of approach to personal conversation. She now concentrated her energy into challenging our religious beliefs and our spiritual state before God. Contrary to Roman Catholic teaching, my sister claimed that Scripture was the only authoritative Word of God and that being in right standing with God was not accomplished by our good works but by faith in

Jesus Christ who had already accomplished our salvation on the cross and through the resurrection. Furthermore, because we were dead in our sins and trespasses and our hearts were set against God, it was necessary to be born again by the Holy Spirit and receive a new heart with new affections.

Such statements were startling to my parents and me. Salvation? Faith alone? Born again? All of these were foreign concepts to us. Yet, what was most disturbing was the claim that the Roman Catholic Church was wrong on such foundational issues like the Bible and salvation. My sister may have found a new and different expression of the Christian religion, but surely she was mistaken to suggest that the Catholic Church had been teaching such serious falsehood for centuries.

As we continued to reel from my sister's theological onslaught, it became apparent that she probably wouldn't be appeased by our polite head nods and dismissive smiles. We would need to go to her church and find out what all the fuss was about.

*A New Church*

So we did. Breaking with years of Sunday tradition, we made our way across town to a small Baptist church. Although there were many things that distinguished this little gathering from our typical experience at Mass, one feature stood out above all the others: the preaching. I did not understand much of what was said from the pulpit, but what I did comprehend intrigued me and provoked some ongoing curiosity. Generally speaking, however, I was mainly caught up in the preacher's homiletic skills, but I wasn't a believer yet. I was like Benjamin Franklin, who, while admiring George Whitefield's ability to captivate an audience with his superior rhetorical talents, wanted nothing to do with the content of his teaching. (George Whitefield [1714-1770] was a famous Reformed evangelist in North America during the colonial period. He was a contemporary of Benjamin Franklin and garnered the praise of this founding father, though not for his doctrine, for Franklin despised Reformed theology and was, for all intents and purposes, a deist.)

But my parents and I continued to attend my sister's little church on a semi-regular basis, jumping back and forth from Sunday Mass, finding ways to excuse our occasional absences from Mass when questioned by concerned friends. Over the next several months, however, it started to become clear that if one were to take the Bible for what it taught, my sister was correct: the Roman Catholic Church was wrong. Salvation was by grace through faith alone, not by works nor by taking the sacraments or by church attendance. And not only was it wrong, in our experience, it had neglected to introduce the matter of salvation altogether. It was in that little church on Rimrock Road in Billings, Montana that we first heard of the concept of salvation and that man is dead in his sins and must be made right with God. So, from a purely objective standpoint, it became increasingly clear that we had a choice to make: remain in the Catholic Church or transfer our allegiance to my sister's church.

### Tradition!

We quickly learned that such a move was easier said than done. My parents had been Catholic for over fifty years and had dense religious and social ties to the Church. Catholic teaching declares that if you break away from the Church then you were choosing to separate yourself from any hope of salvation. The

*Catholic Catechism* states unambiguously, "Basing itself on Scripture and Tradition, the Council teaches that the Church, a pilgrim now on earth, is necessary for salvation: the one Christ is the mediator and the way of salvation; he is present to us in his body which is the Church. He himself explicitly asserted the necessity of faith and Baptism, and thereby affirmed at the same time the necessity of the Church which men enter through Baptism as through a door. Hence they could not be saved who, knowing that the Catholic Church was founded as necessary by God through Christ, would refuse either to enter it or to remain in it" (Part 1, Section 2, Chapter 3, Article 9:846).

Furthermore, most of my parents' friends, business associates, and former schoolmates were Catholic. To leave the Church was to leave everything.

I didn't have nearly the same amount of trouble as my parents did making the decision to abandon the Catholic Church and start attending my sister's church. Although I had no desire to live in accordance with what the Bible taught, it made sense to me that it alone was the Word of God and that we should go to a church that teaches the Bible correctly.

### Justified

Yet, with more exposure to the Bible week after week, my parents slowly but surely came to a full realization of the gospel. They recognized they were sinners and needed a Savior, and they understood the gospel of justification by faith alone. To be justified means to be "declared righteous." The moment a person places genuine faith in Jesus Christ, they are declared perfectly righteous in relation to God's law and are no longer subject to condemnation. God can justify sinners because Jesus Christ fulfilled all righteousness in the believer's place and died to pay the penalty of the believer's sin (see Romans 3:19-26; 4:5).

My senior year of high school, my parents and I were baptized. Wonderful, except one major problem: their son didn't know Jesus Christ.

It should have been clear to anyone that really knew me that I wasn't a born-again believer, despite my baptism. I had no desire to fellowship with other believers (I thought Christians were weird and annoying and too religious), no love for Jesus Christ, and no desire to live in obedience to God's Word. Indeed, the night I was baptized, I went out with friends and committed with vigor the same sins from which I had supposedly turned. My profession of faith was a sham. But the hypocrisy actually began a couple years earlier.

## Hypocrisy

For several years at my high school, the summer going into one's junior year was traditionally marked by a memorable one-week *Young Life* retreat in Michigan called "Castaways." Although "Castaways" was intended to be a time of spiritual refreshment and renewal for students, it was predominately an outdoor sports playground and a seed-bed for immoral relationships. Nevertheless, every evening after dinner we would gather in an auditorium to hear a gospel message. I remember distinctly one female student from our group devastated and angry because the speaker had explained the nature of sin and that, apart from Christ, none of us were morally "good" or in right standing with God.

I was unfazed by such pronouncements—I had heard these things before—but I did want to make a religious display before my friends. So, one night during one of our meetings, when asked by the speaker if anyone wanted to be saved, I stood up, and repeated the phrase, "Today I am giving my life to Jesus Christ."

I reveled in the attention and subsequent pats on the back. By professing faith in Christ, I could distinguish myself from others and appear spiritual and concerned about the "important" things of life. Truthfully, under my religious façade was a deep desire to experience real change on the inside and find peace with God through the gospel. I just didn't know how to get there.

Almost immediately after my return home I was assailed (from my perspective) by my sister and her pastor. "Derek, I heard you professed Christ last week!" my sister exclaimed. "You need to meet with the pastor."

Within a few days, there I was, sitting across the table from our pastor, squirming under the interrogation and pointed exhortations. "Now that you're a Christian, we need to talk about how to live for Christ," the pastor lectured.

I wasn't too excited. "Let's slow down," I thought; I don't want to get too serious about this whole Jesus thing. I don't want to change my life or have to hang out with other Christians.

But I played the part for a while. I went to youth group occasionally during the week and attended church on Sunday with my parents. I debated with my friends about the stark differences between what the Catholic Church taught and what the Bible taught, despite the plain fact that these doctrines were making no difference in my life. Actually, I became so skilled in the rhetoric and language of Christianity that I won an award my senior year for penning a stirring narrative about a teenager who had come to faith in Christ. The story would later be published—a frightening reminder, forever fixed in a book, of how much a person may sound like a Christian and talk eloquently of salvation, yet remain in spiritual darkness and death.

Under the guise of my selective spirituality, however, there brewed a longing to be right with God. I already had a kind of "prayer life," so I would sometimes pray at night for things to go well for me and for my family. I would pray for stuff I wanted and ask for deliverance from consequences I was facing due to my sinful choices. There was, however, a desire, lurking deep within these prayers, to be saved and to end the hypocrisy. Yet, I knew that coming to faith in Jesus Christ required repentance from sin. I had to be willing to give up my current lifestyle and submit myself to Jesus Christ. No longer could I be the Lord and Ruler of my life. I needed to bend my knee to the Lord Jesus Christ and to His will.

## Resistance

There was a problem with the whole repentance thing: I didn't *want* to give up my sin. I loved it. I wanted to keep living for myself and make my own decisions and do my own thing without the hindrance of church or the embarrassment of saying I was "living for Jesus." I started to realize that I couldn't come to Jesus Christ unless God did something major in my life. I found myself praying—hesitatingly, fearfully—that God would bring some event into my life so that I could come to Christ. I wanted salvation... but I didn't. The only way out of the malaise of indecision would be a sovereign interruption into my life by God Himself.

The following year I set out from Billings, Montana for Portland, Oregon. I wanted to go to a small college in a cool town that was just far enough away from my parents to keep them from visiting every weekend. The University of Portland was the place. It wasn't far into my college education, however, that I found myself deep in despair.

Initially, I made friends quickly and reveled in the freedoms of college life. Partying took on a new excitement as I was able to come and go as I pleased, inebriated or sober, and I didn't need to check in with parents or worry about a curfew. This was the life!

## Depression

Soon, however, I started to sense a growing cloud of hopelessness hovering over my life. Saturday mornings were typically the worst, although these onslaughts of depression were indiscriminate in their choice of the day and time they would appear.

I had started my college career as a music performance major. I changed my major to business finance the following semester because I had enough sense to know that pursuing the musician's path would probably not lead to a lucrative future. Frankly, I didn't know what I wanted to do with my life. Once during my freshman year I even suggested casually to my roommate that I wanted to be a pastor. How I had the gall to offer such a ridiculous suggestion of a personal career choice while living in utter immorality I'm not sure. What was clear was that I didn't know who I was or what I was doing with my life. (Interestingly, my unconverted desire for pastoral ministry was also a hint of God's sovereign kindness, as we will see a little later.)

These bouts with depression continued as I found myself living only for the weekend. Thoughts of drinking, partying with friends, and committing immorality filled my mind incessantly.

I slogged through my schoolwork each week by leaning on the hope of an intoxicating weekend. But I would wake up on Saturday morning, hung-over and empty, haunted with the inescapable feeling that my life was meaningless.

Also, because I was away from my parents, my church attendance dropped off completely. This couldn't be helped, I reasoned: I don't have a car and I don't know much about the churches in the area. I will just wait until I get home. My profligate lifestyle and neglect to attend church, however, didn't stop God's pursuit of my soul. He soon invaded my life through a man named Alan.

Alan was with *Campus Crusades for Christ* (now called "Cru"). During freshman orientation earlier that year I had quickly scribbled out a yellow religious affiliation card provided by the school. I said that I was a Christian and checked the box that indicated that I would like to have someone contact me about my faith. Perhaps this gesture would appease my mother who was already pestering me to find a church to attend regularly. Anyway, I didn't think that someone would actually contact me. Alan did.

Alan would call frequently, visit my dorm, and take me out to lunch. I wasn't going to church but at least I was meeting regularly with a Christian; this should tide my mom over, I thought. It did, and for a while I enjoyed meeting with Alan. He would talk to me about the Lord and about Scripture, and he would show genuine interest in my life. He would even come to see me in my room while I was hung over. He wasn't intimidated by my hypocrisy, sinful lifestyle, or my occasional annoyance over his refusal to leave me alone. He was the real deal. Deep down, I wanted to be like him.

My freshman year ended and I went back to Montana. I worked for my dad, partied with high school friends, and maintained a lifestyle similar to the one I kept in Portland. My parents, recognizing that I was now a college student, eased their curfew requirements so that I could stay out nearly as late as did while at school. As my freedoms increased, so did the opportunity to commit sin. And, the more my opportunity to commit sin increased, the less I wanted to go to church.

The hypocrisy was starting to become too great a burden to bear. So long as I could stay away from church I wouldn't have to deal with a conscience that was straining under the weight of blatant contradiction. I had professed Christ and received baptism; I talked like a Christian when it suited me; and I spoke with others about the deficiencies of their religion, but I was walking in rebellion against Christ and his Word. I was a fraud and deep down I knew it. But the desire for deliverance was increasing.

The following semester I was back in Portland. Although I was vice-president of my dorm and adding to my boast-worthy experiences daily, the depression that attended my first year in college was growing. Shortly into my second year, I was dumped by a girl for the first time in my life; I was confronted by our Resident Director for the obvious failure to execute my responsibility as vice-president; and I was wallowing in a general lack of direction.

## Conviction

Nevertheless, I also found that the desire to give my life to Christ was increasing, but I didn't think I would be able to really come to Jesus until after college. The pressure from friends and the ridicule I anticipated persuaded me that I would have to wait until I graduated to repent and trust Christ. Such a life change just wasn't possible right then. I did keep the door open to divine intervention, but short of a dramatic, life-changing event, I was convinced that I couldn't come to Christ.

That winter I went back to Montana for Christmas break. Because our vacation started earlier than many other colleges that my high school friends attended, my friend Rob and I were the only ones in town. The obvious conclusion: let's hang out, drink, and reminisce about the good ole' days. So we did.

That evening, only one day after I arrived in town from Portland, Rob and I grabbed a liter of hard alcohol and tossed shots of vodka with beer chasers in his basement. Although we were content drinking by ourselves, we soon learned of a party in the Heights—about eight miles north of Rob's house. We gathered our brew and stumbled outside.

In the driveway were two vehicles. On the left was my dad's beautiful black Dodge Ram 1500. On the right was Rob's white Volvo, desperately in need of a car wash and body detail. Although we were both drunk, I was less drunk than Rob, so I said I would drive. But, I pressed, I wasn't going to drive my dad's truck in my current state; I would need to drive Rob's Volvo.

At about 12:00 AM we set out for the party. We met some old friends and made a few new superficial acquaintances. We drank some more and talked about who knows what. After awhile it was clear that small talk and cheap beer was about as good as it was going to get, so Rob and I decided to leave. Despite our drunkenness, I was still in better shape than Rob, and so I

was, by default, the "designated" driver. We climbed in the car
and left for Rob's house.

Only a few blocks away from the party, we pulled out onto
Main Street. As I rolled through the green light—careful to obey
all the traffic laws so as not to cause suspicion—I glanced in my
rearview mirror; what I saw brought about instant panic: the
police car behind me had cued his emergency lights.

*Broken*

I drove for a few moments and turned into a nearby parking
lot. The officer approached the car and signaled for me to lower
my window. I obeyed his request but with my heart in my throat.
It became quickly apparent that we had been drinking. A second
officer appeared at Rob's door and motioned for us both to get
out. I was swiftly escorted to the front passenger's side of the
police car.

The police officer who had first come to my door was now
with me in the police car. He said a few words and then put
a breathalyzer to my mouth. I feigned a few weak attempts at
blowing into the breathalyzer, hoping to outsmart the machine.
Undeterred from carrying out his duty, the officer exhorted me to
make a genuine effort to blow into the breathalyzer. I finally did,
and it was immediately apparent that I was well over the legal
limit. The officer read me my rights, cuffed my hands behind my
back, and placed me into the backseat of the police car.

I was cold, frightened, and the heavy reality of what was
happening started to settle upon my mind. My initial thoughts,
however, were not about what this would cost me in terms of
relational turmoil and earthly consequence. The first inclination
was to turn to God and cry out in repentance. This was it. This

was the event for which I had been reluctantly praying. I could repent from my sins and *really mean it.*

The other officer finally corralled Rob into a second police car and both cars left that empty parking lot for the police station. There we were, subjected to further sobriety tests and questioning. After the interrogation, we were allowed to call our parents. While waiting for my dad and mom to pick me up from the station, I asked the arresting officer why he had pulled me over. "Was I swerving or driving poorly?" I asked curiously.

"No," came his semi-amused reply. "You had a broken taillight."

It didn't dawn on me until much later—as I learned more about God's sovereignty in salvation—that had we taken my dad's truck that night, we probably wouldn't have been pulled over. Praise God for that crummy Volvo.

I could now give my life to Christ. In His kindness, God provided a way in which I could stop drinking and call a halt to a life committed to partying. As I returned to Portland for my second semester, I would be able to avoid the party scene by using the excuse of my DUI to convince my friends that I should no longer drink. Later in the semester, I would provide the deeper reason why I had chosen to give up this kind of lifestyle and why I was no longer interested in chasing girls.

### Born Again

Much of this came as shock to my friends, and few could understand what I was doing. Nevertheless, the calling that Christ had put upon my life was stronger than the thought of losing friends and familiarity. And although I grieved that many relationships were now coming to an end, the Lord gave me an unwavering passion to pursue Him at all costs. Through a sweet work of sovereignty, the Lord Jesus had brought me to genuine faith and repentance and rescued me from eternal condemnation and a life of futility.

*A New Way of Living*

Now that I was born again, my latent desires for pastoral ministry blossomed full-bloom, and my longing to study Scripture and devote myself to preaching the truth was almost overwhelming. I completed my year at Portland and transferred to The Master's College (TMC)—a small Christian college north of Los Angeles—in order to study the Bible and prepare for ministry.

The following summer and my first semester at TMC was a time of spiritual bliss. I discovered that a new love for Christians and Christian fellowship had replaced the embarrassment I used to feel around other professing believers. I looked forward to singing praises to God with His people and I enjoyed hearing the preaching and teaching of God's Word, so I made church a priority. My heart, formally only capable of indulging in thoughts of sexual immorality, had been purged by God's Holy Spirit, and a new desire for purity brought me to break with several patterns of habitual sin.

Equally remarkable was the fact that God had dislodged the hopelessness that previously characterized my life by giving me that sense of purpose that all men and women were created to have. The all-consuming call on my life now was to glorify God in everything I did, and I was ready to respond to that call. "I've wasted nineteen years of my life," I reasoned, "I need to make up for lost time."

*An Over-Zealous Disciple*

So, shortly after I arrived to TMC, I sought ways I could serve God and live to the fullest this life He had given me. I went on a local mission trip, joined a Bible study, went regularly with friends to Santa Monica's *Third Street Promenade* to evangelize, over-loaded my class schedule, started playing drums for my church's college group, and even joined the cross-country team—all within the first semester. Yet, my unofficial plan to catapult myself into spiritual maturity backfired, and I soon found myself in a mire of spiritual confusion.

At a time when I should have been growing my roots deep and focusing on the basics of Christian discipleship, I pursued "busyness" in ministry. Partly out of ignorance, but mostly out of pride, I believed that spiritual growth was stimulated primarily by religious activity, and that my maturity was gauged by the sheer amount of such activity. So the busier I was, the better. Unfortunately, it didn't take long to learn that the tender branches of my newly sprouted faith could not bear the weight of such rigorous demands.

Coupled with and enflamed by this misguided pursuit of spiritual maturity was a growing lack of assurance in my salvation. Although God had purified my heart in a miraculous way when I was regenerated, I had not yet learned that sin still indwells genuine Christians (Romans 7:14-25), and that one of the primary responsibilities of the Christian life was to put such sin to death (Colossians 3:5). And, even though I believed the gospel, I was slowly putting more and more confidence in my religious activity rather than Christ. I was coming under the Galatian indictment: "Are you so foolish, having begun by the Spirit, are you now being perfected by the flesh" (Galatians 3:3)? Yes, I was.

Religious busyness, a misunderstanding about the reality of sin in a believer, and doubts about my own salvation conspired to create the perfect storm, and I was caught in the vortex of spiritual depression. I struggled through three more semesters and after my second year at TMC, I asked my parents if I could take a semester off of school, work at home, and take some time to heal my soul. After I insisted that I was committed to completing my college degree, my parents reluctantly agreed to let me take a semester off.

## A Time to Rest

That summer I worked for my dad and sought to remain faithful to church despite the fact that I had come to convince myself that I had committed the unpardonable sin. Nevertheless, even though I was struggling mightily with the assurance of my salvation, I couldn't walk away from Christ. I wanted the Lord more than anything, and the thought of losing Him was a fate worse than death. Through the encouragement of my parents, my family, my pastor, my friends from college, and unrelenting discipleship from Scott, an older brother in Christ who had befriended me two years prior, the Lord slowly drew me out of the quagmire of spiritual depression.

As I returned to TMC for the spring semester, I decided that given my spiritual struggles, pastoral ministry was probably not where the Lord was leading me. I began to think about other career options, and I soon landed on elementary education. I could complete my bachelor's degree in Bible and add an extra year or two to earn my teaching credential and perhaps pursue a master's degree in education.

By God's grace, I graduated in December, 2002 and moved into a friend P. J.'s house near TMC while substitute teaching first and second graders at a nearby Christian school. His parents allowed me to live in their home at little cost while I worked and looked for a place to pursue a teaching credential and a master's degree in education.

The only problem with this plan was that I didn't really want to teach elementary school. Although I valued the work of educators and considered teaching a worthy profession, I longed to serve the Church. I wanted to study Scripture, teach Scripture, and minister the Word to God's people. Yet, given my spiritual struggles only a year ago, I was unwilling to take any active steps toward ministry.

This indecision eventually bred complacency, laziness, and listlessness in my life. I found myself substitute teaching only two to three times a week, while spending most of my free time watching movies, hanging out aimlessly with friends, surfing the Internet, and playing video games. But God would reveal His sovereign care over my life once again.

## An Opportunity for Ministry

Because I had so much time on my hands, I decided to take a week to visit a college friend, Bobby, in the San Francisco Bay Area. He was a high school pastor at a church in the South Bay, and he invited me and another friend up for a few days to check out his ministry and record some music. While there, Bobby informed me that the middle school pastor position had recently opened, and he encouraged me to apply for the job. I hesitated, but Bobby was persistent, and he soon involved another pastor—his supervisor, Cliff—to help persuade me. I obliged his request and applied for the job.

During my initial interview, I indicated to Cliff my reluctance to pursue ministry, the intimidation I felt at the thought of shepherding young souls in the Christian faith, and my desperate need for discipleship in the area of pastoral ministry. Cliff graciously countered all my objections and assured me that he would actively mentor me in my role of middle school pastor. He also suggested that I begin as an intern since I had no experience and much to learn and told me that youth ministry is an excellent place for a young man to gain experience and determine whether or not he is called to vocational pastoral work. So after only two month's at P. J.'s house, I packed up my jeep with all my earthly possessions and moved to the Bay Area.

The Lord used the next four and a half years of pastoral work to not only confirm my call to vocational ministry, but to teach me the value of hard work, the importance of discipleship, and my vital need for humility. I was also blessed during this time to meet Amy, an intelligent, beautiful, winsome, competent woman who would not only become my wife, but my perfect complement. Knowing that I needed someone who was patient, compassionate, sympathetic, and sensitive to others, the Lord provided a woman who balanced my many weaknesses with her many strengths (Genesis 2:18).

### Seminary, Adoption, and Beyond

About two years after we were married, it became clear that if I were going to pursue a life of pastoral ministry, seminary would need to be the next step. So, August 2007, we loaded a moving truck and drove 2,500 miles to Louisville, Kentucky so that I could pursue a M.Div. (Masters of Divinity) at *The Southern Baptist Theological Seminary*. After two years in the program, it became progressively clearer that I should pursue a Ph.D. for the sake of future usefulness in the Church and in the seminaries. After a seven-year journey (three years for the M.Div. and four years for the Ph.D.), I completed my formal theological training.

Our time in Louisville was rich as we met many new friends, served in various capacities in our church, enjoyed the local culture, worked several different jobs, and learned in a deeper way to rely upon the Lord and upon each other. Our trust in Christ was tested most intensely during two adoptions.

After four years in Louisville, we found ourselves on a plane to Ethiopia to adopt our first child—a little boy not even eleven months old. Our path to adoption, however, had been paved with significant difficulty and mingled with some sorrow. Nevertheless, God's sovereign kindness prevailed and we not only brought home a little boy from Africa, but three years later we boarded another plane—this time to the Republic of China— to pick up our second little boy.

Immediately after we arrived home with our second son, we started packing all our earthly possessions in order to move back to the San Francisco Bay Area. I had recently accepted a full-time pastoral position in Sunnyvale, and I needed to report to work within two months. From rebel, to over-zealous Christian, to struggling disciple, to husband, daddy, pastor, and professor, the Lord has graciously guided my every step despite my sin and many weaknesses and failings. His sovereign care brought me from condemnation to salvation, from death to life, from a life of futility to a life of purpose and joy. A sweet work, indeed!

# 16

## *Adopted and Secure*

*"But as many as received Him, to
them He gave the right to become
children of God, even to those who
believe in His name, who were born,
not of blood nor of the will of the flesh
nor of the will of man, but of God"*
*John 1:12-13*

**M**y name is Greg. I was born on June 17, 1986 in Saginaw,
Michigan near Lake Huron—one of the five Great Lakes. Even
though I live in California now, my birth-place explains why I
am a die-hard Lions and Red Wings fan. I actually don't know
anything firsthand about the details of my birth. To this day,
at age twenty-eight, I know nothing about my dad—his name,
his whereabouts, what he does. I have only conflicting stories
to go by regarding my mom, and I've had minimal contact with
her over the years. I have a half-brother but don't have much
of a relationship with him either. From a human perspective I

don't really have a family. I was orphaned the day of my birth, but by God's grace He adopted me through Jesus when I was about nineteen.

## Saginaw

I lived with my birth-mom the first two months of my life and then was taken from her by the government and social services. All I know is that supposedly my mom's lifestyle at the time put my health and safety in jeopardy. Apparently there was alcohol, drugs, unsafe people and unsafe conditions surrounding me. Social services of Michigan gave me to my aunt when I was two months old. She is my mom's sister. She was married at the time with one child when she took me in. I lived with her family for two years and then I was put in an orphanage in Michigan.

## Orphanage Life

This first time in an orphanage lasted about one year. I don't remember anything about it, not even its name or location. At around age three I went to a foster home, where I would end up staying for the next ten years. So within five years, I had lived in three different homes, with three different families. Not until many years later would I realize what tremendous instability this would cause in my growth, development and security as a young child.

The foster home family ended up adopting me in 1992 when I was almost six, along with my younger half-brother. My foster family was traditional Lutheran, so I went to a Lutheran church until I was thirteen. I went to *Peace Lutheran School* and *St. Michael's* from preschool until third grade. I don't have fond memories of those years. I distinctly remember that I did not believe in what they taught in terms of religion. They did not actually teach the Bible, even though they said they believed in the Bible. What they taught was the Lutheran Catechism, much of which was dogma and tradition about the Lutheran Church. Even at church the pastor would not teach the Bible, although he would quote a verse once in a while. By the time I was in third grade I knew I wanted to hear the Bible, not man-made religion. The Lutheran Church was creating spiritual hunger but was not meeting that desire with the human religion they were giving me.

Sadly, the foster home that adopted me turned out to be very abusive—emotionally, but also physically and sexually. There were as many as ten other children that they took into their home, some adopted, some just foster children. Life was chaotic, ungodly and dangerous for me. Older children in the home began violating me in unspeakable ways from the time I was a preschooler. One of the parents routinely beat me physically. The abuse continued unchecked for years. I said nothing for a long time out of ignorance since I was so young. As I got older I knew it was wrong but did not speak up out of fear of retaliation.

At about age ten adults at my school began to notice the regular bruises that were on my body. When I turned thirteen I made a formal complaint to my lawyer and social services about the home I was in. I told them I did not feel safe and that I was being abused. That was sufficient grounds for me to terminate the rights of adoption of the family I had been a part of for ten years. Thankfully I was able to leave that place. It wasn't until later, around age fourteen, when I would divulge more specific details of the kinds of abuse I was subjected to for many years.

## The Pilgrim Life

Upon leaving that home I went to juvenile hall for two days, for the weekend. Then I was transferred to another foster care center for another two weeks. From there I went to a group home for one month called *Muskegon River Youth Home*, ninety miles northwest from my birth-town of Saginaw. This home for teens had been around only about three years at the time. It was a non-secure facility that worked with at-risk youth that emphasized positive reinforcement as well as group support.

I left *Muskegon* and ended up in a hospital for two weeks. The details are foggy but I had to leave for a violent reaction toward one of the residents in the home. By nature I am not an aggressive or violent person, but I did have a natural tendency by the time I was thirteen to want to defend myself if I felt my life was in danger or if someone tried to harm me. I did not trust anyone after all I had been through up to this point. After two weeks in the hospital I was sent to *Bridges Assessment Center* in Caro, Michigan. *Bridges* had a twelve-step program for youth—for those with drug, alcohol or behavioral problems. I was sent there because of my growing erratic behavior. I had never been involved with alcohol or drugs, but by age nine I was regularly seeing a psychologist, therapist and psychiatrist. I was sent to these "specialists" at age nine originally because I was having trouble in school, exhibiting abnormal behavior and was not talking. From age nine to age thirteen I was visiting a therapist twice a month. They said I had ADD, and ADHD with depression. After I was hospitalized I was seeing a therapist weekly.

From age nine to thirteen I vaguely remember having some thoughts about God—but spiritually I was very confused. At age thirteen I began to think about God more seriously and even began to talk with Him very specifically through prayer about my life and problems.

*A Glimmer of Light*

After spending a year at *Bridges* I went to *Boysville*, a private home for boys in Saginaw. *Boysville* started in 1948 as a Catholic boarding school for boys with serious home problems. I was there for almost a year, from 2000 to 2001. I did not have a good experience at this facility; once again I was subjected to bullying by fellow residents. But there was one bright spot—Connie Weaver. Connie came in to *Boysville* to do assessments and IQ tests as an outside counselor. She tested my IQ and I scored a 118—that is above average. That was encouraging. Connie cared for me as a person, became a sweet mother figure to me and even invited me to church. I did visit the church and all I remember is that it was very friendly. This was in stark contrast to my years of attending the dead, boring, irrelevant Lutheran church. This new church was the first positive experience I had with a community of believers. God would use this experience as one way of softening me and drawing me to Himself.

After leaving *Boysville* I was sent to *Pine Rest Christian Mental Health Clinic* in Grand Rapids, Michigan from age fifteen to age nineteen. It was a school and a high security hospital. *Pine Rest* existed to provide behavioral health services for people of all ages and was staffed with psychiatrists, psychologists and social service workers. It tried to minister to the whole person with Christian values as opposed to strictly secular ones. While at *Pine Rest* I was able to have my own room. And I am glad I did. Otherwise I would have been bullied, which seemed to happen everywhere I went. At *Pine Rest* fellow residents did not like the fact that I was honest and up-front. Even though I was not born-again yet I did have a conscience and did not believe in lying. That threatened some people.

From ninth to twelfth grade I went to *East Kentwood High School,* a public school in Kentwood just south of Grand Rapids. *East Kentwood* was a typical public high school. I didn't play football but I went to every game and was a big fan. A local church had an out-reach ministry on campus called "E. K. For Christ." A pastor would come on the campus regularly and try to minister to the students. I was invited and actually went to several of the events, on and off campus. I was becoming more open, sensitive, curious and interested in spiritual matters and more serious about God. I knew God existed. I still had not heard the gospel clearly explained though.

All through my four years of high school the psychological meds continued along with the meetings with therapists, psychologists and psychiatrists—almost weekly they were monitoring my mental behavior. They continued to increase the drugs they would give me and they also continued to pile on the diagnoses as well. They said I was ADD, ADHD, depressed in addition to supposedly having bi-polar disorder, schizophrenia and schizoaffective disorder, among other things. They could not make up their minds and the diagnosis always seemed to be changing. To me, they were schizophrenic in their assessments of me. Much of the diagnosis was based on the fact that many times I simply would not talk.

To be honest, looking back over those years, ten years of medications did not really help me or solve any of my problems. They could not address my real problem. All they did was dull my emotions and made me numb. At the time I didn't mind because I wanted to use them as a crutch. I did not want to face my problems—I did not even know how to. How could a pill fill the void I felt about not knowing who my dad was as a fifteen year old or the sadness I felt about being taken from my birth-mom when I was two months old? No medication in the world could solve that problem or meet that need. As I began to think at this deep level about my life, I also began to think more about God.

## Closure

When I turned eighteen I met my birth mom for the first time since I left her when I was two months old. I wanted to meet her ever since I was thirteen when I first found out that I was adopted. With the help of social services and my lawyer it did not take long to locate her. She agreed to meet with me, but it had to be at the courthouse in Saginaw with my therapist present with me. Leading up to the meeting I was very nervous and did not know what to expect. I was hoping that we could live together as I assumed that maybe she was in better condition now and in better health. She had a reputation of being addicted to alcohol and drugs.

We met face to face for the first time for an hour. The meeting was terribly disappointing for my mom did not even seem coherent throughout the meeting. She seemed obviously intoxicated or high on something. She could hardly talk. It made me sad. My dreams for reuniting were smashed, at least for the time being. I have had minimal interaction with her since that time—it's been ten years. I do talk with her once or twice a year on the phone.

*California*

In April, 2005 I was almost nineteen years old when I moved out of *Pine Rest* to San Jose, California to live with my aunt. This was the same aunt who took me in for a short while when I was two months old. She and her husband graciously let me move into their apartment along with their three children. This was at least the tenth different place I would live in my first nineteen years. Within two weeks of moving to San Jose a knock came on the door one Saturday morning. It was members from *North Valley Baptist Church* going door to door inviting people in the neighborhood to go to church. They had a bus ministry and said they could give me a ride to church on Sunday if I was interested. I hesitated at first but then said, "Sure," because I wanted to get into the local church so I could learn more about God.

True to their word, they came to pick me up and took me to their youth class. I clearly remember the youth minister's Sunday school message that day. He talked about God the Creator, how Adam and Eve sinned and were separated from God, that all humans are sinful and need a Savior. Jesus was the only Savior. This was the first time in my life I heard a clear and complete presentation of the gospel. And I was convicted as soon as I heard it. I knew it was true. The gospel began to work on my heart. For the next two weeks I read my Bible and learned more about what God expected of me as a human and as a sinner in need of Him. The more I read the Bible the more convicted I became.

*Born Again*

About two weeks after hearing the gospel at *North Valley*, in mid-May, I gave my life to Christ as I prayed to God asking Him to save me and I told Him I believed the gospel that *North Valley* just preached. *North Valley* became my home church—my first real church family in my life. I went there for almost four years. I learned much about the basics of the Bible and Christianity. I developed a respect for God's Word. *North Valley* was a friendly church, hospitable and very evangelistic.

After becoming a Christian I noticed some immediate changes in my life and in my heart. I was more sensitive to sin in my life—I hated my sin. I also thought of struggles in my life in a new way. Instead of going into deep depression over trials all around me I realized that I could not control all of my problems, only God could. I also had a real sense that God loved me and that He was willing to forgive all the wicked things in my life based on Jesus' sacrificial death as He promised in Scripture. After getting saved I also had the opportunity to share about Christ with my mom and younger half-brother. My mom was not very receptive and made it clear she did not want to talk about religion when we interact in the future. That has been difficult, but I keep praying for her salvation and transformation.

In August of 2007 I checked myself into *Valley Medical Hospital* because of my anxiety. I stayed there for over a month. After leaving the hospital I ended up staying at *Golden Living Center* in San Jose. It was a care facility that specializes in helping adults recovering from specific illnesses or injuries, including areas of mental health. It was a medium-security facility, meaning I could not come and go without permission or staff supervision. I ended up living there for five months.

Then in April of 2008 I moved to a group home called *Riviera Villa Boarding Care* in San Jose. It was for adults who needed help in many areas of health. I had a roommate there.

His name was Nick. Nick was nineteen, friendly and a believer. Soon he invited me to his church in Mountain View. I had not been a part of a regular church for several months and I knew it was time to get back to the body of Christ. After four years of attending *North Valley Baptist,* out of the blue, they could not provide a ride for me anymore, so I ended up missing for a few weeks.

So it was in about September, 2009 that I made my first visit to *Grace Bible Fellowship of Silicon Valley*—or simply, *GBF.* I loved it! It was smaller than *North Valley* but the people were friendly and welcoming. And they taught the Bible in a way that was clear and practical. The pastors got to know me personally by name. I had never experienced that at a church before. Usually the pastors don't get to know you very well.

There was a very nice older couple there at *GBF,* the Andersons, who lived in San Jose and were willing to pick me up every Sunday to take me to and from church. That was a huge blessing because the church was sixteen miles away. I could take the bus but that would take over ninety minutes sometimes. I continued to go to *GBF* for the next several months and really felt like I was getting to know them like family. I was also learning a tremendous amount about God's Word. Within a year I became a member.

*Orphaned No More*

One of the biggest blessings since becoming a Christian has been learning the Bible. I have been particularly blessed by God's good servant Job. I believe Job was a real person who lived a life just like it describes in the Bible. He faced greater suffering than almost anyone in history yet he remained faithful to God.

Job lost most of his earthly possessions, was afflicted with horrible physical pain and sickness and all ten of his children were instantly killed in a storm but he never got mad at God. In light of all these trials, amazingly Job said, *"Shall we indeed accept good from God and not accept adversity?" (Job 2:10).* And then it says of Job, *"In all this Job did not sin with his lips"* (2:10).

I have had some terrible things happen to me my whole life, many things that just seem down-right unfair. But I still have not suffered as bad as Job. I want to continue loving God and trusting Jesus no matter what is going on in my life, no matter how trying or terrible. God will favor us as long as we keep our eyes on Him. He doesn't give us more than what we can handle through His strength. God is always faithful (1 Corinthians 10:13).

I have also come to learn that a key to dealing with hardships in life is being part of a solid church family. I don't really have a real earthly family and never did since I was two months old. But God has provided me a spiritual and eternal family through the local church where I have real brothers and sisters in Christ who love me. God saved us to be a part of a community, not to be isolated by ourselves. The Church is a family, with God as Father and all believers as siblings. The Church is a temple with all Christians as individual stones or bricks where God dwells. The Church is a Body with all the saints as the individual members joined together. I thank God that He rescued me and adopted me into His family forever.

# 17

## *Jesus, Wonderful Counselor*

*"Jesus said to them, 'It is not those who are healthy who need a physician, but those who are sick; I did not come to call the righteous, but sinners'"*
*(Mark 2:17)*

***I*** was born into a broken and dysfunctional home in San Jose, California in 1956. Much of my childhood memories I'd rather forget. But blessed be the God and Father of our Lord Jesus Christ who is in the business of salvaging, rescuing, saving and restoring fallen and sin-ravaged lives. My gracious heavenly Father has done that for me.

### Deserted

My earliest memories are of me and my two brothers living with my mom in the basement of my grandmother's home. My dad was not around, being that he deserted the family when I was a baby. So during my earliest years we had no man around to be the provider and protector of the family. As I grew older I did have an interest in learning about my dad, but it was made clear that it was taboo to even mention him. To this day I have never met him. The only specific thing I ever heard about him was when I was twelve and was told he was in a hospital because of his addiction to drugs. That was hard to hear, being a young impressionable girl.

When I was five my mom married my step-father. He had four children of his own, so we became a blended family of nine. We moved onto his three-acre San Jose ranch. His ranch housed several semi-trucks, a big house and a smaller house. We moved into the small house and his children lived in the big house. Sadly our new home would not be an abode of refuge and peace, but rather a lair of turmoil and abuse. For the next ten years I became vulnerable to physical, verbal and emotional abuse. I lived in fear in my own home. I did not share the details with anyone as I felt guilty for what was being done to me. From the time I was eight I vividly remember going into a panic every time my mom would leave the house. On Saturdays she would go get her hair done, and as she drove away I would run after her car crying and yelling, "Please don't leave me! Please don't leave me!"

When I was twelve I was shocked to learn that I had a half-sister. My twenty-year-old "aunt" revealed to me at that time that she was actually my sister. I couldn't believe it.

My mom gave birth to my older sister when she was eighteen. While she was in the hospital the doctors discovered my mom had tuberculosis (TB), an infectious disease caused by various strains of mycrobacteria, often attacking the lungs and many times fatal. They kept my mom in the hospital and eventually sent her to a sanitarium where she would receive treatment in an iron-lung for two years. My grandmother took my half-sister in as her own while my mom remained isolated. When I was born eight years later, my sister was called my "aunt." Also during that two year period her father was unfaithful to my mom on repeated occasions, and didn't hide it. This devastated her and hurt her deeply and undermined her ability to be the confident, caring mom she desired to be.

## Spiritually Deprived

The first ten years of my life spirituality was pretty much non-existent, although my mom said we were "Presbyterian." But we didn't go to church, read the Bible, pray or practice any kind of religion in the home. Interestingly, my public school, Orchard Elementary School in San Jose, introduced me to religion, the Bible and prayer! Once a month on Fridays the students were segregated into two groups—the Catholics and the Protestants—and sent across the street for religion class for thirty minutes and they would actually teach us about the Bible. I was a Protestant, so I was in a group with about twenty students while the Catholic students numbered more than sixty. This was the mid-sixties, about the very time the United States Supreme Court began banning prayer and Bible reading in the public schools, state by state.

When I was ten, my mom began sending me and my brothers by bus to the Baptist church for Sunday school and worship. My parents never attended. It was just us kids, about twice a month for about a two year period. The only thing I remember

from this experience was attending the Baptist church dance
for kids. Occasionally during this time of my life I would spend
weekends at my grandmother's house and secretly walk to the
local Catholic church, with a veil on my head, and attend Mass.
My grandmother thought I was going down the block to the
local Presbyterian church. I wanted to go to the church where
all the other kids were going—I didn't like being a minority as
a Protestant.

*Early Marriage*

Despite these short stints of exposure to religion, I did not
learn anything significant about the Bible or the gospel. I was
being more influenced by godlessness going on in my home. I
got to a point where I just wanted to escape and get away...so I
did. In 1971, when I was only fifteen I met my first boyfriend,
dropped out of school and got married. We soon had a child
together. I naively thought my new marriage would be an escape
and a place of refuge, safety and security. The marriage actually
turned out to be full of darkness and fear for me, which was no
improvement over my home-life for the first fifteen years. Life
was good for a few months, but then I realized that this was not
the life that I expected. I was a little girl married to a person that
wanted me and many other women too. I would last ten years
in that situation. We had three boys together.

We married young and were immature. He partied a lot with
friends. Over time my husband and I became very close to one
of his co-workers and his wife. We enjoyed spending time on
the weekends together. Then, out of the blue, when I was close
to twenty-one, that couple got saved—they became crazy "born-
again Christians" who loved Jesus. My husband immediately

cut-off our relationship with them for he wanted nothing to do with their new-found religion. He was not going to have anything to do with a bona fide "Jesus freak." At the time I also said that I would never serve God in such a fashion. They became affiliated with some kind of Apostolic Pentecostal church. It was a combination of being charismatic and also legalistic.

I did not keep my promise though. My apostolic friends tried to convert me and even told me that I was "going to hell." I told them adamantly, "No, I'm not going to hell," and from that point on I did everything I could think of to keep from going to hell. I basically began listening to them, doing things their church prescribed that supposedly would keep me out of hell. So I began to let my hair grow long. I stopped wearing makeup. I stopped drinking alcohol, watching TV and stopped wearing jewelry and long pants and replaced them with long, feminine skirts. They gave me a Bible and I actually began reading it, with a veil on my head. I read it intensely and often. I was learning Scripture for the first time and drank it in enthusiastically. I became vocal at church during testimony time as I would gladly share all that I had recently learned from the Old Testament stories.

## Suffering for Christ

My husband was furious with what was happening to me. He caught wind that I wanted to give my life to Christ and so he showed up at the church the night I got baptized. After church he drove me home, took me into the house to the back room, loaded his 354 magnum, put it to my head and demanded that I renounce Christ on the spot, quit that crazy church and go back to drinking beer and watching TV. He couldn't handle that he would not longer be my god, because that is how he had been conducting our marriage and home-life. It was so ironic that I had purchased the 354 magnum gun for him earlier that year as a birthday present for hunting. There I was in a fetal position, as he threatened my life. I truly thought I was going to see Jesus that very night. I begged for my life nevertheless. For some unknown reason, he suddenly came to his senses, realized what he was doing and sent me out of the room. In shock while standing outside the bedroom, I could hear him removing the bullets from that gun. A few days after the gun incident, he filled up the bathtub and tried to baptize me again...perhaps by drowning me. That didn't work either and for a second time I escaped with my life. God had graciously spared me as He was watching over me.

For the next five years I was committed to the Apostolic church. Despite its legalism, and even some heretical teachings, I believe I got saved when I was twenty-one while going to this church. I fell in love with Jesus and the God who loved me as I read the Bible. I would finally have the Father I always wanted but never had in this life. I had real joy for the first time in my life—I was so happy. And I felt safe when I was with the people at the church. God would now, forever, be my Father. But after getting saved, life did not get easier. In many ways it got more difficult. I began to realize over time that the church I was in was not healthy, but actually dangerous and even cult-like. It was like being in prison. I couldn't think or act on my own free will. I think that after being an abused child, getting married to get out of the house, and then finally joining a controlling, authoritarian religion was all I could take. At about that time the pastor of the church got involved in immorality and the church imploded. The way the indiscretion was being handled was blatantly wrong, and I knew it. I became disillusioned with "the church." So I left.

*Divorce*

To make matters worse, after ten years of marriage I divorced my husband when I was twenty-six. He had become a serial adulterer and despised my faith. When I got divorced I made the worst decision of my life when I agreed to give full rights of my three children to my husband. I caved in to my ex-husband's intimidation and manipulation. He said he wouldn't give me one cent of child support. My lawyer tried to convince me that I could have my children and the house. I was young, scared, and naïve. I didn't have anyone to give me stable advice and tell me to keep my kids and home. I probably couldn't listen to any good advice anyway. In my mind I thought that I shouldn't even have the kids because I was such a bad person. I didn't deserve them. He took them with him and I was allowed to visit on weekends and holidays.

I didn't realize that that decision would torment me for years to come. I also didn't realize how much rejection and pain my boys would endure in their new situation; I couldn't see beyond my own pain at that point. They were subjected to a home that was unhealthy and destructive, and they were so young—ten, eight and one. This decision would eventually destroy my relationship with all three of my boys to the point where I had no relationship with them at all. To this day, as young men they still struggle from the divorce and from not having their mom there for them. They experienced horrific abuse for years, until they were able to escape, one by one, as they each turned eighteen. Next to my salvation, my three boys were the best things that ever happened to me and I became broken-hearted as the years went by as I became aware of their struggles.

But where sin abounds, grace much more abounds (Romans 5:20) and I have seen that truth now decades later with respect to my boys. By God's grace I began to rekindle relationships with the boys, trying to earn their trust and God began making that happen. God is little by little working all things together for good in this area of my family life (Romans 8:28). It's a slow process, but God is truly in control, bringing about real change and progress for His glory and my good. I am so thankful to Him. His grace continues to abound toward me.

*Disco Queen*

Upon losing my boys and losing my church I sank into deep hopelessness and despair. I thought I had no reason to live on. I was not going to church anymore so I tried to escape by living like the world. I began to experiment with the party-life and joined the disco scene and became a disco queen. For almost five years I became a hard- core partier. I thoroughly enjoyed it and thoroughly enjoyed my newfound freedom, having been liberated from the smothering legalism and micro-managing control that the man-made Apostolic church had over me as they tried to control my behavior by external pressure. I was introduced to a darkness I never knew existed. Looking back, I am amazed and so thankful that during that time I didn't kill myself as I put myself in danger. I was spared once again by God's grace.

During this time of compromise I believe I was truly a believer—a disobedient one, but a true believer. As such, living like the world could not continue. When I turned thirty, I knew

I needed God in my life again, in a serious way. Sin was not ultimately satisfying. I still feared hell and I still loved Jesus. I had always remembered how great it was that God existed and that He was good, even though I didn't quite fully understand the Bible yet.

At this time a Pentecostal Christian colleague began ministering to me, encouraging me and challenging me. So I started going to her church in San Jose. It was an intensely charismatic church, and I became immersed in it full-bore for the next ten years of my life. By going to this church I was formally introduced to the highly controversial "Word of Faith" philosophy that dominates much of today's Evangelical charismatic Christianity. One of its main doctrines was the idea that I could just command God to do something—in a prayer— and then He was obligated to make it happen. God had to obey me! If it didn't happen, I was told it was because I did not have enough faith.

For the next several years I would try to serve God through the Word of Faith church. I was still trying to be good and kept failing, and I didn't understand it. Over time, I actually became embarrassed by the doctrines and methods they used in that church that I wouldn't even want my family to come to church. So I wouldn't invite them. I knew in my heart that my family would have thought I was crazy to be at a church like that. And I knew something was just not right, but I couldn't put my finger on it because I was spiritually immature, lacked discernment and did not know the Scriptures enough.

A bright spot during my thirties was when I decided to go back to school to earn my high school diploma. I took a full two years of high school classes in Milpitas and completed all the required courses to earn my diploma. Milpitas had a program allowing adults to finish their high school courses. About seventy-five of us finished together, and there was a full-blown commencement graduation service, the oldest student being almost eighty-five. I was thrilled that I persevered and finished the program.

## More Trials

While attending a church in San Jose, I met a Christian man who was handsome, went to church and was very nice to me. I thought, "This could be the one...finally." So we got married. I was forty years old. At this time in my life I still was not very emotionally healthy or balanced and I was very insecure. I had idealistic ideas going into this marriage. Initially things started out well. We had a beautiful home. My husband had a good job. I was optimistic at the beginning thinking all my problems were left behind...wrong.

My husband wanted to be a preacher but did not want to work and be the provider. He quit his job and wanted to just go to school and study. I tried to help him so I thought of selling our home so we could buy a mobile home with cash. Then he could study while I worked to provide for our family. But things then fell apart—our roles were reversed and I became the provider...I could not handle the pressure. In addition, he became abusive as the marriage went on. About this time I snapped and had a nervous breakdown. I became severely depressed. I could not even get out of bed. I felt paralyzed. Up to that point I never really had anyone to talk to about all that had transpired in my life. The pressures of life overwhelmed me. I was in a stupor for about three months. I first tried to ask my husband to help me but he felt inadequate and refused.

I was now in a place—flat on my back—where I had to deal with all my past issues. We recently had left that Faith Movement church and started attending a Baptist Church in Gilroy. The Pastor there referred me to a Christian counselor to help start the healing process. So I started meeting with her regularly, for a period of two years. During those sessions I was forced to confront the real issues in my life like never before. It was the most painful and challenging time of my life. It was a very slow process, but my husband wanted me well instantly. My counselor explained to him that I needed time to heal, and that he should support me 100 percent, because I needed a support system. He didn't want a sick wife and couldn't wait for me to get well. His controlling behavior over me intensified during this time. My counselor was exposed to it during our sessions together as a couple. His heart became hard toward me and mine toward him. Sadly, after seven trying years of marriage we divorced. My heart broke over my guilt knowing how I let my God down, again.

*A Time of Growth*

The counseling continued. It was difficult. Each time I would go through a session, it was like an elephant was sitting on my chest and I couldn't breathe. She explained so clearly what a biblical healthy life looked like, and gave me the tools (the Bible) to help me progress in the healing process. One of the biggest benefits of the counseling was that I began to see how unhealthy I was in light of what Scripture described the Christian life should be like. I had tried to live the Christian life for decades according to human principles, and my own ways, instead of according to biblical truths. This was a turning point in my life. I wanted in my heart to be healthy and happy and enjoy life in Christ. I wanted to experience and know first-hand "the peace that surpasses all understanding" (Philippians 4:7). I cried out to God and asked Him, "Is it real? Please let it be real!" He began to answer my prayer as I slowly found out.

In addition to learning the Scriptures through my counselors, I was also blessed by the ministry of my Christian uncle who began to speak into my life after my divorce. It turns out he was a godly Reformed Presbyterian, who believed strongly in the sovereignty of God. His perspective was so different than what I had been hearing for years in the Apostolic, Pentecostal and Word of Faith churches.

He was saying things about Scripture I had never heard before, especially regarding God's sovereignty. He made it clear from the Bible that God was completely in control of all things, that humans are inept in and of themselves, and that God is the one who initiates, sustains and completes salvation. Prior to this time I believed I actually contributed much to my own personal salvation. I put myself on the pedestal and was quite puffed up and spiritually proud. I had not fully understood Ephesians 2:8-9 that taught salvation was wholly of God, by His undeserved grace, apart from any human works or endeavors whatsoever. I had an immature understanding of that great truth. I began to spend weekends with my uncle and aunt and he continued with his wise biblical insights that had an indelible impression on my thinking. God was definitely "cleaning house" at this time in my life—and I needed it.

By this time I came to realize that I needed to be a part of a solid Bible teaching church that made Scripture the priority and not human wisdom, emotion or experience. For two solid years I scoured all of San Jose and the surrounding area trying to find a church that taught the Bible. I scrutinized church websites, their doctrinal statements, their philosophy of ministry, and began to get frustrated wondering if there were any biblical churches out there. Finally, in God's providence, I came across a small Bible church in Milpitas that taught meat from God's Word. Through this church I was introduced to the ministry of Pastor John MacArthur, whom God would use mightily to bless my soul, help me grow and stabilize as a believer. This went on for five years. I am now at a place in my life where I finally feel spiritually healthy, emotionally balanced and practically stable. I believe it was the power of God's truth that brought me to this point. His Word is living and active, piercing the soul and attending to the innermost being of a person (Hebrews 4:12).

*For His Glory*

It took many years, but I finally learned that living a content Christian life begins with me getting my eyes off myself, all my problems and struggles, and keep them focused on God and His glory. It's all about Him, not me. And I also know it's about getting my eyes off myself and onto others and their needs—me asking God how I might serve and bless others. Today God has me learning His Word in accountability with other godly women in a regular Bible study, discipling younger women in my local church, praying for others who are in need, loving my family by being a servant to them, and continually praising God for not giving up on me. Now it makes so much sense to me that my journey was not just a waste of time and energy. I know that I have made so many wrong choices in my life, and I have been hurt and have hurt others along the way, but God was with me through them all. Because of His Word, I have a clear view of my journey now. I know that good days will come as well hard days.

God has rescued me from so much. I'm forever grateful to Him. I'm especially overwhelmed on how He continues to restore the broken relationships in my life. Through the grace of God, I have been able to grow with my children and have received their forgiveness. It is not perfect, but nothing is. I'm learning to make room for forgiveness, and to accept forgiveness from others. Nowadays, the healing continues to be an everyday lifestyle for me. I have seen God's hand carry me through many of life's trials and tribulations. I have learned through God's Word that nothing can snatch me from my Father's grip. After all, He holds the world in the palm of His hand, and His grace has been more than I could have ever imagined. I've lived it every day and I know this is true.

# 18

# *Mission Accomplished*

*"Jesus said, 'Father... I glorified You
on earth, having accomplished the
work that You gave Me to do"
John 17:1, 4*

**B**y delivering His people from sin's power and penalty, God has given every Christian a testimony—a story of sin and grace; justice and mercy; failure and redemption. Yet, a personal testimony of salvation in Christ is unique to all other stories we can tell. We might have warm-hearted stories of time spent with family or riveting stories of adventure and friendship. Our testimony of salvation in Christ is unique, however, for it is the story through which all our other stories find meaning and significance.

In this way, our testimony is both a blessing and a stewardship. It is a blessing because it reminds us of God's grace in our lives and renews our assurance of salvation. Our testimonies are a stewardship because they serve as evidence of

God's continued work in the lives of sinners. We have been given a story *to tell*, not to keep to ourselves. Indeed, Jesus told His disciples, just prior to His ascension, that they were to be His witnesses (Acts 1:8). The word used here for witnesses is also translated in the New Testament as "testimony." When a person gives a testimony of salvation, they are standing as a witness to the power of the gospel and the reality of Jesus Christ.

We are grateful for the wise stewardship exercised by each of these contributors. By freely offering their testimonies for public readership, these writers are seeking to fulfill Jesus' commandment to be His witnesses. And, by obeying Christ, they are also serving others. Those who already believe the gospel will have found in these pages cause for much joy and encouragement; those who do not yet trust in Jesus will have discovered, I trust, good reasons to consider the claims of the gospel. Still, I am convinced that both sets of readers will be helped by considering how each of these testimonies demonstrates three essential truths about the nature of salvation.

### A Complete Salvation

The first truth underscored by these testimonies is this: God's salvation is a *complete* salvation. In the retelling of their experience of salvation, each of the contributors demonstrated that God's grace was active and effective both in their conversion and in their life following their initial faith in Christ. In no case did God draw someone to Himself only to leave this new Christian with conversion and nothing more—as though the promise of heaven after death would be enough to stave off the inevitable temptations to sin and despair that these believers would encounter. In many cases, there were profound physical, emotional, and spiritual trials following conversion; but God remained faithful, providing everything needful for a life of faith and obedience.

According to the Bible, salvation promised is salvation provided, both now and in the future (Romans 8:28-39). Where God gives genuine conversion, He provides enduring faith in the gospel, desire for Christ, longing for Christian fellowship, passion for Scripture, love for the saints, gifts for ministry, and perseverance through suffering (Hebrews 10:39). While our affections may ebb and flow and our progress in godliness occasionally sputters and threatens to stall, the Spirit who first ignited faith in Christ promises to keep our hearts kindled with steadfast hope in a merciful God (Philippians 1:6).

## A Diverse Salvation

The second truth highlighted by these testimonies relates to *how* God conducts His saving mission. Not only is it clear that God's salvation is a complete salvation; we also see in these testimonies that God's salvation is a *diverse* salvation. Now, by "diverse" I do not refer to salvation's Author and Founder: Jesus Christ, who is the only way, truth, and life, and no one comes to the Father apart from Him (John 14:6). He is the only Savior of the world, and forgiveness of sin, justification, and deliverance from eternal judgment is only found by repenting from one's sin and placing conscious faith in Christ alone. Clearly, there is only one Savior (Ephesians 4:4-6).

Rather, by "diverse" I refer to the varied ways that people are brought to believe the gospel. Some are rescued after walking through a series of life-threatening events, finally moved to trust

Christ by the prayers, letters, and testimonies of other faithful Christians. Others grow up in the Church and enjoy a genuine relationship with Christ from a very early age. Some are delivered from external, man-made religion, others from paganism. Prior to their conversion, some are attracted to Christianity at some level, while others are repulsed by any thought of it. Some live many years under the pretense of a false conversion; others believe in Jesus the first time they hear the gospel.

Yet, this diversity of God's methods of drawing His people into salvation is not exclusive to the testimonies found in this book; this variety is showcased in the biblical narrative as well. Paul, previously a violent persecutor of the Christian Church is leveled by Christ in a dramatic conversion on the road to Damascus (Acts 9:1-19). Lydia, immediately upon hearing the gospel, places her faith in Christ as the Spirit opened her heart to understand the message the apostles spoke (Acts 16:13-16). A government official from Ethiopia, after studying the scroll of Isaiah on his chariot-ride back from Jerusalem, trusts in Christ after receiving clarifying instruction from Philip as to the identity of the Suffering Servant (Acts 8:27-38). Cornelius, a soldier in the Italian Cohort, is visited first by an angel and then by the apostle Peter; the latter bringing the gospel message to this eager, God-fearing Gentile (Acts 10:1-33). Paul's ministry apprentice, Timothy, was led to Christ as a result of the early biblical tutelage he received from his faithful and godly mother and grandmother (2 Timothy 3:14-15).

Examples could be multiplied. Still, the above cases suffice to illustrate Jesus' mysterious statement to Nicodemus recorded in the Gospel of John. After explaining the necessity of spiritual rebirth to this reputed teacher of Israel, Jesus concludes His discussion with an enigmatic sentence: *"The wind blows where it wishes, and you hear its sound, but you do not know where it comes from or where it goes" (John 3:8)*. While Nicodemus and the other Jews desired a predictable religion they could control and dispense through extra-biblical rule and ritual, Jesus spoke of something infinitely better: a sovereign Spirit that descends upon whomever He will, who is neither deterred by someone's religious, ethnic, social, or educational background, nor obligated to action by the same. The Spirit saves whomever He desires, however He desires, uncontrolled by human methods. Often, we find that He saves those whom we least expect. Indeed, He delights to do so (see 1 Corinthians 1:18-31).

Yet, God is also a God of means, and He is pleased to use a myriad of different circumstances to draw people into relationship with Christ. Actually, while it may be tempting to conclude that God started working toward our salvation at a specific point in our life—perhaps after a family crisis or an evangelistic encounter that really got us thinking about spiritual things—the truth is that God has been orchestrating the salvation of His elect since before creation, from eternity past! God the Father *"chose us in Him [Christ] before the foundation of the world" (Ephesians 1:3)*. Our upbringing, our geographic location, our personality, our jobs, our families, our friends, and our experiences are all vital aspects of our testimony because they are what God used to bring us to repentance and faith in Christ (Acts 17:26-27). To give our testimony of Christ's grace in our lives is to exalt the sovereignty of God.

> *I have told the glad news of deliverance*
> *in the great congregation;*

*Behold, I have not restrained my lips,*
*    as You know, O LORD.*
*I have not hidden Your deliverance within*
*    my heart; I have spoken of Your*
*    faithfulness and Your salvation;*
*I have not concealed Your steadfast love*
*    and Your faithfulness from*
*    the great congregation*
*(Psalm 40:9-10).*

### A Compelling Salvation

The third truth that these testimonies illustrate is that God's salvation is a *compelling* salvation. While some people may be unwilling to investigate Christianity on its own terms because they doubt the Bible's veracity or because they find little power in erudite, rational defenses of Scripture's truth claims, it is unlikely that they will remain unmoved in the face of a genuine testimony of God's life-changing grace. A clear testimony of one's recognition of their sin, repentance, and faith in Jesus coupled with a presentation of the objective truths of the gospel can serve as a powerful means to encourage faith in others.

Apologetically, these testimonies demonstrate the reality of Christ and the truth of the gospel. Jesus has truly risen from the dead and He is in the business—right now—of changing lives for eternity. Although we believe unashamedly that Scripture is sufficient in and of itself to turn a sinner to Christ, we also thank God that He has seen fit to use our personal testimonies as a means to draw attention to the truth of God's Word and the beauty of the gospel.

*Testimonies Encouragement Evangelism*

As we consider the three biblical truths highlighted by these testimonies, we should find ourselves encouraged to share the gospel with others. If there is one thing we hope you take away from this book, it is this: God can save anyone! There is no heart too hard, no hypocrisy too entrenched, no life too lost, no lifestyle too sinful, that God is unable to break through the wall of unbelief and, by His grace, rescue those for whom His Son died. *"And this is the will of Him who sent me,"* Jesus proclaimed to His listeners centuries ago, *"that I should lose nothing of all that [the Father] has given Me, but raise it up on the last day"* *(John 6:39).* Nothing can stop Jesus from building His Church, not even the powers of hell (Matthew 16:18). Those whom God draws to Christ will believe the gospel and, despite the worst of trials, come safely into His eternal kingdom (Romans 8:30).

Over the years you may have allowed yourself to become convinced that there are friends, family members, and colleagues in your life who are beyond the hope of God's grace. If so, let these testimonies and the truth of God's Word realign your mind and heart. We have concrete proof of God's power to save in the previous pages. The stubborn unbelief of your dad, co-worker, or neighbor is no match for the God who will unfailingly fulfill His purposes, the Christ who freely shed His blood for his sheep, and the Spirit who blows upon whom He will. God can save anyone (Romans 10:13).

*Many Stories, One Gospel*

It is essential to keep in mind, however, that the foundational reason we can celebrate a diversity of salvation stories is because there is one and only one gospel. Jesus did not commission us with good news that is relevant only to particular cultures and limited to particular eras of history; the gospel is vitally relevant for *everyone at all times*. But how can this be? How can a message delivered some two-thousand years ago carry significance today? The gospel itself answers that question.

The God who created this breathtaking universe and abundant earth also created man in His image (Genesis 1:26). Sadly, God's image-bearers, though originally created without sin, soon turned to disobedience, away from trust in their Creator. The first man and woman each took and ate fruit from a tree from which they were forbidden (Genesis 3:6-7). They had believed the lie of God's enemy Satan who had told them they would not die if they took from the tree in question; a direct contradiction to what God had previously told Adam: *"And the LORD commanded the man, saying, 'You may surely eat of every tree of the garden, but of the tree of the knowledge of good and evil you shall not eat, for in the day you eat of it you shall surely die' " (Genesis 2:16-17).*

That day in the Garden of Eden, mankind fell into sin and ruin, and the effects of their disobedience were immediate. Adam and Eve were, for the first time, ashamed of their nakedness. Recognizing that something wasn't right, they attempted to cover themselves with self-made loin coverings. The man who was expected to lead and protect his wife, sat passively by while she was beguiled by Satan, and then blamed her (and ultimately God, for He had given her to Adam) for their mess. The woman, also not willing to share any of the blame, pointed her finger at the serpent, in effect saying, "The devil made me do it!" (Genesis 3:8-13).

As a result and reminder of their sin, God cursed the entire creation, including the man and the woman. Difficulty, stress, and futility would now attend work; pain would now be a regular aspect of child bearing. Man's proclivity to passivity and the woman's desire to rule over her husband would now constantly threaten to undo the harmony of every marriage and the family structure (Genesis 3:16-19). Soon, envy, hatred, and murder would enter God's world through Adam and Eve's children (Genesis 4:1-16). And, even if you could avoid murder from an angry neighbor or relative, you would eventually die (Genesis 5:1ff).

But mercy would prevail. Even before the pronouncement of the curse, God promised the man and woman that He would send another man—the offspring of a woman—to crush the serpent. This rescue mission, however, would be costly and the One tasked with crushing the serpent would suffer. Yes, He would be victorious—He would destroy the serpent (Romans 16:20)—but He would not escape the fray unscathed. The serpent would, as the text says, *"bruise his heel" (Genesis 3:15).* Deliverance from sin and its dreaded effects was certainly on the way; but even here, in the earliest chapters of the Bible, we find hints of a suffering Savior.

God would carry out His promised deliverance over many centuries, first by drawing specific people to Himself (like Noah, Abraham, Isaac, and Jacob—later named Israel), then by rescuing an entire nation from the clutches of Egyptian slavery so that they would be His people and He would be their God (Jeremiah 32:38).

As His chosen people, God provided the nation of Israel with a multitude of pictures—all embedded into their religious and civil life—of a coming Deliverer. Israel needed an upright King would to lead them (2 Sam 7:1-17), a sinless High Priest to intercede for them (Psalm 110:4), a selfless Shepherd to protect them (Ezekiel 34:15-23; Psalm 23), a trustworthy Prophet to speak God's words to them (Deuteronomy 18:18), and a righteous Substitute to die for their countless transgressions (Isaiah 53:1-12). Not only this, but Israel also looked forward to the time when God Himself would come down from His heavenly throne and fulfill the many promises He had made to His people over the past several centuries (Isaiah 9:6; 64:1).

Finally, at the perfect time, He came (Galatians 4:4). The Deliverer God had promised entered into the world through the womb of a virgin. Only the very Son of God could fulfill the numerous roles described above, so God's Spirit fell upon Mary, a young Jewish girl in the line of David, and she conceived a child (Luke 1:30-35). The eternal Son of God, formally enthroned in glory with his Father from all eternity would become a human being and enter the world through a miraculous conception (Isaiah 7:14).

But He wasn't what Israel expected. He didn't descend upon the earth in a glorious entourage of angels, ready to defeat Israel's earthly enemies in one victorious flash. He came as a baby, a baby born in a dirty stable suitable only for animals and feed—the most unlikely of places for a triumphant king. And His name would be Jesus, for He had come to save His people, not from earthly enemies, but from that which had cast the world into ruin many centuries ago; He had come to save his people from their sin (Matthew 1:21).

Because Jesus didn't fit the description of what many of the Jews expected of their coming king and savior, He wasn't warmly embraced by the religious leaders. Besides, not only did He not fit the Jews' notion of what their deliverer should look like, He further aggravated their discontent by challenging their spiritual apathy, confronting their hypocrisy, and denouncing their self-righteousness (Matthew 23). He called for repentance from self-reliance and self-justification, and He offered salvation to anyone who came to Him looking for rest from the burden of religious requirements to earn God's favor. Jesus was their King, but as in the case with David, Israel's most famous monarch of old, suffering would come *before* glory.

Neither Jesus' message of true righteousness nor His plan to suffer on the behalf of His people sat well with the Jewish leaders. While some appeared to believe in Him on a superficial level, most of them joined in a conspiracy to kill this itinerant preacher (John 7:1). After three years of teaching, healing, and disciple-making, Jesus' time had come.

One of Jesus' twelve apostles, Judas, having feigned loyalty during the entirety of Jesus' ministry, finally ended his façade and sold his Master to the religious leaders for thirty pieces of silver. A covert arrest, a set of false charges, and a mock trial would eventually land Jesus into the hands of Pilate, the Roman prefect of Judea (Mark 15:1). Caving to the pressure of the Jewish leaders and buckling under his fear of Caesar, Pilate acquiesced to the demands of those who sought Jesus' demise. "Crucify Him!," the fickle mob cried only days after many of them had cordially greeted Jesus' entrance into Jerusalem (Mark 15:13). Pilate complied. Having already been scourged and beaten, Jesus would then be nailed to a cross alongside two criminals outside Jerusalem's city limits.

Some would write Jesus and His apostles off as a rogue group of religious zealots whose plan went awry, disquieted by the untimely death of their leader. Jesus, seemingly unwilling to talk His way out of an assortment of exaggerated accusations, was now dead, the victim of His own silence. With a little clean up and preemption, His short-lived but troublesome movement could be quickly laid to rest.

What the Jewish leaders couldn't see, blinded as they were by their own rage and self-righteousness, was that the God (whom they claimed to worship) had brought about the entire ordeal. Although the people who conspired against Jesus and lobbied for His execution were guilty of great sin—for they had acted freely out of their own evil desires—it had been God who planned from before the beginning of time that his Son would die in the place of sinners (Acts 4:27-28). It would please the Father to crush His Son because His Son's willing death would secure the salvation of God's people while simultaneously upholding God's righteousness. God would remain just while justifying those who put their faith in Jesus (Romans 3:26).

Essential to God's plan to justify sinners, however, was a component to Jesus' mission that neither the Jewish leaders nor Jesus' own disciples recognized, despite Jesus' clear and repeated teaching on the subject. In order to defeat man's three great enemies—sin, death, and Satan—Jesus had to rise again from the dead.

By living a life of flawless obedience to His Father as their representative and taking the punishment they deserved, Jesus had landed a decisive blow to Satan, for the adversary could no longer accuse God's people of their unrighteousness. Those who believed the gospel now possessed a perfect righteousness that was found, not in themselves, but in Christ alone (Romans 3:21-26). Plus, by freeing His people from the condemnation they had incurred for breaking God's law, Jesus removed the dominion of sin over their life. At the cross, sin was soundly defeated because sin's power, the condemnation of the law, had been dismantled by Jesus' substitutionary death (Colossians 2:13-14). But these two glorious realities could only come to full realization if Jesus defeated man's third great enemy, death.

From the moment that Adam and Eve disobeyed God's commandment in the Garden of Eden they were subjected to physical and spiritual death. Death was God's penalty for disobedience (Genesis 2:17), and in their refusal to trust God's good Word, the first man and woman opened the floodgates of mortality upon the entire human race (Romans 5:12). The promised Deliverer, then, in order to crush the serpent and rescue mankind from eternal misery, had to bring death to a complete end.

So, in another garden, approximately two-thousand years ago, a few of Jesus' closest disciples would discover an empty tomb. Yet, one of His followers, Mary Magdalene, would find more than an abandoned grave:

> *Mary stood weeping outside the tomb and as she wept she stooped to look into the tomb. And she saw two angles in white, sitting where the body of Jesus was laid, one at the head and one at the feet. They said to her, "Woman, why are you weeping?" She said to them, "They have taken away my Lord and I do not know where they have laid him." Having said this, she turned*

*around and saw Jesus standing, but she did
not know that it was Jesus. Jesus said to her,
"Woman, why are you weeping? Whom are you
seeking?" Supposing him to be the gardener, she
said to him, "Sir, if you have carried him away,
tell me where you have laid him, and I will take
him away." Jesus said to her, "Mary" (John
20:11-16a).*

The Savior was no longer dead; He was alive! Jesus had
completed His mission by taking the place of His people,
fulfilling every righteous requirement of the law in their place,
bearing the penalty of their sin by dying on the cross, and rising
bodily from the grave.

Now seated at the right hand of His Father, Jesus calls
sinners to receive a sure and irrevocable pardon from heaven.
He calls you to stop using sophisticated excuses to hide from
God. He pleads with you to be done with your attempts to mask
your sin with the threadbare coverings of religious ritual and
good works. He invites you to trade an unfulfilling life of self-
indulgence for the satisfying life of faith in Christ and ministry
to others. He commands you to repent from your hypocrisy,
self-righteousness, self-seeking, and self-reliance and believe
in a gospel of grace and truth (Acts 17:30-31).

If you place genuine faith in Jesus Christ, you will find in
him a *complete salvation*. You will find justification, forgiveness
of sin, reconciliation with God, hope for the future, power over
sin, strength for ministry, and wisdom for living a life that
truly pleases God. And, although you will inevitably face trials
and persecution for your allegiance to Jesus, don't worry. The

troubles of this life are but a mere moment when compared to the eternity of unspeakable joy that Christ has in store for those who love Him.

> *Come, everyone who thirsts, come to the waters;*
> *and he who has no money, come buy and eat!*
> *Incline your ear, and come to Me;*
> *hear, that your soul may live…*
> *Seek the LORD while He may be found;*
> *call upon Him while He is near;*
> *let the wicked forsake his way,*
> *and the unrighteous man his thoughts;*
> *let him return to the LORD, that He*
> *may have compassion on him,*
> *and to our God, for He will abundantly pardon*
> *Isaiah 55:1, 3, 6-7.*